Celebrity Fans and Their Consumer Behaviour

Ever since the dawn of the Hollywood star system in the early 1920s, consumers have been fascinated by film stars and other celebrities and their seemingly glamorous private lives. The public demand for celebrities has become so pervasive that it is arguably an essential element of our everyday culture and market economy, and the focus of increasing study.

This book explores the widespread phenomenon of celebrity fandom and provides a deeper understanding of why individual consumers develop an emotional attachment to their favourite celebrity and what this parasocial fan relationship means in their life. Based on an in-depth insider study of a consumer's fan relationship with a film actress, the book provides unique insights into the celebrity-fan relationship, revealing the meaning it has for the consumer in everyday life, and how it evolves and expresses itself over time.

While this book is primarily located within the field of consumer research, fandom and celebrity are of interest to a variety of academic disciplines. It will appeal to an interdisciplinary audience from marketing and consumer research, film studies, media studies, cultural studies, and sociology.

Markus Wohlfeil is a Lecturer in Marketing in the Marketing and Retail Division at the University of Stirling, UK. Previously, he has also been a Lecturer in Marketing at the University College Cork and the University of East Anglia, UK. As a self-confessed film buff and devoted fan, his research interests are in the fields of celebrity fandom, the experiential consumption of films, film marketing and the film industry in general.

Routledge Interpretive Marketing Research
Edited by Stephen Brown
University of Ulster, Northern Ireland

Recent years have witnessed an 'interpretive turn' in marketing and consumer research. Methodologies from the humanities are taking their place alongside those drawn from the traditional social sciences.

Qualitative and literary modes of marketing discourse are growing in popularity. Art and aesthetics are increasingly firing the marketing imagination.

This series brings together the most innovative work in the burgeoning interpretive marketing research tradition. It ranges across the methodological spectrum from grounded theory to personal introspection, covers all aspects of the postmodern marketing 'mix', from advertising to product development, and embraces marketing's principal sub-disciplines.

Celebrity Fans and Their Consumer Behaviour

Autoethnographic Insights into the Life of a Fan

Markus Wohlfeil

LONDON AND NEW YORK

First published 2018
by Routledge
2 Park Square, Milton Park, Abingdon, Oxon OX14 4RN

and by Routledge
711 Third Avenue, New York, NY 10017

Routledge is an imprint of the Taylor & Francis Group, an informa business

British Library Cataloguing in Publication Data
A catalogue record for this book is available from the British Library

Library of Congress Cataloging in Publication Data
Names: Wohlfeil, Markus, 1969- author.
Title: Celebrity fans and their consumer behaviour : autoethnographic insights into the life of a fan / Markus Wohlfeil.
Description: Abingdon, Oxon ; New York, NY : Routledge, 2018. | Includes bibliographical references and index.
Identifiers: LCCN 2017048537 (print) | LCCN 2017054616 (ebook) | ISBN 9781351173483 (eBook) | ISBN 9780815387275 (hardback : alk. paper)
Subjects: LCSH: Consumer behavior. | Fans (Persons)–Psychology. | Celebrities. | Marketing.
Classification: LCC HF5415.32 (ebook) | LCC HF5415.32 .W64 2018 (print) | DDC 306.3086/21–dc23
LC record available at https://lccn.loc.gov/2017048537

ISBN: 978-0-8153-8727-5 (hbk)
ISBN: 978-1-351-17348-3 (ebk)

Typeset in Times New Roman
by Wearset Ltd, Boldon, Tyne and Wear

MIX
Paper from
responsible sources
FSC® C013056
www.fsc.org

Printed and bound in Great Britain by
TJ International Ltd, Padstow, Cornwall

I dedicate this book to my parents, my late grandma, my brother Sven, my sister Katja, my niece Hannah, my nephew Felix and, in particular, to Ms Debbie Malone and Ms Jena Malone.

Contents

Figures

Acknowledgements

In the academic literature, conducting a research project is often compared to going on a journey of discovery in order to advance the knowledge in a specific area of study. Even though this may be true, in many cases this type of journey will also take the researcher on a quest of self-discovery through which s/he ultimately becomes a different, more enlightened person at the end. However, as with any other journey, the researcher has to acknowledge that he would have lost his path on so many occasions, if it weren't for the support, help, encouragement, wisdom or simply the comfort of some important people along the way.

I would, therefore, like to acknowledge the major academic and personal support, trust and commitment I have received from my supervisor Dr. Susan Whelan during my MBS and PhD at Waterford Institute of Technology. I would like to thank Susan for accompanying me on the first parts of my journey into academia that went from uncharted territory into the complete unknown, for making sure that I did not get stuck somewhere along the way and/or distracted by some other adventures, and for giving me the intellectual freedom to explore, develop and establish my own path into academia. Next, I would like to thank Emeritus Prof. Morris B. Holbrook, Columbia University, Prof. Stephen J. Gould, Baruch College, City University of New York, Emeritus Prof. Sebastian Green, University College Cork, and Prof. Anthony Patterson, University of Liverpool for sharing their incredibly vast experience with me, proof-reading and advising me on my papers and, also, acting as my mentors during this exciting journey and beyond.

Other important people who have shared their huge experience with me and I have had great discussions with include Dr. Donncha Kavanagh, Dr. Brendan Richardson, Dr. Finola Kerrigan, Emeritus Prof. Darach Turley, Prof. Douglas Brownlie, and Prof Thorsten Hennig-Thurau. Very special and warm thanks go to my friend Dr. Wided Batat, University of Lyon. Further thanks go to Ms Jacqueline Curthoys and Ms Laura Hussey at Routledge for taking on this project and publishing this book – never mind their valuable advice along the way.

Of course, I shouldn't forget my family. Thus, I would like to thank my little sister Katja for her patience, support, advice and the occasional kick in the butt. A special thanks go to my nephew Felix and my niece Hannah, who once in a while allow me to talk to their mummy for a few minutes on the phone and keep me on my toes (aka young) during my yearly Christmas visits. I would also like to acknowledge my father, Eckhard, and my mother, Beatrix, for their understanding and support; even though we have not always agreed on the path I was taking and have had lots of heated debates. But at the end, I'm grateful that you are always there for me. A very big gratitude goes to my late granny, who was always standing behind me ever since I was a little boy – until her death a few years ago. Thanks for all that you have done for me!!!

I would also like to thank Mr. Andre Pause for being such a great friend in all those years. Last but not least, I would especially like to thank Ms. Debbie Malone for being one of the best friends I ever had and for giving me all the great advice, encouragement and support. And, finally, my very special thanks, obviously, go to Ms. Jena Malone for inspiring me, although without knowing it, to this incredible research journey.

1   In Our Nature

The phenomenon of celebrity fandom

Why studying consumers' fan relationships with celebrities?

Ever since the dawn of the Hollywood star system in the early-1920s, consumers have always had a keen interest in the creative performances, public appearances and private lives of film stars, athletes and any other famous people (Barbas 2001; Geraghty 2000). We only need to open our daily newspapers, browse the Internet, turn on the TV, read the glossy magazines at our dentist, barber or hairdresser, shop in the supermarket, walk down the street, wait at the bus stop or talk to our friends, peers and colleagues at school, university or work these days in order to meet and read about consumers, who love to indulge in and comment on the latest creative works, achievements, life-stories, gossip, misdemeanours and scandals of celebrities (Hermes 2006; Hermes & Kooijman 2016). Therefore, it is only fair to say that film stars, directors, rock/pop stars, athletes, novelists, artists, models and even reality TV stars have without any doubt become an essential part of our contemporary cultural fabric (Barron 2015; Turner 2004) and market economy (McCracken 1989; Thomson 2006).

Of course, most people tend to have only a fleeting interest in celebrities per se and enjoy primarily the exchange of gossip with other like-minded individuals (Hermes 2006; Stacey 1994). Some consumers, however, experience a much stronger interest and admiration for a specific male or female celebrity and, subsequently, become what are commonly known as *fans* (Henry & Caldwell 2007; Leets et al. 1995; O'Guinn 1991) or *celebrity worshippers* (McCutcheon et al. 2003). Hence, since celebrities seem to play such an important role in so many consumers' daily lives, it is both surprising and disappointing that, until very recently, hardly any academic research has actually sought to develop a deeper understanding of how individual consumers' fan relationships with their favourite celebrities express themselves in everyday consumption experiences and practices (O'Guinn 1991; Wohlfeil & Whelan 2012).

As it so happens, I'm one of those … *fans*. Ever since I purchased the DVD of the indie-film *Saved!* (US 2004) in a 3-DVDs-for-€20-sale back in April 2005, I have been a devoted fan of the very talented, intelligent and beautiful actress Jena Malone, who mainly features in lesser known, yet much more interesting and challenging independent films like *Donnie Darko* (US 2001), *The United*

States of Leland (US 2003), *Into the Wild* (US 2007), *The Ruins* (US 2008), *The Messenger* (US 2009), *Five Star Day* (US 2010), *In Our Nature* (US 2012), *10 Cent Pistol* (US 2014) or *Neon Demon* (US 2016), and sometimes also in bigger films like *Pride & Prejudice* (UK 2005), *Sucker Punch* (US 2011) or *The Hunger Games: Catching Fire* (US 2013). What is hereby particularly curious is that I have never really experienced this kind of admiration and devotion for a specific film star, rock star or any other celebrity before; though, like probably most other people, I have enjoyed watching films since my early childhood for the pleasure that their audio-visual storytelling provides (Holbrook & Hirschman 1982; Kerrigan 2010).

As films have always meant much more to me than mere short-term entertainment, I have been collecting films for more than 35 years by now on VHS, DVD and, more recently, as iTunes downloads. Similar to collectors of artworks (Chen 2009), literature (Brown 2006) or vinyl records (Holbrook 1987), I take care and pleasure in displaying my *'little treasures'* for the eyes of the occasional visitor, and especially for my very own private enjoyment (Belk et al. 1989). But more importantly, on an emotional level, the experiential consumption of films has always provided me with both an exciting way to escape temporarily from a dull and lonely life, and a source of inspiration for pursuing a *'better way of life'* (Wohlfeil & Whelan 2008). Thus, instead of being just a passive form of short-term entertainment, my enjoyment of films actually derives from the active mental immersion into the film narratives (Batat & Wohlfeil 2009; Green et al. 2004) and the identification with film characters (Cohen 2001; Wohlfeil & Whelan 2008) that give me the opportunity to live out my hopes, dreams and fantasies in my imagination.

However, despite this emotional investment in films, I have never really viewed and described myself as a fan before, nor have I ever felt a strong interest in a specific celebrity, or celebrities in general, either. Of course, there were those moments in my life, when I felt momentarily attracted to a particular talented and/or physically attractive film actress like Alyssa Milano, Winona Ryder, Claire Danes or Natalie Portman, whose films I preferred to watch on those occasions more often than others.[1] But while my temporary interest in them was usually awoken by my enjoyment of a specific film or TV show they were featuring in, it often involved little more than just watching the respective actress in a few other film or TV roles and perhaps reading the occasional article about them. Furthermore, I never really developed a genuine emotional attachment to any single one of them and paid virtually no attention to their private lives or anything else that was not related to their performances. As a consequence, my interest in each of them usually evaporated within a few months again just as quickly as it began. At least, that has always been the case until, by chance, a young, very talented and beautiful actress named Jena Malone unexpectedly caught my eye and, somehow, captured my heart...

Ever since the moment I saw Jena Malone, I have experienced a completely different and more intense emotional relationship with her. In addition to having all of her films in my personal collection, I also feel this strong desire to learn more about her as both a creative artist and a real person behind the public image (Wohlfeil & Whelan 2012). Moreover, Jena Malone's original hand-signed photo autographs, especially those ones that she has dedicated to me personally, are my most cherished *'treasures'*. In a strange way, Jena Malone has *'Saved!'* (US 2004) me from the dull, lonely and frustrating life as an unwilling single by filling it with some meaning and a sense of purpose (Wohlfeil & Whelan 2012). My emotional attachment to Jena Malone, therefore, presents us also with some interesting questions that, in my opinion, warrant further academic investigation. For instance, what is it exactly that attracts an ordinary consumer like me to become and remain the devoted fan of a film actress (or any other celebrity for that matter)? Why does a consumer like me experience such a strong emotional attachment to one particular film actress or any other celebrity, but remains indifferent to many other equally talented and physically attractive ones? What does the everyday lived fan relationship with one's admired film star or celebrity mean to the individual consumer? And how does it manifest itself in everyday consumer behaviour?

Since these are indeed some interesting and valid questions, it is quite surprising and also disappointing that hardly any academic research prior to this study has actually sought to address them. Even though a growing interdisciplinary body of literature from such diverse academic disciplines as consumer research, marketing, media studies, cultural anthropology, sociology, social psychology, sports and leisure research has been dedicated to fan studies in recent years, earlier research has focused mainly on the symbolic (and sometimes obsessive) consumption practices of certain, more *'extreme'* subgroups of fans commonly associated with cult media texts (Hills 2002; Jenkins 1992; Kozinets 2001) or sports spectatorship (Derbaix et al. 2002; Richardson and Turley 2006, 2008). Methodologically, these studies have been limited to an *outsider-looking-in* perspective (Smith et al. 2007) that has provided researchers primarily with the opportunity to establish and reinforce a sociological ideology-informed distinction between *'US'* (the normal, rational, socially desirable mainstream) and *'THEM'* (the abnormal, irrational, socially undesirable deviant) by looking from some obscure *morally superior* high ground down on the non-conform *'OTHER'* within culture and/or society (Duffett 2013). However, because the interpretation of what a fan is seems only too often to be highly dependent on the underlying agenda of the respective researcher examining the phenomenon (Smith et al. 2007), it is no wonder that the present literature still lacks even a coherent understanding of what exactly constitutes fandom in the first place (Wohlfeil & Whelan 2012). What is clear, though, is that both academic literature and popular media tend to place fans consistently on the receiving end of ridicule, negative stereotyping and *'bad press'* (Barbas 2001; Duffett 2013; Jenson 1992).

As desired, fans are thereby conceptualised either as uneducated, gullible, dull and vulnerable *'numbs'*, who are easily controlled and manipulated by a dangerous and *'evil'* popular mass culture (Boorstin 1961; Gabler 1998; Schickel 1985), or as subversive and creative rebels against the corporate establishment, who poach commercial media texts to create their own textual products (Barbas

2001; Jenkins 1992; Turner 2004). Some scholars portray fans as members of neo-religious cults, who worship celebrities like *'gods'* through shared rituals and the sacralisation of associated profane items within like-minded communities (Kozinets 1997; O'Guinn 1991). Others describe them as geeks and alienated, lonely social misfits, who experience for various reasons deficits in their social skills and/or networks (Kozinets 2001). While often being well-educated, creative and quite successful in school or at work, these consumers often feel in their private lives lonely, rejected and stigmatised especially by those others, who may be less imaginative and intelligent, but are much more privileged in terms of social skills, status and/or physical attractiveness (Cusack et al. 2003). Thus, fandom would provide them with a means of compensation and social interaction with similarly isolated individuals. In following Munsterberg's (1916) legacy, however, a small group of social psychologists have recently set out on a deliberate quest again to confirm the century-old and sensationalist popular stereotype that fans are *'cognitively inflexible'*, gullible, uncreative and dull individuals (McCutcheon et al. 2003) or, worse, delusional, pathological-obsessive stalkers (McCutcheon et al. 2006). In fact, McCutcheon et al. (2003, 2006) have even gone so far to imply that *'celebrity worship'* would actually constitute a (sic) *'serious mental illness'*; even though their own published statistical data strongly contradict such claims.

In light of such a devastating portrayal of fans, it may seem to be a very unwise move to admit here publicly to my personal infatuation with the film actress Jena Malone and risk being branded with one of these common stereotypes or, worse, to be declared as *'cognitively inflexible, gullible, dull and obsessive'* – at least if the findings by McCutcheon et al. (2003, 2006) are anything to go by. But as none of these conceptualisations either describes or fully captures many facets of my own everyday lived fan consumption experiences, I cannot stop wondering whether there is maybe much more to a consumer's fan relationship with one's admired film star or celebrity and the resulting consumption practices than previous research has uncovered so far. This suspicion is further strengthened by the knowledge that all earlier studies have paid little attention to the everyday lived fan experiences of the *'normal'* fan in one's daily life and/or explored the true nature of fans' personal relationships with the subject of admiration. Instead, their focus has always been either on the symbolic relationships and social dynamics that consumers experience with other fans within their specific consumption subcultures (Hills 2002; Jenkins 1992; Kozinets 2001; Richardson & Turley 2006) or on the psychological well-being of *'gullible, pathological-obsessive celebrity worshippers'* (Leets et al. 1995; McCutcheon et al. 2003). This inadvertently meant that, in the process, the admired subjects of fandom have often been reduced to the mere status of an interchangeable, non-consequential commodity.

A closer look at the brief autobiographical account of my own fandom, however, would suggest that an alternative conceptualisation of fans and fandom may be needed, which focuses instead on the fan's dyadic relationship with the subject of their fandom. Hence, I set out on my own research journey back in

2005 to gain a deeper understanding of what meaning(s) the fan relationship with a film star or celebrity has for the individual consumer and how it manifests itself in everyday consumer behaviour. Since addressing the raised questions in an appropriate manner requires a research methodology that gives the consumer a real voice (Stern 1998) and allows us to explore from a fan's *genuine insider* point of view (Smith et al. 2007) what it really means for the individual consumer to be the devoted fan of an admired celebrity within one's daily life, I have used an autoethnographic research method (Ellis & Adams 2014; Gould 2008; Holbrook 1991, 1995) embedded within an existential-phenomenological framework (Merleau-Ponty 1962; Thompson et al. 1989).

By drawing on narrative transportation theory (Gerrig 1993; Green et al. 2004), I describe and examine how my own personal fan relationship with the film actress Jena Malone has developed, evolved and expressed itself in my everyday lived consumption experiences over a period of 21 months (Wohlfeil & Whelan 2011, 2012). The emphasis is hereby placed less on the factual recollection of observable consumption practices that could have easily been observed via a less controversial research method, but much more on how my everyday lived experiences (i.e. inner feelings, thoughts, sensations, daydreams and fantasies) derived from or translated into my fan relationship with Jena Malone. This book is a research monograph that presents a detailed account of this extended research journey, on which I now invite you, the reader, to join me. But before we set off, it may be a good idea to explain first the study's background, rationale, underlying epistemological foundations and methodological approach.

Origin of my research journey into the world of celebrity fandom

While the issues and questions I have just raised in relation to celebrity fandom are quite clearly of interest, my research journey did not commence with them in mind, but actually emerged by a fortunate coincidence from my initial research idea. Inspired by Holbrook's autoethnographic work about his own personal consumption experiences stemming from his love for jazz music (1986, 1987, 1995, 2011) and photograph collections (2005, 2006), I planned in spring 2005 to study the experiential consumption of films from an individual consumer's autoethnographic insider perspective (Batat & Wohlfeil 2009; Wohlfeil and Whelan 2008). Due to my long-running love for films and losing myself in their imaginary worlds, I felt at the time that such a topic would make for an interesting and insightful contribution to consumer research. In contrast to conventional product or service brands, film brands must be understood as composite artistic brands that consist of a complex tapestry of various other brands, which include among others the involved actors and actresses, director, producer(s), scriptwriter(s), cinematographer(s), editor(s) and the soundtrack composer(s) as individual human brands in their own rights (Hart et al. 2016; O'Reilly & Kerrigan 2013; Wohlfeil & Whelan 2008). The film's brand image and success, therefore, influences and, simultaneously, is influenced by the personal image and *'value'* of each involved human brand (Albert 1998; Beckwith 2009; Wallace et al. 1993). Therefore, I initially looked at the admiration for film stars and celebrity fandom as little more than just one of many relevant factors contributing to consumers' enjoyment of films (Batat & Wohlfeil 2009; Wohlfeil & Whelan 2008).

But when my personal admiration for the film actress Jena Malone intensified during the summer of 2005, a number of interesting questions began to intrigue me as a result of my own personal fan experiences that begged for closer examination and presented me with a research opportunity that was just too good to ignore. For example, why do I feel emotionally attached to Jena Malone instead of any other celebrity, who might be more *'popular'*, and/or *'media-friendly'* and/or *'prettier'*? What is about her that fascinates me so intensely, while I usually remain rather indifferent towards other celebrities or celebrity culture in general? And while I describe myself as a Jena Malone fan, what exactly does it actually mean to be a fan in the first place? The focus of my autoethnographic research project has subsequently shifted towards understanding the widespread phenomenon of celebrity fandom – with a particular emphasis on film actors/actresses. In so doing, I have recorded and examined my own everyday lived consumption experiences as a Jena Malone fan as primary data to provide genuine insights into celebrity fandom from a fan's insider perspective. All the findings eventually emerged iteratively from the collected autoethnographic data without me having a prior knowledge of the relevant interdisciplinary academic stardom, celebrity and fandom literature. While this may sound straightforward, the research's new focus and overall approach has actually been a huge gamble on two fronts that easily could have backfired under unfortunate circumstances.

First of all, there has always been the danger that my admiration and fan interest in Jena Malone could have evaporated at any time as quickly as it began. In other words, I could have ended up with insufficient autoethnographic data to obtain meaningful insights. Fortunately, my emotional attachment to this film actress has persisted with varying degrees of intensity not only throughout the period of data collection, but continues to this very day. Second, and more crucially, my knowledge of the fandom, celebrity and stardom literatures was virtually non-existent at the time of the data collection. In fact, I only started reading up on either literature after I had completed the 16 months of contemporaneous self-observation and began to transcribe the recorded diaries (more details are covered later in this chapter). The obvious advantage of this approach is that I would neither consciously nor unconsciously be able to influence the recording of autoethnographic data in the diary against or in favour of a certain conceptualisation of celebrity fandom in the present literature, if I do not know about them in advance.

The major downside, however, is that all the findings emerging iteratively from the autoethnographic data could have already been covered in detail by earlier studies and, thus, failed to make a contribution to the literature. Fortunately, it has turned out that celebrity fandom is still a largely neglected and underdeveloped field of research within the wider interdisciplinary study of fandom, as I will show later in Chapters 2 and 3 of this book, that – apart from a few individual pioneers (Henry & Caldwell 2007; O'Guinn 1991; Thomson 2006) – has only in recent years gained some slow momentum following my own research (Wohlfeil & Whelan 2011, 2012) and those of a few others (i.e. Banister & Cocker 2014; Hills 2016; Radford & Bloch 2012). In fact, by offering a genuine insider perspective into a consumer's real-lived fan experiences with the subject of one's admiration, I propose an urgently needed reconceptualisation of fandom.

Overall aim(s) of this book's research journey into celebrity fandom

The general idea behind pursuing academic research is to contribute to the growing body of knowledge in a specific discipline or area of interest by investigating phenomena that call for scholarly explanation. The romantic image that we thereby usually have of research is that of a *journey of discovery*, where a researcher ventures into uncharted territory to explore observed phenomena of interest and, after some time, returns home to report the findings. But if this travel metaphor is accurate, then it seems that most researchers select the phenomena they investigate akin to package tourists walking sightseeing on the beaten path from one tourist attraction or landmark to the next highlight of the tour. And regarding the so-called *'armchair scholarship'* common in economics or sociological theory, scholars even appear to be content enough with merely reviewing the existing literature in order to theorise about distant phenomena without ever actually leaving the safety of their desks – which is pretty much the scholarly equivalent of writing a travel book without ever having been to the very country or culture in question. And as it so happens, this is especially true with regard to the study of fans and fandom.

With the exception of some ethnographic studies, where the researcher has visited a certain group of (often *'hardcore'*) fans at least temporarily within the exceptional situational context of fan-clubs (Henry & Caldwell 2007; O'Guinn 1991), conventions (Jenkins 1992; Kozinets 2001) or online communities (Kozinets 1997; Richardson & Turley 2008), the vast majority of critical scholars have theorised fans and fandom through an ideological lens without ever actually engaging in person with the very people and phenomenon they claim to investigate. In either case, their detached *'outsider-looking-in'* position has allowed them, under the pretext of objectivity and scientific rigour, to examine and discuss fans and fandom by imposing their own preconceived, abstract and only too often prejudiced meanings onto this phenomenon and to differentiate fans as the *'deviant other'* from what is idealised as being the *'normal'* in society (Smith et al. 2007). And since fan studies have often treated the subjects of fans' admiration as interchangeable commodities (Duffett 2013), we still lack a genuine understanding of how and why a consumer experiences this special emotional bond to a specific celebrity.

Hence, my overall aim with this book is to provide the reader with some holistic insights from a genuine insider perspective into what meaning(s) a consumer's personal fan relationship with one's admired film actor/actress or celebrity has for the individual and how it manifests itself in everyday consumption experiences and practices. In taking an existential-phenomenological perspective (Merleau-Ponty 1962), I am occupying the dual role of both the researcher and the sole informant in this autoethnographic study by describing, examining and interpreting my own everyday lived experiences as a devoted fan of the film actress Jena Malone and how they manifest themselves through my consumption of her films, autographs and other collectible items and my daydreams, thoughts and feelings. Or in other words, my research journey has required me to explore the uncharted territory of celebrity fandom as a native backpacker with an open mind and as little baggage of preconceived abstract ideas, stereotypes and prejudices as possible in order to investigate the phenomenon from a genuine insider's point of view. And you, the reader, are now invited to join me on this journey as a side-participant and to experience celebrity fandom through the eyes, ears and words of a real-living fan.

As an early point of departure, the autoethnographic research journey in this book commenced with the following initial objectives in mind that derived from the questions and issues raised earlier:

- To explore the nature and extent of a fan's emotional attachment to one's favourite film star/celebrity. By gaining first-hand insights into what exactly it is that attracts an ordinary consumer like me to become and remain the devoted fan of a film actress like Jena Malone, we would be able to understand why a consumer may experience such a significant level of interest, admiration and devotion for a particular celebrity, while not experiencing similar feelings of attraction and attachment towards other equally talented, interesting and/or physically appealing celebrities.
- To develop a genuine understanding of what meaning(s) the everyday lived fan relationship with one's admired film star or celebrity has for the individual consumer within the context of one's personal life-world (Thompson 1998). In examining the meanings that being a devoted fan of Jena Malone has for my personal subjective quality of life experiences, this book seeks to provide you, the reader, with a true insider perspective to understand in particular what it really feels like for individual consumers to be the fan of a film star. Furthermore, by giving a real fan, who happens to be me, his own voice of representation (Stern 1998), it should surely be quite interesting to explore through his eyes and words how and in what different forms the experienced emotional fan relationship with his admired film star is occupying both a mental and a physical space within his daily life.
- To examine how a consumer's emotional attachment to one's favourite and admired film star/celebrity expresses itself in everyday consumer behaviour. As it is highly unlikely that an ordinary consumer like me would ever get to know one's admired film star/celebrity as the real private person behind the

public persona in the media (Dyer 1998), this book may enable us to gain a deeper understanding of how an individual consumer may create or enhance the personal feeling of the admired film star's/celebrity's physical and emotional presence in one's everyday life through the acquisition and consumption of tangible possessions, such as autographed photos, posters, DVDs, articles and other collectibles (Wohlfeil & Whelan 2011, 2012).

Keeping in mind that these initial objectives are only early points of departure, they were never intended to serve as the foundation for some preconceived, deductive hypotheses or their confirmation. Instead, all the obtained insights and findings of the study presented in this book have emerged iteratively from the extensive and thorough hermeneutical analysis of the collected autoethnographic data (Gadamer 1989; Thompson 1997).

Into the Wild (or the research's epistemological and methodological foundations)

In general, the research methodology provides the road map and technical equipment for an academic journey of discovery into a phenomenon that calls for scholarly explanation. The question, therefore, is why I have taken an existential-phenomenological perspective and followed an autoethnographic research methodology in this study instead of any traditional, more established and less controversial one. The film *Into the Wild* (US 2007), in which Jena Malone has happened to feature in a support role, may hereby offer an excellent analogy for the existential-phenomenological approach that has guided my research journey. Just like the lead character Chris McCandless, we too need to get out of the comfortable trap that is our established path in academic scholarship, leave the *old* (= what is known and/or how it became known) behind and walk with an open mind into *'unknown territory'* to obtain genuine insights into the human condition (Batat & Wohlfeil 2009). Indeed, by studying only individual elements of a consumption phenomenon in isolation, the traditional scientific (or rather *scientistic*) methodologies that still dominate most of academic research in the social sciences have usually failed to appreciate its holistic context and complexity.

The research methods that have informed much of the fandom and stardom literature tend to examine film stars and their fans as purely separate and isolated texts, on which they impose their ideology-informed and preconceived meanings from a detached outsider-looking-in position (Barron 2015). But in order to gain a truly holistic understanding of celebrity fandom, we must give the individual consumer a voice by focusing from a real insider perspective on the consumer experience in the way it presents itself to consciousness (Merleau-Ponty 1962; Thompson 1997). If we, like Chris McCandless, look hereby into our own individual subjectivity, we may even learn a few unexpected things about ourselves as human beings (Gould 1991). And although he eventually met his doom at the unforgiving hands of Mother Nature, I hope that, at the end of my journey, I may be spared a similar fate at the hands of academia.

To describe and understand the underpinning ideas behind phenomenology in a crash course is not easy, as it is essentially a research philosophy, a paradigm and a methodology. In the 1910s, Husserl (1985, 1986) developed phenomenology as an anti-foundationalist approach to knowledge that is centred in the certainty of conscious thought and rejects the foundationalist notions of Cartesian duality, absolute truth and its criteria of evaluating knowledge claims (Hirschman & Holbrook 1992). Key to understanding phenomenology is Husserl's (1985) argument that material objects, despite their real physical existence in the external material world, only appear to the individual in one's conscious thought as *'intentional objects'* rather than being perceived correctly as the things they are. By defining objects not as things in themselves but as *'phenomena of consciousness'*, Husserl (1985) concluded that *'all consciousness is consciousness of something'* and that all thoughts are always directed at some phenomena of interest. Hence, Husserl (1985) proposed to *'go back to the things themselves'* in order to understand the true *'essence'* of a particular phenomenon in its ideal form and the context of its appearance.

But in order to comprehend phenomena with certainty, researchers would be required to bracket out their own preconceptions of the external world and to focus only on the contents of consciousness, which Husserl (1986) called the *'lived experience'*. The role of the researcher, therefore, is to interpret the everyday meanings and structure of the world as *'lived'* by the individual person; the so-called *'life-world'* (Husserl 1986). The foundation of human understanding emerges thereby from an underlying field of pre-reflected lived experiences like practical knowledge, emotional experiences and an intuitive understanding of the individual's socio-cultural way of life (Thompson 1998). Other phenomenological scholars such as Heidegger (1927), Merleau-Ponty (1962) or Gadamer (1989) have built on Husserl's thoughts by injecting existentialist ideas and proposing that the life-world is the structure of fundamental relationships that shape an individual's everyday lived experiences and private meanings s/he ascribes to them (Thompson 1997).

These proponents of existential-phenomenology have argued that the life-world is a hermeneutic construct that provides an analytical framework through which holistic comprehensions of phenomena arise iteratively from the interpretive interaction between the developing understanding of consumers' life narratives and life-world categories (Thompson 1998). In borrowing from Gestalt psychology, Heidegger (1927) proposed that knowledge manifests itself in its existential *'Gestalt (figure)'* or *'Dasein (being there)'* and should offer insights into human life experiences as the individual's *'being-in-the-world'*. Merleau-Ponty (1962) suggested that the pre-reflected perceptual experiences serve as the foundation for conceptual knowledge claims and must be understood as a process of *'seeing-as'* metaphors. Human experiences that have traditionally been viewed as unconscious are hereby described as both reflected and unreflected and as being located only in the present life-world rather than as being determined by historical antecedents (Merleau-Ponty 1962; Thompson 1998). As reflective meanings thereby emerge from the background of unreflected experiences, their relationship to each other can be explained through the figure/ ground metaphor (Thompson et al. 1989).

Thus, human experiences must be seen as a dynamic process, where at any one point in time certain aspects stand out as a figure from the ground, while receding back into the ground at another point in time when other aspects become figural instead (Thompson et al. 1989). As a result, the figure is never independent from its contextual ground, as they constitute each other and neither can exist without the other (Heidegger 1927). Furthermore, all human experiences such as thoughts, feelings, fantasies, memories, perceptions and imaginations are intentional phenomena that are directed towards some focal point of interest (Merleau-Ponty 1962; Thompson et al. 1989). This means that because consumers' behaviour patterns cannot exist in isolation, they also should not be studied independently of their social and environmental contexts. Thus, existential-phenomenology seeks to describe human experiences in the very way they are *'lived'* within the context they emerge from, whereby the world of lived experience does not necessarily have to be identical with the world of objective observation and description (Gadamer 1989; Thompson 1997).

According to Merleau-Ponty (1962), the individual's life-world consists of four core categories, which are one's *'perceptions of the cultural context'*, *'emotional relationships to others'*, the *'lived body'* and the *'historicised self'*. First, based on the assumption that meanings of specific experiences always emerge within the individual's socio-cultural life (Thompson 1998), the life-world analysis is primarily interested in understanding how the individual makes sense of his/her surrounding social and cultural environment. Second, as personal relationships comprise not only the social fabric of everyday life, but are also vital to an individual's sense of belonging to a social community, every social relationship (including parasocial ones) and interpersonal contact provides a stream of meaning (Merleau-Ponty 1962). In contrast to the traditional economic-rational paradigm, which defines relationships as sets of rational cost-benefit decisions between two parties, the life-world concept holds that interpersonal (and even parasocial) relationships are emotionally charged with symbolic significance for the individual, which include all those emotions like feelings of care, love, jealousy, anger, frustration, disappointment, happiness, sadness, etc. as essential facets of human experience and existence (Gadamer 1989; Thompson 1998).

Third, rejecting the old Cartesian idea of the body being only a container for the human mind, Merleau-Ponty (1962) ascribed two unique functions to the lived body. On the one hand, the body is the essential *'instrument of human experience'* through which the individual experiences the external world. But, on the other hand, the body is also an object in the world, which like any other material object is subject to external forces and can be experienced, controlled and monitored (Hirschman & Holbrook 1992). Thus, the body plays a vital role in the construction of the individual's self-identity and self-perception (Gadamer 1989). Any voluntary or involuntary alteration to one's body (i.e. make-up, haircut, body decorations, injuries or even rape) has the potential to affect the way in which one relates to all other aspects of the life-world (Thompson 1998). Finally, the historicised self refers to the living legacy of cultural practices, beliefs and meanings that provide the transcendent, intersubjective ground of human experience where history becomes a meaningful event through personal and culturally-shared stories that express the cultural way of life (Thompson 1998). Because the individual's self-identity is the reflection of one's personal history and socio-cultural background, one's life and consumption stories express a personal subjective history of holistically experienced cultural meanings in one's life-world.

As I stated before, in taking an existential-phenomenological perspective, the aim of the research in this book is to obtain holistic insights into a consumer's everyday lived fan experiences with one's admired celebrity through this individual's eyes and words (Gadamer 1989; Heidegger 1927). But due to the perceptual and experiential differences that naturally exist between the researcher and the informants, the ultimate form of understanding human experiences within their situational and personal contexts would be achieved by a *'fusion of horizons'* (Gadamer 1989) that involves the researcher taking on the dual role of the researcher and the informant. It is for that reason that I followed a narrative form of autoethnography as my data collection method. Holbrook (1986, 1987, 1991, 1995) introduced autoethnography to consumer research back in 1986 and, since then, its application has further been advocated by Gould (1991, 1995, 2006), Brown (1998a, b), Ellis (1991, 1995, 2002), Rambo (1992, 1996, 2005), Patterson (2005, 2009, 2012) and, lately, by myself.

In its purest form, autoethnography is an *'extreme form of participant observation that focuses on impressionistic narrative accounts of the writer's own private consumption experiences with a phenomenon from the viewpoint of an informed and deeply involved insider'* (Holbrook 2005: 45), where the researcher is often the sole informant. Although autoethnography has often received a rather hostile reception due to more or less deliberate misconceptions endorsed by its critics (Wallendorf & Brucks 1993; Woodside 2004), many of the raised issues have already been discussed and dealt with extensively in the literature (i.e. Brown 1998b; Ellis & Adams 2014; Gould 1995, 2008; Holbrook 1995, 2006). One of its major advantages, however, is that it allows the researcher an unlimited 24-hour access to an insider's everyday lived experiences with the investigated phenomenon without having to wrestle with ethical concerns regarding the informant's privacy (Brown 1998b). Moreover, autoethnography enables the researcher to explore the subjective nature of human feelings, daydreams, sensations and streams of consciousness related to consumption (Gould 1991) in the very way they are experienced by the individual, but have remained inaccessible through traditional scientific and qualitative research methods (Wohlfeil & Whelan 2012).

For this research, I therefore provide autoethnographic insights into my own personal lived consumption experiences as a devoted fan of the film actress Jena Malone over a total period of 21 months of self-observation. My lived fan experiences in the period from April to 10 September 2005 were obtained as retrospective data in a 36,000-words essay, which was written in early September 2005 to describe how I became a fan of Jena Malone in the first place. Then, during the period from 11 September 2005 to 31 December 2006, I collected all my everyday lived fan experiences with Jena Malone as raw contemporaneous data while they occurred in real time in order to ensure a high degree of *'data accuracy'* (Wallendorf & Brucks 1993). Contemporaneous introspective data field the unique advantage of supplying a large pool of pure emotional data on consumption experiences that would be inaccessible to any other scientific or qualitative research method that is based on retrospective recall or pure observation and, thus, inevitably lost forever (Wohlfeil & Whelan 2008, 2011). To collect them, I used thought-watching exercises that are relatively similar to the ones described by Gould (2006), whereby I observed within me how my thoughts, feelings and/or fantasies in response to Jena Malone-related stimuli – both external (i.e. acting performances, interviews, photos or articles) and internal (i.e. daydreams or imageries) – developed, progressed, receded and even led to different emotional responses and physical reactions.

Still, my overall approach is closer to the narrative autoethnography championed by Holbrook (1991, 1995, 2005), Ellis (1995, 2002) or Rambo (1996, 2005), where autobiographical stories provide us with a lens for looking into the human condition of our mundane everyday lives. To ensure data accessibility for external review, I have recorded all the contemporaneous hand-written data systematically, unfiltered and on the spot in a specifically assigned diary (Patterson 2005). The emphasis has thereby been less on the factual recollection of observable consumption practices and much more on how my everyday lived experiences (i.e. inner feelings, thoughts, fantasies and daydreams) derived from or translated into my emotional attachment to Jena Malone. In total, I obtained more than 150,000 hand-written words as raw data, which were supplemented by 50 photographs taken during the same time to offer further holistic insights, for a thorough hermeneutic part-to-whole analysis.

Consistent with the existential-phenomenological research tradition, I have devised a data interpretation process that largely draws on Thompson's (1997) proposed hermeneutical-narrative model of understanding. Thompson suggests that the phenomenological process of hermeneutic circles involves a part-to-whole analysis of each informant's accounts through an interactive process, whereby five key aspects of consumer stories need to be analysed. First, individuals structure narrative contents by plotlines that present events according to a temporal movement in order to highlight goals, motives and envisaged outcomes. Second, the consumer narratives reflect symbolic parallels between the meanings of different events. Third, they also present us with intertextual relationships, in which the meanings of different consumption stories become integrated in consumers' narratives of personal history (Hirschman & Holbrook 1992). Fourth, consumer narratives express existential themes by which consumers negotiate their self-identity through reflections on consumption experiences, rituals, treasured possessions and life choices (Thompson et al. 1989).

Finally, consumer narratives reflect and draw from socio-cultural codes of shared meanings and conventionalised viewpoints (Thompson 1997).

But as such hermeneutic analysis normally works with retrospective data that have been obtained in a number of interviews from various informants (Thompson et al. 1989), I have had to make a few adjustments to meet the unique requirements of this research. First, despite being merely a sample of one, I have generated a large data set of more than 190,000 words in total rather than smaller data units. Second, only the retrospective essay would meet the plot criteria of a consumer narrative. While the contemporaneous data represent the accurate chronological sequence of events, a structured plot is subsequently absent. Nevertheless, the contemporaneous data can still be considered as a collection of smaller interlinked narrative fragments. But to get some distance between my role as a researcher and my role as informant, the hermeneutic data analysis first began a year after completing the data collection and nearly four months after finishing the data transcription. The temporal, mental and emotional distance also enabled me to bracket out any preconceptions that I may have had about myself.

The first step of the hermeneutic analysis involved a repeated full reading of the entire autoethnographic data transcripts to gain a first sense for the overall picture. Due to the *'plotless'* nature of the individual instances that I have collected over the full 21 months of self-observation, I have summarised the autoethnographic data in the extensive consumer narrative presented in Chapter 4 of this book, which reflects the chronological order of events while staying true to the emotional consumption experiences and feelings, to gain a better overview. Based on the early impressions, I have broken the contemporaneous data set down into more manageable, logically coherent chunks to be examined individually as *parts*. I, thereby, discovered that the best way of achieving it is the identification of different phases, through which the fan relationship has moved over time. On the surface, all identified phases seemed to share issues like the search for the latest information about Jena Malone, enjoying her acting performances in films, the purchase and collection of Jena Malone-related items (i.e. DVDs, magazine articles, posters and signed autographs) and her constantly experienced *'presence'* in my everyday life. However, their nature, the importance and emphasis placed on them and, most of all, the experienced, emotional intensity seemed to vary significantly within the context of each identified phase. A further part-to-whole reading supported the chosen breakdown of the data into (in themselves conclusive) temporal phases.

The next step involved acquiring a feeling for any ideas expressed within the accounts of the individual phases in order to understand them fully in their contextual complexity. At this point, I found that drawing on narrative transportation theory (Gerrig 1993; Green & Brock 2000) and, by extension, parasocial interaction theory (Horton & Wohl 1956; Rubin et al. 1985) as conceptual frameworks from social psychology and communication research would really help us to understand how and why a consumer may feel attached and devoted to a particular celebrity. In the third step, I started to *'extract key statements'*

(Goulding 2005) within the context of each individual fandom phase by identifying key sentences, specific phrases, wordings and even metaphors I used as an informant to describe a particular situation and/or Jena Malone fan experience. In so doing, I examined whether the extracted statements would indicate certain patterns and themes by comprehending them as the outcome of figure-ground relationships within their respective situational contexts. The emerging meaningful key themes were then brought in context with each other and the overall consumer narrative to be scrutinised further in order to identify key patterns of meaning (Goulding 2005; Thompson 1997).

While iteratively clustering recurrent significant statements into meaningful themes, however, I sought to prevent the abstraction and generalisation of the emerging emic themes into etic constructs, which would only inhibit us from understanding the true essence of an individual consumer's everyday lived fan experiences with one's admired film star/celebrity. Instead, I sought to integrate the emerging emic *'surface level'* themes into a coherent, thick and meaningful description (Geertz 1973; Goulding 2005) of my everyday lived fan relationship with Jena Malone as an emic *'higher level'* theme based on identified intertextual linkages between my own life-text and the mediated Jena Malone text (Wohlfeil & Whelan 2008, 2012). The aim is to reduce the thick description to the essential structure that would offer an explanation for the experienced fan relationship within the socio-cultural context of the individual's (= my) life-world, which includes my personal perceptions of the cultural settings, the lived body, the historicised self and my relationships to other people such as family, friends, colleagues and, obviously, Jena Malone in particular (Thompson 1998).

As the reader, however, you need to keep in mind that any interpretations that have emerged iteratively from the data through a hermeneutic analysis never represent the final and absolute findings, but can only be viewed as a snapshot of the phenomenon at a certain moment in time that continues to evolve further with every new reading and knowledge obtained after the initial study was completed (Gadamer 1989; Heidegger 1927). Moreover, any interpretations also represent only one set of possible explanations. Nonetheless, the hermeneutic interpretation of the autoethnographic data enables the research in this book to examine whether the findings offer any evidence that might support, question or challenge pre-established stereotypes, assumptions, (mis)conceptions and other popular beliefs about consumers' fan relationships with film stars/celebrities that scholars have in the past imposed on them while theorising fans and fandom from the convenience and safety of their distant outsider positions.

A brief road map for the next chapters of the book

The purpose of this book is to provide you, the reader, with truly holistic insights into the popular phenomenon of celebrity fandom from a genuine insider's perspective. Using my own fan relationship with film actress Jena Malone as a case study, I will in the following chapters describe and examine in the presented research how a consumer's everyday lived fan relationship with an admired celebrity develops, evolves and expresses itself over a period of time and what personal meaning(s) this emotional attachment to the celebrity may have for the respective individual. For that reason, the present book is in its essence also both a symbolical and literal journey of (self-)discovery. Now, to provide our journey with a sense of direction, here is a brief travel map through the rest of the book.

Before we can delve deeper into the different facets of a consumer's fan relationship with one's admired celebrity, it might be a good idea to give you first a critical overview of the current interdisciplinary fan studies literature. Chapter 2, therefore, takes a closer look at how fans have been portrayed, conceptualised, stigmatised, celebrated and studied across a variety of different academic disciplines and in the popular media. Following a brief introduction to the intertwined roles of the creative entertainment industries, celebrities and fans within our contemporary society, I critically examine how fans have been studied across a variety of academic disciplines with a view of presenting the first comprehensive and truly interdisciplinary taxonomy of how fans have been conceptualised in academic research. In so doing, I also investigate the historical origins and underlying ideological agendas behind some of the prevailing popular stereotypes, prejudices and misconceptions of fans in the popular and academic discourse. Finally, the chapter concludes with the suggestion that an alternative conceptualisation of fans is urgently needed, which puts the emphasis of fan studies back on the intricate relationship that fans form, experience and foster with the subject of their fandom.

Due to the lack of literature on celebrity fandom, I thoroughly examine in Chapter 3 how film stars and other celebrities have been conceptualised across such different academic disciplines as marketing, consumer research, film studies and media studies as well as what is already known in the academic literature on how film stars appeal to consumers. Because the study of film stars, by its very nature, is intrinsically linked to the study of film, I start the chapter by elaborating in detail on how the consumption of films has been studied across a number of different academic disciplines, whereby particular attention is obviously paid to film studies. Then, I examine how film stars and celebrities have primarily been constructed, conceptualised, studied and *'consumed'* as textual consumption objects or *'human brands'* by the film studios, managers/agents, film and media scholars, the media, consumers and even by some celebrities themselves rather than as real human beings. I conclude the chapter by proposing the use of narrative transportation theory as an alternative approach to obtain a genuine understanding of the lived meaning(s) that the personal engagement with a film star or celebrity may have for the individual consumer.

In Chapter 4, I present you, the reader, with the extensive autoethnographic consumer narrative of my own personal fan relationship with the film actress Jena Malone and how it has developed, evolved and manifested itself in my everyday life over a period of nearly two years. The purpose of this chapter and, especially, the presented consumer narrative as a genuine case study of real-lived celebrity fandom is to take you, the reader, on a narrative journey into the real life of a fan, which enables you to immerse yourself as a side-participant into a consumer's fan relationship with the admired film star/celebrity in everyday life and experience the emotional attachment in the same way as it is experienced by the fan. I believe that this way allows the reader to judge independently and without having already been inundated with readymade explanations and interpretations, as would normally be the case with traditional research approaches, whether the research findings that I discuss afterwards in Chapter 5 (or, alternatively, any previous fan conceptualisations examined in Chapter 2) would indeed offer insightful explanations that account for the concrete observed real-life fan experiences.

Based on the case study of the presented autoethnographic consumer narrative and data, I offer in Chapter 5 an alternative explanation as to how an individual film star/celebrity appeals to individual consumers as a real human being. Instead of treating film stars and celebrities just as *'semiotic receptacles of cultural meaning'* (Dyer 1998; McCracken 1989), as the film studies and celebrity endorsement literatures do, I conceptualise them in this chapter as real human beings and performers with a multi-constituted, polysemic consumer appeal, as revealed by the findings from the hermeneutic analysis of the autoethnographic data. In so doing, I unpack in this chapter the heteroglossia of how individual constituents of a celebrity offer a specific personal parasocial appeal to each individual consumer. Drawing thereby on the consumer narrative of my own everyday lived fan relationship with the film actress Jena Malone presented in Chapter 4, I explain how an individual film star or celebrity attracts the personal interest of individual consumers by appealing to them as (a) the creative performer, (b) the perceived *'private'* person behind the public performer, (c) the *'tangible manifestation'* of either through products, and (d) the social link to other like-minded consumers.

Based on this alternative explanation of the celebrity's polysemic, multi-constitutional consumer appeal, I discuss in Chapter 6 how and why individual consumers may develop an emotional attachment to a specific film star or celebrity. Drawing on and unpacking the individual facets of my own fan relationship with the film actress Jena Malone presented in Chapter 4, I critically examine and explore how a consumer's personal lived fan experiences derive from and engage with the admired celebrity's personal polysemic appeal under the corresponding headings (a) admiring the celebrity as a performer, (b) adoring the celebrity as the perceived private person, (c) 'taking possession' of the celebrity as a tangible manifestation, (d) sharing versus non-sharing the celebrity in participatory fandom, and (e) 'living' with the celebrity as an important part of one's everyday life. Drawing thereby on narrative transportation theory, I provide an explanation of how a consumer's parasocial fan experiences derive from one's personal engagement with the admired film star's films, acting performances, public appearances and *'private person'* based on the presented case study (and the corresponding observations with other celebrities). The latter would essentially be the consumer's own intertextual reading and interpretation of what s/he perceives to be relevant and *'reliable'* media texts. This can even lead to a feeling of *'knowing'* the celebrity like a personal friend.

Chapter 7 brings our journey of discovery into celebrity fandom and the everyday lived experience of a fan finally to its conclusion by reiterating why a reconceptualisation of fans is needed. This reconceptualisation would put the emphasis of fan studies back on the emotional attachment that consumers form, experience and foster with their precious subject of admiration – and away from the narrow traditional focus on participatory fandom or, worse, pathology that have dominated the fan studies discourse exclusively for decades. Moreover, I suggest that it is also time for stardom and celebrity scholars to put the actual human being and artist back into the film star, rock/pop star and any other celebrity and to discuss them as real-living, complex individuals rather than merely as interchangeable, culturally-constructed semiotic textual constructs that serve mainly as canvasses for ideological discourses. Hence, I also reiterate the benefits of taking a insider perspective in order to gain a genuine understanding of what meaning celebrity fandom has for the individual consumer. Finally, although this book is not directly concerned with serving the managerial interests of managers and talent agents, I still outline in this chapter what implications my research's findings may have for our understanding of celebrity endorsements or the management of creative talent and their interaction with their audiences and, especially, their fans.

But now, the time has come for us to go onto our backpacker journey of discovery by walking on unbeaten paths into the uncharted territory of celebrity fandom ...

Note

1 The same is also true for my temporary attraction to female musicians like Nena, Susanna Hoffs, Heather Nova or Alizee, whose music at the time I enjoyed listening to.

2   The Dangerous Lives of Fans

Stereotypes and stigmas

Creative industries, celebrities and fans in contemporary culture

Ever since the early days of the film, music and professional sports industries, film stars, athletes and any other celebrities have captured the imagination of their audiences and played an important role in our popular culture (Turner 2004). But as incredible as it may sound, despite the broad attention that both celebrities and their fans generally receive in our popular media discourse, academic literature dedicated to the study of celebrity fandom has remained scarce to this very day. This deficit is the more disappointing, as the creative entertainment industries have not only played an essential role as acculturation agents in many societies' popular culture (Barbas 2001; Hirschman 2000a), but have also consistently been some of the commercially biggest and most successful industries in the world (Epstein 2005, 2012; Hennig-Thurau & Wruck 2000). And in addition to their very own production outputs, these industries have also spawned, feed into and depend on a network of other billion dollar industries, which range from glossy gossip magazines and publicists over various kinds of merchandising products to theme parks and tourism (Beeton 2015; Hackley & Hackley 2015) and which have all prospered from satisfying our general public interest in the *'glamorous and scandalous'* lives of film stars and starlets, rock/pop stars, athletes, models and any other celebrities (Gabler 1998).

Celebrities, therefore, perform not only a vital role as the creative industries' most visible faces, but their strong media presence also gives a good indication of how important to contemporary consumer culture they have become (Marshall 1997). Contradicting Boorstin's (1961) much-cited derogatory definition that celebrities are merely *'people who are only famous for being famous'*, their respective claims to fame are actually quite diverse and based on either their artistic-creative talent, their professional occupation, their personal relationships with (other) famous people (i.e. spouse, offspring or love affair) or their mere notoriety for an *'outrageous'*, *'scandalous'* public life-style (Barron 2015; McDonald 2003). But whatever their personal claim to fame may be, each individual celebrity's popularity and success is still dependent on the personal relationship that they develop with their most loyal admirers – their fans.

Despite a certain tendency in the popular discourse to stigmatise fans as *'gullible'* and *'odd'* (Jenson 1992), celebrity fandom is actually quite a common social phenomenon. When engaging with celebrity culture, most consumers obviously tend to have only a fleeting interest in the glamour, scandals and private lives of film stars and celebrities per se and enjoy primarily the exchange of gossip with other like-minded individuals (Hermes 2006) – rather than to invest any strong feelings in the admiration for a specific celebrity. However, some consumers do indeed develop and experience a stronger emotional attachment to their favourite celebrity and, subsequently, become what are commonly known as *fans* (Leets et al. 1995; O'Guinn 1991). We just need to take a careful look around us to find the fans of film actors, rock/pop artists, TV personalities, athletes, models, novelists and reality TV stars virtually everywhere and across all walks of life. They even have the audacity to admire the creative works of their favourite celebrity in broad daylight and full public view, share with each other the latest information and gossip obtained from the media, wait for hours at premieres to catch a glimpse of their idols and passionately collect the beloved celebrity's hand-signed autographs and any other memorabilia (Barron 2015; Henry & Caldwell 2007). Furthermore, these consumers do not hesitate to come to the aid of their adored celebrity in *'times of need'*, such as receiving bad reviews, relationship problems, illnesses, addictions, court hearings and even to protect them against the threat of abusive stalkers (!) – as we could witness in the cases of Michael Jackson, Robert Downey Jr., Maire Brennan, Jade Goody, Owen Wilson, Lindsay Lohan, Anne Hathaway, Jennifer Lawrence or Taylor Swift to name just a few. Hence, it is only fair to say that fans may play an equally important role in our contemporary culture as the very film actors, musicians, athletes and all other celebrities that they so enthusiastically, if not at times even obsessively admire.

Fans: the rise of evil?

It should therefore come as no real surprise that fans have also become a *'soft target'* for the very same cultural critics (i.e. Adorno & Horkheimer 2006; Boorstin 1961; Gabler 1998; Schickel 1985; Thorp 1939) and their many followers, who have pretty much since the early days of the creative industries been on a tireless crusade to portray popular media consumption and, especially, celebrity culture religiously as the apocalyptic embodiments by which today's *'excessive capitalist consumer culture'* is dulling our minds and, thereby, threatening our freedom and the very fabric of our social, cultural, intellectual and psychological well-being. Their efforts in convincing us of popular culture's inherent perils have been so relentless, especially over the past 40 years, that we could easily come to the conclusion that we are about to face another Sodom and Gomorrah, if we do not repent our ways towards a more *'natural'* and puritan mode of consumption that ideally takes place outside the *'exploitative'* capitalist marketplace (Gabler 1998; Schickel 1985).

Hence, the very notion that there are actually consumers out there, who would voluntarily choose to forfeit the *'educated spiritual-intellectual'* appreciation for the high arts and invest instead a large amount of their mental energy, time and financial resources into the *'primitive, dull and tasteless'* popular mass culture (Boorstin 1961; Bourdieu 1984; Giles 2006), must really be a terrifying idea for these critics. For them, the only acceptable logical explanation to make sense of such *'irrational'* behaviour, therefore, is that the consumers in question (= *fans*), due to their *'inherent gullible nature'* and overall *'lack of critical awareness'*, must obviously have fallen prey to the manipulative powers of the popular mass media (Adorno & Horkheimer 2006; Gabler 1998; Schickel 1985). Underpinning their line of argument is the concept of the *'vulnerable audience'*, which implies that consumers would be highly susceptible to the influence of media images and the *'false values'* they provide (Boorstin 1961) and that, with increasing consumption, they would even no longer be able to distinguish between the *'fictive media content'* and the *'real world'* (Baudrillard 1970; Gabler 1998).

Given that cultural critics have expressed such vocal disgust and contempt for fans, celebrity culture and the popular media overall, it seems quite ironic, if not even strange, that much of their critical discourse is voiced and spread through the very same popular media they despise – often with the primary aim of enhancing their own reputation (= *'fame'*). At the same time, the popular media, too, have welcomed, embraced and promoted, if not even often initiated these derisive images of celebrities and their fans in an effort to increase their circulations with sensational stories about celebrity-obsessed teenagers screaming in front of hotels and at film premieres, childish nerds at ComicCon and SciFi conventions, violent football fans and psychopathic stalkers (Duffett 2013; Jenson 1992); even though they are, in the process, criticising and ridiculing in essence (parts of) the very audiences on which they commercially depend (Barron 2015). Therefore, while the tabloids and entertainment press regularly slam popular art, celebrity and fan cultures self-righteously as anti-social and dangerous to society, they also stimulate, feed and profit heavily and quite openly from them.

But the tabloids and gossip media are not the only popular media that have embraced these representations of fans, as the very same stereotyped images of fans often serve as story or character material for the film and TV industries, whose entire commercial existence, ironically, is largely dependent on the fans' appreciation and true enjoyment of their products (Barbas 2001). Apart from the much-cited *Saturday Night Live* sketch, in which guest host William Shatner is pestered with Star Trek-specific questions by some exaggerated, stereotypical nerdy *'Trekkers'* (= Star Trek fans), who seem to live in their parents' basements, know even the most irrelevant miniscule detail of every episode and buy everything related to the show, until he responded with the now famous phrase *"Get a life!"* (Jenkins 1992), Lewis (1992) shows how several film stories have portrayed fans as childish nerds (i.e. Jerry Lewis's gullible Anita Eckberg fan in *Hollywood or Bust*, 1956), as social misfits whose fandom severely interferes with a romantic love life (i.e. Jimmy Fallon's baseball fan in *The Perfect Catch*, 2005) and much too often as dangerous psychopaths (i.e. Desiree Nosbusch in *Der Fan*, 1982, Robert De Niro in *The Fan*, 1996, and Kathy Bates in *Misery*, 1990).

A particularly dominant and curious feature of this critical discourse is that ideology-informed cultural critics seek to present a dichotomy between what they view as the *'worship of false heroes'* in today's *'excessive, corrupted and sexualised'* capitalist consumer culture and a romanticised past, where consumer behaviour adhered to puritan moral values and public acknowledgement was granted based on great achievements and special skills (Boorstin 1961; Thorp 1939). Both academic literature and popular media have thereby discussed fandom and the *'obsession'* with celebrities always as quite recent, contemporary social phenomena that pose a growing menace to our culture and society. But contradicting this common belief, fandom is, historically speaking, anything but a new phenomenon and, in fact, at least as old as most creative entertainment industries themselves (Barbas 2001; Schmidt-Lux 2010). Indeed, ever since the motion pictures began in the mid-1890s to show convincing impressions of life on the silver screen, consumers across the world have imagined the film industry as a dream factory, where nothing seems impossible and even the wildest dreams may come true (Gaines 2000).

Although their enthusiasm may have shifted over time from an initial technology-focused curiosity[1] over a fascination with the art of filmmaking to an obsession with the glamour of Hollywood, film fans also have in all those years felt enchanted by the magical worlds and aesthetic images that films offer them (Barbas 2001; Cousins 2011). Moreover, although consumers have been fascinated with the acting performances and private lives of film stars since the very early days of the Hollywood star system (Studlar 2016), leading theatre actors on Broadway or the London West End have already enjoyed the support of loyal and enthusiastic followers in the mid-19th century, while novelists, poets, opera singers, composers or the infamous castrati were adored by audiences in Italy, France, Germany and Austria throughout the 18th and 19th century (Gabler 1998; Glass 2016). But despite the film industry still being in its infancy, it was film audiences in particular that caught the wrath of social reformers like the Christian Temperance Union in the US, and were picked by them as a *'soft target'* in a desperate attempt to stem the tide of social and cultural change that came with economic progress in industrialised societies.

To support their condemnation of films as an *'evil menace'* that corrupts people's souls and their moral integrity, the social reformers cited numerous news reports, in which watching films had supposedly tempted young women into a life of promiscuity and vice, dissuaded young men from *'doing the right thing'* and literally scared *'decent folk'* to death with their realistic images on screen (Barbas 2001; Gabler 1998). But although it turned out that, in absence of any real evidence, the Christian Temperance Union had actually fabricated and planted most of these reports in numerous local newspapers themselves, their claims gained credibility by having some prominent psychologists among their ranks like the Harvard Psychology Professor Hugo Munsterberg (Barbas 2001). To provide solid *'scientific support'* for the social reformists' ideological views, Munsterberg (1916) proposed and advanced his theoretical concept of the *'vulnerable audience'* by which he portrayed all film audiences[2] indiscriminately as impressionable, uneducated, uncritical and passive viewers that, *'like little children'*, would easily be deceived by films into mistaking the fake film realities for the real world; a view that has dominated the ideological critical discourse on media audiences and, especially, fans ever since.

Munsterberg (1916), a devoted puritan, was convinced that films are *'like a drug'* that heighten emotions, reduce inhibitions, alter the senses and cause pathological delusions among the *'addicted'* viewer. Historical evidence, however, clearly shows that even the first film audiences were already well aware of how the films' visual effects work, exchanged their knowledge of film technology with each other and discussed how visual effects or other facets of the film-making process could be improved in a growing number of self-published fanzines (Barbas 2001). They thereby laid the foundation for some of today's highly regarded film journals and the academic discipline of film studies. But although there has actually never been any empirical evidence to support the vulnerable audience concept, it has not stopped cultural critics from taking up and reiterating its central ideas with astonishing regularity as 'undisputed facts' ever since (i.e. Adorno & Horkheimer 2006; Boorstin 1961; Gabler 1998; Schickel 1985). And since those ideas are constantly recycled, they are nowadays taken as 'proven facts' in our academic and popular discourse and shape our stereotyped conceptualisations and views of celebrities and fans.

Fan or fanatic: what actually is a fan?

While the term *'fan'* is often used quite liberally by the media these days to cover all kinds of audiences, spectators or mere buyers of CDs/DVDs, and concert- or cinema-tickets, it is still the devastating picture of fans, which the academic and popular discourse has historically painted, that is still dominating the common public image of fans. Due to the stigma attached to fandom, it is hardly surprising that consumers often feel the urge to distance themselves from this fan image (Cusack et al. 2003). Indeed, when asked to explain or justify their own dedication to a certain TV show, film or music, or their strong emotional attachment to a certain celebrity or sports team, many consumers tend to reply immediately with statements like *"I'm not one of THOSE fans who ..."* in an effort to highlight their *'normality'* and to distance themselves from the *'other, abnormal fan'* (Brooker 2005; Grossberg 1992). And, as the autoethnographic narrative in Chapter 4 shows, I responded in a similar way on several occasions – especially in my first year of becoming a Jena Malone fan. Even the fact that I am *'confessing'* to my own fan relationship with the film actress Jena Malone carries some connotations to a *'coming out'* or attending an AA meeting.

However, during the course of my research, I have also received a number of *'well-meaning'* suggestions from reviewers, who felt so uneasy with the study's topic, content and approach that they advised me, *'for my own good'*, to close this research sooner rather than later, leave my *'fannish inclination'* behind and devote myself instead to *'proper'* and *'worthier'* personal and academic pursuits.

Since these kinds of responses can partially be explained by the negative connotations that seem to come with the term *'fandom'* itself, it is necessary to clarify now what a fan actually is and what the etymological and historical origins of the term are. According to Leets et al. (1995), the most popular, undisputed and widely shared public belief is that the term *'fan'* is an abbreviation of the word *'fanatic'*, which in return derived from the Latin word *'fanaticus'* – meaning *'inspired by a deity'*. This view seems to gain additional credibility by the fact that the Greek translation of fanatic is *'entheos'*, from which the contemporary word *'enthusiasm'* originates (Smith et al. 2007). And because the term *'fanatic'* refers since the 1650s to individuals who subscribe to extreme religious or political views with zealous and intense uncritical devotion (Thorne & Bruner 2006), it requires little imagination to see where our negative pictures of fans come from.

The only problem with this popular association between *'fan'* and *'fanatic'*, however, is that, historically, it is false and was in fact conceived, advanced and spread by the Christian Temperance Union in the late-19th century with the aim to discredit, first, spectators of the new sport baseball and, later, film audiences (Barbas 2001). The true origin of the term *'fan'* stems instead from the English word *'to fancy'*, which means *'to experience an intense liking for someone or something'*, as in the late-18th century boxing aficionados among the English and Irish working-classes were often called *'fancies'* or *'fances'* – meaning 'people who like ("fancy") to watch and bet on boxing fights' (Dickson 1989). During the mid-19th century, Irish immigrants brought the term *'fances'* to the US, where it shortened over time to *'fans'* and referred initially to boxing spectators, but was soon extended to the audiences of popular theatre productions as well. A particular group of such popular theatre audiences, the Bowery Boys, may have in light of the so-called Astor Palace riots of 1849 the dubious honour to be probably the first hooligans in history[3] (Gabler 1998).

Nonetheless, the contemporary concept of a *'fan'* (or *'fandom'* in general) emerged in the late-19th century and referred, at first, to enthusiastic supporters of the new US sport baseball (Dickson 1989; Leets et al. 1995) and, soon thereafter, all other team sport supporters around the globe – especially in relation to soccer. It is at this stage that social reformers of the Christian Temperance Union sought to establish a mental association between fans and fanatics – and succeeded, as even the Oxford Dictionary accepted this definition for fact. The unintended irony is that the social reformers were the true 'fanatics'. With the emerging film industry in the 1890s and the arrival of the Hollywood star system in the 1920s, the term *'fan'* expanded from sports spectators also to enthusiastic admirers of the performing arts, popular culture and celebrities (Gabler 1998). Nowadays, it is only fair to say that everyone has, at least once in their lifetime, been a fan of something – be it a specific sports team, an athlete, a rock/pop star, a film star, any other celebrity, a particular TV show, film or any other kind of leisure pursuit (Duffett 2013).

While many consumers are fans of specific novelists like JK Rowling or Stephen King (Brown 2007), even literary icons like Jane Austen, James Joyce or Lewis Carroll who passed away a long time ago, are still admired by devoted fan communities (Brooker 2005). But due to their adherence and sense of belonging to high-brow culture coupled with an inherent *'snobbish'* disdain for popular culture, these committed devotees of literary icons prefer to call them-selves *'connoisseurs'* or *'aficionados'* who meet each other in serious *'societies'* (Brooker 2005). Nonetheless, despite this blunt effort to distant themselves from *'those other fans'* that belong to low-brow culture and meet up in gullible fan-clubs or at conventions (Kozinets 2001), they actually engage in very similar behaviours such as the devoted collection of cherished works, artefacts and memorabilia associated with the sacred subject of desire (Belk et al. 1989), a hunger for gathering and updating one's knowledge of the subject and even going on a pilgrimage to the homes, landmarks or other sites associated with the writer or his/her work (Brooker 2005; Hede & Thyne 2010).

Thus, some useful definitions proposed by Thorne and Bruner (2006) may help us to differentiate between fans and fanatics. Thorne and Bruner (2006) define a *'fan'* as *'a person with an overwhelming liking or interest in a par-ticular person, group, activity, artwork, fashion-style or idea, whose behaviour is typically viewed by others as unusual or unconventional but does NOT violate prevailing social norms'*. In sharp contrast, they define a *'fanatic'* as *'a person with overwhelming or excessive liking or interest in a particular person, group, activity, artwork or idea that exhibits extreme behaviour viewed by others as dysfunctional, dangerous and violating social norms'*. However, while Thorne and Bruner (2006) define *'fandom'* as a subculture composed of like-minded fans with a shared interest, other scholars (i.e. Barbas 2001; Kozinets 2001; Wohlfeil & Whelan 2011, 2012) disagree and view it instead as an umbrella term that comprises all fan activities, practices and experiences of individuals and communities. For that reason, I define *'fandom'* hereby as *'the overwhelming interest, liking or emotional attachment to a particular person, group, activity, artwork, fashion-style or idea expressed in personal or communal consumption activities, practices and experiences'*. Nevertheless, despite this clear objective distinction between fans and fanatics, we are still left with the question of why fans continue to be on the receiving end of ridicule, stereotyping and bad press within both the academic and the popular discourse. Thus, a closer look at how different academic disciplines have studied fans and fandom and with what underlying agenda may provide some explanations.

Fans and fandom as subjects of academic research

Apart from the occasional sociological-theoretical essays and treatises by cul-tural critics and psychologists (i.e. Adorno & Horkheimer 2006; Baudrillard 1970; Schickel 1985; Thorp 1939) that sought to expand Munsterberg's (1916) concept of the vulnerable audience onto popular consumer culture in general, academic scholars had until recently shown very little interest in the actual study of fans and fandom – despite having been such a widespread, global consump-tion phenomenon for more than 140 years. Eventually, it was events like the rise of hooliganism in British football during the 1970s, John Hinckley's assassination attempt on US President Ronald Reagan in order to *'prove his love'* for the actress Jodie Foster (Krämer 2003) or the murders of John Lennon and Mexican singer Selena Quintanilla by self-proclaimed fans in the early 1980s that suddenly caught the eyes of academic scholars from such diverse academic disciplines as social psychology, sociology, forensic sciences, sports studies, media studies, marketing or consumer research (Duffett 2013). Because of their different backgrounds in terms of areas of expertise and academic schools of thought, however, those scholars have thereby investigated fans and fandom not only from very different perspectives and with very different research agendas in mind, but also relied on very different research methodologies that are dominant in their respective disciplines and range from scientific inquiry over critical discourse analysis to ethnography.

Due to the long history of sports spectatorship, the study of sports fans is the primary focus of scholars in the academic fields of sports psychology, sports studies and leisure research. While early research looked at hooligans and sports fans engaging in compulsive behaviour, most contemporary studies seek to understand the motivations and social dynamics among sports spectators (Murrell & Dietz 1992). On the other hand, it is no secret that marketing and business scholars are mainly interested in identifying the economic value that fans may promise to deliver them as brand-loyal consumers (Thorne & Bruner 2006). Hence, marketing researchers tend to study fans primarily as homogeneous, very brand loyal and commercially attractive market segments that seem to represent ideal target audiences for a host of marketing activities (Hunt et al. 1999).

Academic research of fans within the field of social psychology closely builds on Munsterberg's (1916) original work on the vulnerable audience and, thereby, pays very close attention to extreme types of celebrity fans. Indeed, in light of the earlier mentioned events, social psychologists started to develop an interest in identifying, investigating and profiling the rationales of psychologically disturbed fans for approaching, harassing and even causing bodily or mental harm to celebrities with the aim of preventing potential future threats or attacks (Dietz et al. 1991). While those original studies went to great lengths to differentiate between this miniscule minority of psychotic, delusional fanatics and the absolute majority of normal fans (Dietz et al. 1991; Leets et al. 1995), however, the later research of *'celebrity worshippers'* within the discipline of social psychology failed to make such distinctions and generalised the findings instead to all fans indiscriminately (McCutcheon et al. 2003, 2006). In fact, those later (rather dubious) studies even argue that being a fan would indicate an inherent character flaw within the individual that is linked to some form of mental illness and may even be genetic (Maltby et al. 2004). Their obvious intention is to cater to the century-old popular stereotypes of fans being gullible nerds or pathological-obsessive psychopaths presented by the popular media (Jenson 1992) and even promoted by the film industry itself (Lewis 1992).

Since the academic discipline of film studies essentially evolved from the discourse among early film fans more than 100 years ago (Barbas 2001), this heritage would normally imply a certain interest among film scholars to study the fans of films and/or film stars as dedicated film audiences. Yet, film scholars have paid virtually no attention to either of them at all. One possible explanation for this scant interest might be that film scholars have sought for some time for film to be recognised and included into the canon of high-brow culture as an equal to literature, theatre, opera and the arts in terms of aesthetic status and cultural value. And because fandom has traditionally been viewed as a working-class phenomenon strongly linked to the *'tasteless'* consumption of popular low-brow culture, a research interest in such *'uneducated'* audiences (Bourdieu 1984) would just be counter-productive to achieving this overall goal. Moreover, film studies focus exclusively on examining films within the context of the cinematic experience, while media studies are primarily concerned with popular mass media and television (shows).

Therefore, fan studies have been *'delegated'* in their entirety to the *'unwanted offspring'* of media studies. While much of the early research of media audiences and fans was dominated by the ideology-informed views of cultural critics (i.e. Adorno & Horkheimer 2006; Boorstin 1961; Bourdieu 1984; Schickel 1985) that portrayed them as gullible nerds, deprived working-class and vulnerable victims of popular culture, Horton and Wohl's (1956) parasocial interaction theory inspired media scholars since the 1980s to investigate how and why TV viewers form and maintain emotional relationships either with newscasters and TV personalities (Houlberg 1984; Rubin et al. 1985) or with TV shows and fictional characters (Bielby et al. 1999; Rubin & McHugh 1987). From the early-1990s, the research focus shifted towards the social dynamics within the participatory fandom associated with specific cult films and cult-TV shows as well as the special and unique nature of the often visibly expressed fan behaviour, whereby *Star Trek* has attracted most of the scholarly interest (Jankovich 2002; Jenkins 1992) rivalled only by *Star Wars*, *The X-Files* or *Doctor Who* (Hills 2002; Shefrin 2004).

However, despite celebrity culture being their central area of research, it is interesting to note that media scholars studying fans of celebrities have remained extremely rare, while the celebrity literature has barely dedicated more than a paragraph to fans until recently either (Barron 2015; Redmond 2014). Instead, fans are usually presented as engaging and relating virtually exclusively with the media characters rather than the actual actors who portray them (Hills 2002; Jenkins 1992). But while film scholars completely rely on critical theory approaches to study film and stardom, media scholars have been open to other research approaches besides the still dominant critical theory, with ethnography being a common alternative. Following similar patterns as sports and leisure studies or media studies and often borrowing from those literatures, consumer researchers have also begun at the same time to show a growing interest in both sports and media fans, but with a much stronger emphasis on co-creative, participatory consumption subcultures (Derbaix et al. 2002; Kozinets 1997, 2001) that is influenced by a growing interest in consumer tribes (Cova 1998; McAlexander et al. 2002). Nevertheless, besides my own publications and this book, only a handful of individual studies in consumer research (Banister & Cocker 2014; Henry & Caldwell 2007; Hewer & Hamilton 2012a; O'Guinn 1991; Radford & Bloch 2012) have actually taken a look at the fans of film stars, pop stars or other celebrities.

It should therefore come as no surprise that, because the conceptual understanding of fans and fandom is driven by the underlying personal and disciplinary agenda of the respective academic scholars (Smith et al. 2007), the current interdisciplinary body of fan studies literature still lacks a coherent interpretation of what actually constitutes fandom in the first place. Also, to describe it as *'interdisciplinary'* is only true in the sense that fans are a subject of research in different academic disciplines, but fails to notice that very little cross-referencing is actually happening between different academic bodies of literature. Indeed, most fan scholars are deeply rooted within the discipline-specific research agenda and tradition of their own respective academic fields and fail to look beyond their boundaries.

Approaching a taxonomy of fans

Although the present study in this book is located within the marketing and consumer research literature, such a research of a consumer's emotional attachment to one's beloved celebrity calls for a truly interdisciplinary examination beyond its disciplinary boundaries by bringing together the current knowledge of fandom from across a range of other academic disciplines. Hence, a comprehensive overview of how fans have been conceptualised across all the different discipline-specific bodies of literature is now required. Unfortunately, the few existing fandom taxonomies tend to be restricted to specific academic disciplines like marketing or media studies and are usually limited to either ranking the different levels of fan commitment or providing a historical overview of paradigm developments within the context and boundaries of that specific academic discipline. For that purpose, I have reviewed the fan studies literature across various academic disciplines and eventually identified within them seven distinct conceptualisations of fans, which I present now in the following taxonomy.

Fans as target markets

Despite having traditionally paid scant attention to the study of film consumption, film stars and any other celebrities, marketing and business research has recognised the existence and economic value of fans as consumers for some time (Thorne & Bruner 2006). However, marketing practitioners and academics alike tend to regard fans merely as a commercially attractive, homogeneous and very brand-loyal market segment that would represent an ideal target audience for a host of marketing activities (Hunt et al. 1999). Indeed, fans are not only understood as being extremely brand loyal to the subjects of their admiration, but also as willing to spend large amounts of time, money and other resources on their devotion (Thorne & Bruner 2006), which would involve the continuous and indiscriminate hunt for and acquisition of relevant material objects (Banister & Cocker 2014; Derbaix et al. 2002). The fan, then, tends to cherish and sacralise these material possessions as a physical link to the admired celebrity (Newman et al. 2011), to the supported sports team (Derbaix et al. 2002) or the media text (Brown 2007; Elberse 2014). Hence, with regard to celebrity fandom, marketing researchers are primarily focused on identifying opportunities for positioning a celebrity's products in a way that meets the needs of his/her fans (Brown 2005; Thomson 2006). For example, in the case of a new film's forthcoming release, the fans of individual cast members or the director should be made aware well in advance through strategic media coverage (i.e. film trailers, official websites, press releases, cast interviews on TV and in magazines, etc.) to arouse their interest and expectations, so that they do not want to miss the film (Kerrigan 2010). In addition, marketers are obviously reminded by these studies that they must never forget to tie-in the film with appropriate merchandising to be sold across various retail outlets (Brown 2005; Elberse 2014).

The vast majority of marketing and business scholars, however, still find it extremely difficult, if not impossible, to view films and celebrities as brands in themselves – and not just as mere convenient promotion vehicles. Therefore, it is hardly surprising that most marketing and business studies focusing on fans as target markets are seeking to exploit their emotional attachment to their favourite celebrities for the marketing of other, completely unrelated products (McCracken 1989; Thomson 2006). The underlying assumption is that fans would show such a high enduring involvement in their favourite celebrity or film star that they constantly and indiscriminately search for any information connected to the subject of their admiration (Thorne & Bruner 2006) and thereby happily process any product information positively, which is either directly or indirectly brought into context with their admired celebrity (Banister & Cocker 2014; Thomson 2006). While the direct approach of bringing products into context with celebrities is through endorsement (McCracken 1989; Erdogan 1999), the indirect approach usually involves product placement in films or TV shows (Russell & Stern 2006; Wiles & Danielova 2009). The major problem with academic research that conceptualises fans merely as target audiences is that they provide no explanation for or any real insights into fandom as a consumption experience, what encourages a consumer to develop an emotional attachment to a particular film star or celebrity in the first place or how fandom expresses itself in consumer behaviour. Due to the primary focus on the commercial exploitation of fandom, marketing researchers are primarily interested in the segmentation of fans into specific categories based on general demographic or psychographic variables (Hunt et al. 1999). Thorne and Bruner's (2006) study of the characteristics of consumer fandom and fanaticism and Thomson's (2006) study of the antecedents of consumers' emotional attachment to celebrities have been the first few exceptions to-date.

Fans as spectators and supporters

The public media discourse has always had the habit of using the words *'spectators'*, *'supporters'* and *'fans'* synonymously to describe all audiences attending sports events or rock/pop concerts, listening to a musician's records or reading a novelist's books. Because of the long historical link between sports audiences and their teams, scholars within leisure research, sports studies and sports psychology were the first to equate spectators with fans. Sports fandom is thereby understood as a strong enduring interest in a certain sport or sports in general, which is expressed in the spectatorship of professional sports (Dietz-Uhler et al. 2000). Although hooliganism and violent sports 'supporters' commanded at the beginning the most attention from academics, the emphasis changed by the early-1990s and quickly shifted towards two more *'normal'* forms of sports fandom – sports participation and, in particular, sports spectatorship. In the process, fandom relating to sports spectatorship has received growing attention among marketing (Fillis & Mackay 2014; Hunt et al. 1999) and consumer researchers (Derbaix et al. 2002; Richardson & Turley 2006, 2008) as well.

Having left the extremism of hooligans behind, most sports scholars are nowadays interested in the motivations of sports fans for supporting specific sports and teams, whether gender differences influence such support, in what way fandom is expressed towards insiders and outsiders, or how it manifests itself in consumer behaviour. Hunt et al. (1999) found that sports and, especially, team support develops at an early age through acculturation and is influenced by a child's exposure to specific sports, by a child's ability to play the sport, by the preferences of parents, siblings and/or friends and by local media attention to the sport. Since sports fandom seems to continue through most of an individual's life (even up to seniority and retirement), sports scholars have proposed two main theories to explain different levels of identification and passion among fans. The first theory understands the consumer's emotional attachment to a sports team as an extension of one's self (Richardson & Turley 2006). An identification with a specific sports team, often from the local area where the consumer has grown up, is essentially a means for fans to express among others their belonging to a certain social group within a region (i.e. AC Milan supporters come from Milan's middle-class, while Inter Milan supporters are from Milan's working-class) and their loyalty to their hometown represented by the team (Murrell & Dietz 1992; Richardson & Turley 2006). The identification with the team is subsequently signalled to other supporters and outsiders through the wearing of team-related merchandising, such as official replica team-jerseys, scarves, flags and the sacralised team colours (Derbaix et al. 2002).

Since the strong identification with a sports team expresses and even enhances one's self-concept, it also involves a certain degree of self-monitoring, whereby the fan perceives the success or failure of the supported sports team as a reflection of one's own self-identity (Hyman & Sierra 2010; Richardson & Turley 2008). Hence the second (and widely popular) theory is the intertwined idea of

BIRGing and *CORFing* (Murrell & Dietz 1992). BIRG stands here for *'basking-in-reflected-glory'*, which means that fans identify themselves with successful teams or athletes to enhance their own self-esteem. As fans view themselves and their support as an extension to the team or athlete, which gives the players strength and courage on the pitch to fight on and to try even harder (in soccer often called *'the 12th man'*), they experience and celebrate positive outcomes for their team as their personal successes as well and associate themselves even more with the team (Richardson & Turley 2006, 2008). Indeed, many great sports teams often attract a strong following of supporters in times of success, who in turn are extremely despised as *'gloryhunters'* by hardcore fans (Derbaix et al. 2002; Richardson & Turley 2008). If the team suffers negative outcomes, however, fans who aim to enhance their self-esteem engage in *'cutting-off-reflected-failure'*, which means that they disassociate themselves from the losing team or athlete due to disappointed expectations like rats leaving a sinking ship (Murrell & Dietz 1992).

But although the theory of BIRGing and CORFing sounds somewhat convincing, Richardson and Turley (2006, 2008) have found that it fails to account for the fandom of true supporters, who often stand by their team in good times and in bad times. Indeed, sports fans, who strongly identify with their team as an extended part of the self, are unlikely to CORF on their team and feel even closer to other hardcore fans due to a shared commitment. Whether fans now identify with their favourite team to express their self-identity and social belonging or whether they identify with the team to nourish their self-esteem through BIRGing strongly depends on the nature and intensity of their commitment. Being a team supporter is thereby not only driven by different motivations (intrinsic in the former case and extrinsic in case of the latter) but also reflected in different types of fans. Hunt et al. (1999) distinguish between five categories of sports fans – temporary fans, local fans, devoted fans, fanatical fans and dysfunctional fans.

Temporary fans do not view *'being-a-fan'* as important to their self-identity and, therefore, show only a high situational involvement in the team or sport that only lasts for the time of the match or competition (including the media coverage) (Hunt et al. 1999). Afterwards, these supporters return to other things in their ordinary lives (Fillis & Mackay 2014). Therefore, internalising a team's success through BIRGing seems to come naturally to this type of fans. Similarly, they would have no difficulties in case of failure to distance themselves from the team again. For that reason, they are also strongly despised by hardcore fans as *'gloryhunters'* (Derbaix et al. 2002; Richardson & Turley 2008). Local fans, on the other hand, are geographically bound, as they understand their fan support for the local team primarily as an expression of loyalty towards their hometown. However, while Hunt et al. (1999) argue that leaving the area would lead to a diminished enthusiasm for one's home team, I would rather suggest that the longer the distance and time away from one's hometown the stronger would the consumer's identification with one's home team become part of a nostalgic attachment to one's roots (Holbrook 1993).

Devoted fans feel strongly attached to their favourite team and like to communicate this passion to others. Because of their high enduring involvement in the favourite team and the sport in general, devoted fans enjoy the search for and discussion of new and old news with like-minded fans in public (Richardson & Turley 2008). Moreover, material possessions associated to the team and their systematic collection play an important role in the devoted fan's life (Belk et al. 1989). While BIRGing may occur to some extent, devoted fans are unlikely to engage in CORFing (Murrell & Dietz 1992). Fanatical fans go even a step further than devoted fans. While devoted fans place their fandom within the context of having an everyday life beyond the team or sport, the team, sport and fandom play a central role in the fanatical fan's existence (Hunt et al. 1999). Fanatical fans not only buy and collect team-related memorabilia, but also dedicate shrines to their team or turn even an entire room into a fan museum (Holt 1998; Richardson & Turley 2006). Fanatical fans are thereby willing to invest substantial amounts of time and money into their fandom in order to obtain relevant or even rare team-related items (Richardson & Turley 2008). While the consumer behaviour of fanatical fans can be called obsessive and out of the ordinary, they are unlikely to cause any harm other than putting maybe some strains on their social relationships with less enthusiastic family members and friends (Hunt et al. 1999).

Dysfunctional fans, however, virtually build their entire existence around their favourite sports team as their only method of self-identification and, subsequently, have severe difficulties in living an everyday life outside fandom (Hyman & Sierra 2010). Thus, Hunt et al. (1999) differentiate between fanatical and dysfunctional fans not so much by the degree to which they engage in fandom, but more by the degree to which the expressed devotion to the team is anti-social, disruptive, deviant or even violent. Since dysfunctional fans readily justify their disruptive behaviour under the pretext of their fan support for the team, they pose a serious threat to other fans and non-fans alike (Thorne & Bruner 2006). The intention behind defining these different fan categories was either to identify concrete market segments for targeted marketing purposes (Hunt et al. 1999) or to identify potential troublemakers at an early stage to prevent similar tragedies like the Heysel Stadium disaster in 1985, where 39 Italian football fans lost their lives after being attacked by dysfunctional Liverpool fans and pressed against a stadium wall that collapsed over them.

In addition, sports and leisure researchers have examined whether gender differences among sports fans exist and how they may express themselves. Dietz-Uhler et al. (2000) found that, although male fans identify themselves much stronger, both males and females are equally likely to describe themselves as sports fans. The underlying motivations seem to differ slightly, as male fans' interest in sports often stems from an active desire also to participate (or wishing to participate) at some level in their favourite sport, while females favour more the social environment and atmosphere at sports events (Dietz-Uhler et al. 2000). Also, James and Ridinger (2002) found that males and females differ in terms of the teams and sports they support. For instance, the motives for sports spectatorship regarding both men's and women's basketball were found to differ in relation to their aesthetic appeal (James & Ridinger 2002). Male fans appear to appreciate the athletic and graceful beauty of both men's and women's basketball more, while female fans find women's basketball aesthetically more appealing. Yet, fans of both genders have named the action of the sport as their prime motivation for their sports fandom (James & Ridinger 2002).

But although academic studies into sports fandom have offered a decent blueprint for the study of film and media fandom, some shortcomings also undermine their transferability to the study of celebrity fans and fandom. Despite sports scholars looking at the motivations for sports fans' emotional support for their favourite team or sports in general, scant research has examined why fans attach themselves to one specific sport/team instead of another one, especially when the team is not a local one. In line with traditional fandom research, sports fan studies have also neglected so far the subjective, personal experience of the individual fan *'on the ground'* in favour of abstract generalisations. Items and scales often measure what scholars deduct from the literature and think to be relevant rather than what can actually be observed in the field (Dietz-Uhler et al. 2000; James & Ridinger 2002; Murrell & Dietz 1992). While some consumer researchers have adopted ethnographic approaches involving participant observation and in-depth interviews (Derbaix et al. 2002; Fillis & Mackay 2014; Richardson & Turley 2006, 2008), they often (for logistic reasons) provide an outsider-looking-in perspective into a more *'extreme'* subset of sports fans within the special context of fan-clubs, fan-blogs and supporting the team live from the *'fan-blocks'*.

Fans as victims of popular culture

Ever since social reformers like the Christian Temperance Union have singled them out as their prime target, the most popular conceptualisation of fans is still the one portraying them as uneducated gullible, dull and vulnerable *'dupes'* that have fallen victim to the manipulative powers of the dangerous and *'evil'* popular mass media culture (Duffett 2013; Gabler 1998; Thorp 1939), which is thereby often presented as an oppressive instrument of neo-liberal capitalism (Adorno & Horkheimer 2006). The bulk of literature relating to this conceptualisation of fans is mainly located within the fields of sociology and media studies, which are dominated by an ideology-informed, sociological-theoretical critical discourse that builds on Munsterberg's (1916) concept of the vulnerable audience and those cultural critics that followed (i.e. Adorno & Horkheimer 2006; Boorstin 1961; Bourdieu 1984; Schickel 1985). Just like films and film stars by film scholars, media scholars view fans and their fandom as texts that can be read, analysed and interpreted in order to explore the triangular dynamics between fan texts, the social culture as their author and society (including the scholar) as their reader (Sandvoos 2007).

The difference to critical approaches in film studies and sociology lies in the position of the fan in the triangle. While traditionally the fan is seen as the reader and, thus, consumer of the text, the critical approaches on fandom view the fan – much like the film actor in the stardom literature – as the text that is produced and given meaning by broader cultural forces within society (Sandvoos 2005). Hence, apart from Munsterberg's vulnerable audience, the fandom literature is strongly influenced by the neo-Marxist ideology of the Frankfurt School (Adorno & Horkheimer 2006; Baudrillard 1970; Lowenthal 2006; Weber 2006) and, in particular, by Pierre Bourdieu's (1984) work on cultural capital (Browne 1997; Fiske 1992; Jankovich 2002). In essence, Bourdieu (1984) has transferred Marx's theory of the economic and social relationship between access to capital, production and worker's alienation to the supposed nature of our contemporary culture.

Bourdieu (1984) has defined culture as a capitalist economy in which people invest and accumulate capital in the form of socially and institutionally legiti-mated cultural products (Fiske 1992). The cultural system, however, promotes and privileges certain cultural tastes and artistic competences (*'high-brow arts/culture'*) over others (*'low-brow'* or *'popular arts/culture'*) through the society's cultural institutions like the education system, museums, art galleries, state theatres and concert halls. Thus, the value of any individual cultural product is determined by its compliance with the legitimated cultural taste and competence (Grossberg 1992) and inclusion in the *'canon'*, which is the set of privileged texts from music, literature, and the performing arts that is considered to be *'worthy'*, *'valuable'* and *'tasteful'* (Bourdieu 1984; Fiske 1992). Popular culture, on the other hand, is vehemently rejected and derided as inherently *'unworthy'*, *'worthless'* and *'tasteless'*.

Yet, as with the economic system, access and resources within the cultural system are unequally distributed and, thus, lead to a class distinction between the privileged and the deprived (Bourdieu 1984; Duffett 2013; Jankovich 2002). High culture can therefore only be *'properly accessed'* by those privileged ones, who possess cultural taste and, subsequently, are in the position to appreciate its true value (Browne 1997). And since the possession of taste and the access to high culture also produces a social return in the form of enhanced social pres-tige, access to political influence and better jobs, Bourdieu (1984) argued that social mobility can only be achieved by obtaining cultural taste through personal investment in and acquisition of education. But because the privileged elite with access to cultural capital regard themselves as the guardians of *'proper'* cultural taste (Fiske 1992), they not only show their strong contempt for popular culture but also seek to deny those people access to the canon, who they deem to lack the ability to appreciate and judge the true aesthetic value and pleasure of high culture appropriately (Winston 1995). And since the access to cultural capital and education go hand-in-hand with the access to economic and social capital, the culturally rich elite attempt to protect their privileges by suppressing the ambition of the masses through meaningless popular culture (Bourdieu 1984).

Given their own critical Marxist ideology, it is ironic that scholars in liter-ature, film, media or cultural studies often rely on Bourdieu's (1984) theory to justify or even advance their own distinction between high-brow and low-brow culture, whereby they cherish the former and despise the latter. While high culture is viewed as unique, beautiful, tasteful and of aesthetic value, popular culture as its binary opposite is mass-produced, ordinary, tasteless and only of functional value (Holbrook 1999; Winston 1995). With regard to their critical discourse on fandom, this translated essentially into two main points of view. The first point of view looks at fans from the scholarly perspective of high culture and, hence, portrays them in line with the social reformist and Munsterberg's (1916) tradition as a bunch of uneducated, tasteless and mindless dupes, who are (un-)willingly manipulated by the capitalist popular mass media culture (Adorno & Horkheimer 2006; Baudrillard 1970; Schickel 1985).

Following Marcuse's Marxist criticism of rational industrialism as a one-dimensional society void of any true prospect for change, Sandvoos (2005) and Winston (1995) claim that popular culture would only provide consumers with the illusion that a genuine polysemy of meanings could be discovered in popular texts. In reality, however, consumers would only be distanced from the true meaning and richness of cultural capital by the promise of simple pleasures and instead fed with meaningless entertainment (Bourdieu 1984; Sandvoos 2005). According to this viewpoint, popular culture is understood as a means of turning consumers into passive, mindless and often addicted media zombies (Munsterberg 1916; Schickel 1985). Thus, the very fact that media fans are even willing to devote themselves on their own accord to some particular media text is a frightening thought for the sociologists, cultural critics and media scholars adhering to this high culture perspective. Their common explanation for such behaviour is that media fans, because of their poor education and subsequent lack of cultural taste, must have innocently fallen victim to the evil trappings of popular culture (Baudrillard 1970; Gabler 1998; Thorp 1939).

While the first perspective is based on a disdain for *'capitalist consumer culture'* and, subsequently, for fans as consumers of the inferior popular culture, who are accused of a deliberate devotion to *'tasteless banality'* and a stubborn refusal to better themselves through the *'tasteful appreciation'* of the artistic canon of true cultural and aesthetic value (Gabler 1998; Thorp 1939; Winston 1995), the alternative perspective suggests that the privileged social elite deliberately deprives the majority of consumers of their rightful access to cultural capital (Bourdieu 1984; Fiske 1992; Holt 1998). Fandom is therefore understood as the (sub)culture of the society's culturally alienated and disempowered masses, who have created for themselves a cultural shadow economy within the official cultural system through the sacralisation and aesthetic appreciation of profane mass commodities (Browne 1997; Duffett 2013; Jankovich 2002).

Being denied the legitimate access to education as a mobility agent to true cultural capital, media fandom becomes a means for the society's deprived masses to express their sense of self and their communal relations to others by constructing an alternative cultural world out of superficial popular mass media texts that to some extent is as rich and intricate as the official cultural system (Fiske 1992; Jankovich 2002). In so doing, fan communities develop and establish their own cultural value system, which in its structure mirrors pretty much the dominant cultural system by privileging certain popular texts (i.e. specific films, TV shows, musicals, comics or popular literature) as being of higher aesthetic value than others (Browne 1997; Duffett 2013). While true social mobility and prestige is unattainable, the individual fan is still enabled to grow one's reputation and social prestige among peers through the devotion, knowledge and systematic accumulation of certain popular media texts that within the community are deemed to be of particular aesthetic value (Jankovich 2002).

That sounds like an interesting discourse, but does this conceptualisation of fans hold up in the context of real everyday life? Personally, I think that this whole idea of fans being mindless victims of popular mass culture – be it enforced by a cultural elite or by the individual's own stupidity – is preposterous and seriously flawed; and not only because of its dodgy origins within the religious fanaticism of the Christian Temperance Union and other self-proclaimed social reformers (Barbas 2001). First, none of the sociologists, cultural critics and media scholars behind this conceptualisation of fans has actually ever engaged in any form with actual *'real-living'* fans, fan culture and their fandom in a real everyday life context, which is strongly reflected in their ideology-informed theoretical writings that clearly emerged from the safety of their desks without ever having personally been in the *'actual field'*. Instead, they seem primarily to be interested in advancing their personal ideology regarding both high and popular culture by applying abstract social theories, such as the vulnerable audience (Munsterberg 1916), to specific contemporary phenomena without providing any empirical support from studies of real-existing fans, fan cultures and fandom.

Second, the idea that popular culture in general is aesthetically and culturally inferior to high culture – or even a menace to society – appears not only to be arrogant, but also pretty ignorant of our cultural-historical heritage, since most of today's canon of high culture, such as Shakespeare, Schiller, Goethe, Lord Byron, Mozart, Beethoven, Schubert, van Gogh, Jane Austen, Charles Dickens, Turner, Wagner, Ravel and the performing arts in general, were originally little more than popular entertainment and only gained their high culture status at a much later time – usually posthumously. Therefore, to say that the consumption of and even devotion to popular culture is either a sign of the individual's stupidity or lack of taste resulting from a lack of education and subsequent access to cultural capital is rather narrow-minded – to say the least.

Finally, while fans are portrayed as being dumb, childish and uneducated due to their devotion to *'tasteless'* and *'unworthy'* popular media texts, a few historical (Glass 2016) and ethnographic studies (Brooker 2005; Hede & Thyne 2010) have found that members of the cultural elite express a very similar emotional devotion and consumption behaviour towards high-brow cultural icons like James Joyce, Lewis Carroll or Jane Austen, which involves the systematic collection of authentic or relevant items and the ritualistic pilgrimage to sites and homes associated with the author and his/her work. Nonetheless, cultural critics and media scholars still prefer to call the latter *'aficionados'* or *'connoisseurs'*, whose devotion to high culture icons and their creative artworks is obviously the consequence of a rational, educated appreciation, as opposed to *'fans'*, whose devotion to popular media icons and their creative artworks is just irrational, emotional, uneducated and tasteless (Baudrillard 1970; Bourdieu 1984; Winston 1995). The biggest irony, however, is that the intense devotion of today's sociological-theoretical scholars and cultural critics to the works of social critics and philosophers such as Derrida, Adorno, Marcuse, Bakhtin, Baudrillard, Foucault, Boorstin or Bourdieu is – in a way – also an expressed form of fandom.

Fans as subversive rebels

While the conceptualisation of fans as victims of popular culture portrays media (and also celebrity) fans as oppressed consumers, who are content with the inferior social status and prestige that their fandom reflects, Jenkins (1992) has drawn on De Certeau (1984) to propose an entirely different and revolutionary conceptualisation of fans and their fandom that caused, in the process, a deep rift within the disciplines of media and cultural studies. Being strongly influenced by the postmodernist movement, this new conceptualisation of fandom completely rejects the traditional stereotype of fans as passive and mindless cultural dupes, who are manipulated by the popular mass media, and instead argues that in fact quite the opposite would be true. Fans are thereby portrayed as creative, highly imaginative and subversive rebels against the corporate establishment (Hills 2002; Jenkins 1992), who engage with media texts by *'making them their own'* (Bielby et al. 1999) and creating their own new textual products. Instead of consuming popular media texts merely within the boundaries of pre-authored meanings and contexts, fans are seen as being active producers and creative, skilled manipulators of media texts (Lanier & Schau 2007).

Because consumers in postmodern societies are portrayed as the producers of their own self-representations by using the fragmented meanings of numerous brands as their raw materials, media fandom is driven by the fragmentation and reassembly of media images according to the consumers' individual designs of their self-identities (Hills 2002). Hence, fandom within this conceptualisation is usually associated with the two terms *'participatory fandom'* (Brower 1992; Hills 2002) and *'textual poaching'* (De Certeau 1984; Jenkins 1992) that essentially refer to the same underlying idea of fragmenting and reconstructing media texts. In contrast to the commonly held view that fans would just mindlessly consume media texts and, at best, imitate characters, this conceptualisation holds that fans actually assign their own personal meanings to them and, subsequently, claim ownership of these media texts (Bielby et al. 1999; Shefrin 2004). The idea that fans claim ownership of their favourite media texts has already received empirical support from numerous ethnographic and structuralist studies (i.e. Bielby et al. 1999; Jenkins 1992; Lanier & Schau 2007).

Fans' claim to ownership of media texts has been found to take two distinct forms that can both be witnessed in today's YouTube and (illegal) file-sharing culture (Hennig-Thurau et al. 2007; Sinclair & Green 2016). On a basic level, fans feel that they are entitled to have a say on the content, structure and narrative development of the media text as *'co-producers'* because of their devotion and emotional investment in the media text (Bielby et al. 1999; Shefrin 2004). The underpinning argument is that, due to having got much closer to the media text, its characters and the plot than any TV executives or the film studio holding the legal rights ever will, fans would be in a much better position to judge the authenticity and credibility of narrative developments or new character introductions (Brower 1992). In order to voice their opinions publicly, fans have actually interacted with other fans and the producers of media texts ever since the early years of the film industry by writing fan-letters to the film/TV studios and official publications, publishing their own fanzines, setting up their own fan-sites and leaving comments on websites (Barbas 2001; Hewer & Hamilton 2012a; Kanai 2015).

During Hollywood's golden years from 1919 to 1950, the major film studios had set up departments whose job it was to screen fan-letters for feedback on their films and stars as well as for ideas and suggestions for new projects. In fact, studio bosses like Carl Laemmle, Jack Warner, Samuel Goldwyn, David O Selznick or Irvin Thalberg were known to have spent one day per week reading fan mail to stay in touch with their audiences (Barbas 2001; Epstein 2005) – a practice that today's studio executives would do well to reintroduce again instead of putting their faith in some questionable economic theories and advice (De Vany 2004; Elberse 2014). However, the issue of media text ownership has not only sparked academic debates, but also resulted repeatedly in legal disputes between media producers and their media products' devoted audiences. Shefrin (2004) has thereby examined how different film studios in the age of the Internet dealt with participatory fandom with regard to the productions of *Lord of the Rings* and *Star Wars: The Phantom Menace*. While the latter sought to discourage fan participation beyond the official competitions on their website and even filed copyright lawsuits against individual fans, the former actually invited fans to participate by sharing their opinions in relation to storylines that differed from the original novel and networked with unofficial fan-sites via links to/from the official website.

Jenkins's (1992) concept of textual poaching, however, goes even a step further than the fan's feeling of entitled ownership. In his intensive ethnographic research of various fan communities from *Star Trek* to *Twin Peaks*, Jenkins (1992) found that the fans of media texts behave similar to nomadic poachers with regard to constructing their very own cultures by borrowing storylines, characters, ideas and images from commercial media texts to create their own fictional media products. Fans, thereby, not only interpret their own meanings into a given media text, but actually produce new creative texts out of fragmented media images, which feature known characters, environmental settings and situational contexts participating in new self-imagined narratives (Kanai 2015). One of the oldest forms of poaching, which developed as early as 1900, is the writing of fictional stories that involve the characters, plots and settings of an existing, admired media text, which often tend to be published in specific unofficial fanzines and later online fan-sites (Lanier & Schau 2007).

The emergence of Super 8 film cameras in the 1960s and video cameras in the 1980s has enabled creative fans to shoot their own fan-fiction films, which have nowadays become even easier to make with the availability of affordable digital camcorders, editing software like Windows Movie Maker, iMovie, Video Studio, Final Cut or Premiere Pro and YouTube as a free distribution platform (Turner 2004). The amateur writers and filmmakers either have new story ideas to add or feel that the original media text's official storyline and solution is insufficient and needs to be altered (Jenkins 1992). Due to the growing popularity of queer theory as a critical approach within media studies, the so-called *'fan slash'* genre has received some attention in recent years. *'Fan slash writings'* are fictional erotic, sometimes pornographic stories that take the popular media text, its characters and situational context as their point of departure and develop a romantic/sexual relationship between the lead characters (Cicioni 1998). While most fan slash deal with imagined homosexual relationships between male characters (i.e. Kirk/Spock), they are nearly exclusively written by females (Cicioni 1998; Jenkins 1992). Another form of creative fan expression is *'filking'* (Jenkins 1992), where fans perform self-written songs with lyrics about media texts and characters within their fan community. Many songs follow the melody of familiar folk or pop songs, but some are self-composed.

Fans as members of neo-religious cults

As several US TV shows and films like *Star Trek, Bonanza, Star Wars, Twin Peaks, Picket Fences* or *The X-Files*, which have attracted particularly devoted fan communities, have had strong religious overtones, it comes therefore as no surprise that some scholars have investigated fan culture and fan communities as neo-religious cults (Jindra 1994; Rojek 2006). Although Hills (2002) argues that these studies represent *'voices in the wilderness'*, several ethnographic studies in consumer research have also identified some forms of (neo)religious behaviour within fan communities (Kozinets 1997; O'Guinn 1991; Schau & Muniz 2007). Furthermore, research of fan communities as neo-religious cults is not only limited to TV shows, films or novels (Hills 2002; Jindra 1994; Kozinets 1997), but is one of the conceptualisations of fans that also extends to celebrities too (Henry & Caldwell 2007; O'Guinn 1991; Schau & Muniz 2007).

The conceptualisation of fans as neo-religious cult members suggests that, like organised religion, fan communities form a canon of textual elements in relation to the admired media text or celebrity, which are deemed to be authentic and true, lay out regularised rituals and practices that determine the *'right way'* of cherishing the media text or celebrity and form a member hierarchy (Rojek 2006). By sacralising the otherwise profane media texts or celebrities through shared meanings (Belk et al. 1989), fans give them a special position in their life and even define their self through them (Henry & Caldwell 2007). As with sports fandom described earlier (Richardson & Turley 2008), the sacralisation of a media text or celebrity can reach such an extent, where fans devote a shrine in their living space (or even an entire room) to their admired TV show, film or celebrity (Henry & Caldwell 2007; O'Guinn 1991). Within this context, fans of celebrities can sometimes be heard saying that they *'worship'* their beloved idols and in some cases even credit them with some air of divinity – as O'Guinn (1991) and Henry and Caldwell (2007) have found in their ethnographic studies of Barry Manilow and Cliff Richard fan-clubs. After all, we have nowadays become used to referring to some film and rock/pop stars as *'gods'* – though obviously not in a literal sense (Rojek 2006).

Besides the private sphere, the conceptualisation of fan communities as neo-religious cults focuses on the communal and pseudo-institutionalised facets of their expressed fandom in particular. In this context, fan-clubs are essentially understood as the equivalent to the traditional churches (Jindra 1994; Rojek 2006), which might also explain the contempt voiced by religious social reformers. Both institutions are in essence set up for the purpose of worshipping the divine; whether it is a god, a hero, a celebrity or any other media text does not really matter (Hills 2002; Jindra 1994). While the fan community defines and celebrates the canon that lays out the true content of authentic faith through ritualised practices (Kozinets 1997), another function is to share stories with each other that attribute divine qualities to the worshipped celebrity or media text (Henry & Caldwell 2007; O'Guinn 1991; Schau & Muniz 2007). Acquired and sacralised merchandise as well as other authenticated memorabilia are collectively cherished like sacred relics, especially when the celebrity or a genuine media text representative (i.e. an actor of the TV show) has blessed them through their personal presence, such as a hand-signed autograph, a personalised item or used towel (Newman et al. 2011).

Ethnographic studies by O'Guinn (1991), Henry and Caldwell (2007) or Schau and Muniz (2007) have also found evidence of a missionary spirit among devoted fan community members. Like the followers of most religions seeking happiness and salvation through serving their god, fan communities regard it as their duty to recruit new members, to protect their idol, media text and faith from the harm of bad press and/or *'bad fans'* and to *'be there'* for the subject of their fandom at all times. Despite being an atheist and having a certain dislike for religion of all sorts, I cannot deny that numerous fans and fan communities express a behaviour that in some circumstances resembles religious practices. Also, in contrast to some other fan conceptualisations, this one is actually backed up by solid interpretations of ethnographic data. But most of the research merely studied a specific subgroup of fans for a limited period of time under very special circumstances, i.e. Star Trek conventions or fan-clubs. Hence, there are currently little data available on whether and how these findings also translate to a fan's ordinary daily life outside the community.

Fans as alienated social misfits

While I have some personal difficulties as an atheist to associate myself with the idea of fandom being some form of neo-religious expression, I have to admit that I feel a positive inclination towards the conceptualisation of fans as lonely geeks and alienated social misfits, which has strongly influenced the contemporary fandom discourse in both academic literature and popular media. The German satirist Wiglaf Droste (1995) once said that the general problem with stereotypes and clichés is that to some extent they are often true. His point seems to ring especially true with regard to the popular view that fans are loners, nerds, geeks and other social misfits, just like they are often portrayed within popular media texts (i.e. *The Big Bang Theory*, where highly competent science geeks also happen to be gullible comic and science-fiction fans). After all, there must be something wrong with fans, when they devote so much time, money and effort in mass-produced media commodities, such as TV shows (Jenkins 1992; Kozinets 2001), video games (Cova et al. 2007), music (Herrmann 2012; Holbrook 1987), literature (Brooker 2005; Brown 2006), films (Barbas 2001; Shefrin 2004) and even celebrities (O'Guinn 1991; Stacey 1994; Wohlfeil & Whelan 2012), instead of *'doing much worthier things'* like *'normal people do'* (Jenson 1992) – as I have been reminded many times.

Furthermore, the data from ethnographic research by O'Guinn (1991), Jenkins (1992), Kozinets (2001) or Cusack et al. (2003) provide striking evidence that, unlike sports fans, media and celebrity fans are very often not exactly the most popular guys in school, university or at work. In fact, most fans in those studies reported that they *'somehow don't fit in with the mainstream'*, feel themselves being misunderstood by others, have hardly any friends, report feelings of social isolation and loneliness, and much too often experience numerous forms of stigmatisation, bullying and discrimination (Cusack et al. 2003; Kozinets 2001). There is also some evidence that many of them do not exactly do well in sport, are regularly shunned by the *'in-crowd'* and rarely invited to parties, social events or on dates. But strongly contradicting the popular stereotype of fans being unintelligent, gullible, dull and boring individuals, who consistently fail to succeed in real life and, thus, seek refuge in popular culture fantasies (Gabler 1998), ethnographic research (Cusack et al. 2003; Hewer & Hamilton 2012a; Kozinets 2001) has found that the majority of fans are in fact highly intelligent people, who tend to be quite successful in school, university and their professional careers (just like the lead characters in *The Big Bang Theory*).

It is in their social and private lives, however, where they feel very lonely and socially isolated because of their *'experienced'* lack of social skills and social relationships with others (Cusack et al. 2003). Several fans in Kozinets's (2001) study even reported that they feel they are constantly being stigmatised and socially rejected especially by those others, who tend to be less intelligent, imaginative and creative than they are, but who are much more privileged or blessed in terms of social skills, status and physical beauty – and, thus, more popular. Their fandom, therefore, allows these individuals to escape their frustrating, lonely everyday lives and social isolation for a while by keeping their minds occupied with the deliberate search and collection of specific media texts of interest (i.e. films, TV shows, theatre performances, magazine articles, books, music, games or even celebrities) and immersing themselves into their narratives.

In relation to this context, Horton and Wohl (1956) observed already during the early days of television in the 1950s that TV audiences would often develop an emotional attachment to anchormen, TV celebrities and soap characters. They also suggested that, in particular, TV personalities like anchormen or show masters would actually encourage such an attachment by interacting indirectly with TV viewers through the camera as if they are in an actual face-to-face dialogue. Horton and Wohl (1956) have referred to this illusionary and/or simulated conversation as *'parasocial interaction'*. Once individual audience members extend their parasocial interaction with their favourite TV celebrities far beyond the initial TV show encounter (i.e. by watching their appearances in other shows or media, by reading about them in magazines, etc.) over a longer period of time, they begin to engage with the celebrity in a *'parasocial relationship'* (Horton & Wohl 1956).

Since then, Horton and Wohl's theory has not only become one of the most influential papers in media studies and social psychology with regard to celebrity fandom and audience research (Alperstein 1991; Houlberg 1984; Rubin et al. 1985; Rubin & McHugh 1987), but unfortunately also one of the most misinterpreted ones (as we will see in the seventh conceptualisation of fans). Indeed, the latter has led to the widely-held belief that the parasocial relationships that fans form with their favourite celebrities are clear proof of the individuals' inherent social deficiencies or even for their pathological-obsessive mental disorder (McCutcheon et al. 2003); although Horton and Wohl (1956) actually said the opposite and described them as being very healthy and complementary to normal social life. In fact, Horton and Wohl (1956) argued that parasocial relationships with film stars, TV personalities, celebrities and even soap characters would serve as particularly beneficial, compensatory emotional substitutes for those people, who experience only a rather restricted social life for various reasons, such as being geographically or socially isolated, physically or mentally disabled, timid, elderly, inept in forming social bonds or because they feel otherwise unpopular and rejected by others. In their own words:

> Nothing could be more reasonable or natural than that people, who are isolated and lonely, should seek sociability and love wherever they can find it. It is only when the parasocial relationship becomes a substitute for autonomous social participation, when it proceeds in absolute defiance of objective reality, that it can be regarded as pathological.
>
> (Horton & Wohl 1956: 223)

In other words, celebrity and media fandom provides consumers with a healthy means of compensating for experienced emotional and social deficits; as long as it does not turn into an addiction and the individual's sole purpose of life (Leets et al. 1995). And this is exactly what fans have reported as their personal emotional experiences in several ethnographic, structuralist and naturalistic studies (i.e. Henry & Caldwell 2007; Kozinets 2001; O'Guinn 1991; Schau & Muniz 2007).

Fandom, therefore, seems to offer many of those otherwise lonely individuals the opportunity to interact socially with other like-minded consumers, who not only share with them a similar interest in a certain media text or celebrity but also similar feelings of social isolation, alienation and rejection (Cusack et al. 2003; Kozinets 2001). With increasing social interactions and the exchange of media text knowledge or private experiences among like-minded media or celebrity fans, so-called fan communities emerge, develop and provide these media or celebrity fans with a place, where they can come together and share their interest with each other. These fan communities can thereby take various shapes and forms ranging from infrequent, informal gatherings over Internet chat-rooms and fan-sites to highly organised conventions and institutionalised fan-clubs (Henry & Caldwell 2007; Hewer & Hamilton 2012a; Kozinets 2001; O'Guinn 1991).

Either way, fans of media texts or celebrities, who would normally experience themselves as social misfits (*'not fitting in with the mainstream'*), seem to find within these fan communities the very kind of social acceptance, companionship, status and appreciation that they have been craving for in their private lives, even if they are only of a temporary or virtual nature (Herrmann 2012; Kanai 2015). Furthermore, fan communities also provide individual fans with the opportunity to share their own creative, self-designed outputs, such as fanzines, fan-sites, poems, songs, paintings or self-directed home-made films, with a supportive and appreciative audience of like-minded peers (Barbas 2001; Hewer & Hamilton 2012a; Lanier & Schau 2007). In contrast to another conceptualisation of fans, the production, presentation and exchange of self-made creative products (including the re-sampling of commercial media texts) is not understood as a liberating exercise in *'sticking it to the Man'* (Jenkins 1992), but as a liberating means of gaining other fans' approval and even admiration by paying a loving homage to a shared interest (Barbas 2001; Kanai 2015).

And this behaviour is not only limited to fan communities devoted to popular media texts or celebrities, but also to those devoted to the high arts (Chen 2009). While they may call themselves aficionados and connoisseurs, admire high-brow cultural texts or icons and meet in societies rather than fan-clubs, at the end of the day, members of James Joyce, Lewis Carroll or Jane Austen societies have often joined them in the same way and engage in similar practices and rituals as the members of media, sports or celebrity fan-clubs (Brooker 2005; Hede & Thyne 2010). But irrespective of whether these fan communities centre around a celebrity, popular media text or high-brow culture, each of them can essentially be viewed as a brand community (McAlexander et al. 2002) or at least as a consumer tribe (Cova 1998). It is therefore not surprising that especially the participation and social dynamics within fan-clubs, conventions and fan-sites have received the most attention from consumer researchers. Unfortunately, this particular research focus on fan communities has reached such a level of exclusivity in the scholarly discourse that *'being-a-fan'* is automatically conceptualised as participatory fandom and solely about the social interaction between community members, as evidenced by Thorne and Bruner's (2006) definition of fandom. In fact, I have been told by peer reviewers and fellow scholars on several occasions during the course of my research that I *'cannot be a fan'* of Jena Malone, simply because I do not participate in a dedicated (online) fan community, where I would share my knowledge and appreciation for her with like-minded others. My admiration of her acting performances and my infatuation with her as an attractive young woman were considered to be irrelevant.

Fans as irrational, pathological-obsessive, delusional stalkers

Unfortunately, the conceptualisation of fans as lonely, alienated social misfits has also (re-)invited the much more extreme conceptualisation of fans as pathological-obsessive and delusional stalkers that has always been very popular with the tabloids (Jenson 1992) – and at a fictional level with the film industry as well (Lewis 1992). Ever since the late-1890s, when social reformers like the Christian Temperance Union created, planted and popularised the image of fans as misguided, irrational, deviant and hysterical lunatics (Barbas 2001; Gabler 1998), the academic and popular literature on fans and fandom is haunted by popular and sensationalist stories and images of the socially inept and deviant fanatic, whose excessive, deranged behaviour clearly borders on the mentally insane (Jenson 1992). Since the 1980s, this conceptualisation of fans has enjoyed a renewed popularity among social psychologists and media scholars in response to the high-profile tabloid media coverage of the fan hysteria surrounding the latest teen pop sensation (Jenson 1992) or the often cited, infamous real-life examples of John Hinckley's attempted assassination of Ronald Reagan in order to impress the film actress Jodie Foster (Krämer 2003), Mark David Chapman's assassination of John Lennon (Gabler 1998), the murder of TV actress Rebecca Schaeffer, the murder of Selena Quintanilla by the chairlady of her official fan-club and, much more recently, the murder of the young singer Christina Grimmie.

Strongly grounded in Munsterberg's (1916) original theory of the vulnerable audience and heavily inspired by a severe misinterpretation of Horton and Wohl's (1956) parasocial interaction theory, some social psychology and media scholars have thereby developed a disproportionally strong interest into the darker and extremist sides of fandom (Maltby et al. 2004; McCutcheon et al. 2003, 2006) – even though it merely represents an exceptionally tiny minority of individuals, and most of whom are actually not fans at all (Dietz et al. 1991; Leets et al. 1995). As I have discussed within the previous conceptualisation, Horton and Wohl (1956) portrayed fans' parasocial relationships with their favourite celebrities quite clearly as something that supplements normal social relationships and that provides a healthy alternative for those individuals who experience deficits in their social lives for various reasons. Only when an individual becomes so obsessed with one's parasocial relationship with a particular celebrity that s/he loses his/her grip of reality and can no longer distinguish between fact and fiction, they argued, can such fan behaviour be regarded as pathological and delusional – but only then. However, especially within the field of social psychology, numerous academics have ignored Horton and Wohl's

(1956) original, detailed distinction completely and focused right from the start exclusively on the pathological side of fandom – often apparently with the primary purpose of getting a term or concept like the *'celebrity worship syndrome'* credited to their name (i.e. McCutcheon et al. 2002, 2003).

Due to their different underlying research paradigms and agendas, academic scholars within media studies and social psychology look at pathological fandom from slightly different viewpoints. Media scholars, thereby, identify two distinct images of pathological fans, which can be characterised as (a) the hysterical member of a crowd, and (b) the obsessive, stalking loner (Jenson 1992) – both of which reflecting quite clearly their social reformist heritage. The study of fan pathology in relation to frenzied crowd members emerged in response to the crowds gathered at the funeral of the actor Rudolph Valentino in 1925 (Barbas 2001; Hansen 1986) and has ever since been associated with mostly female (teenage) fans of film and rock/pop stars (Ehrenreich et al. 1992). Indeed, since the 1950s, the popular tabloid press have not been the only ones to connect the images of screaming, weeping and hysterical teenage girls, who gather in large crowds at film premieres, hotels, airports or concert halls to catch in person a glimpse of their idols (even if it is only for a second), rigorously to the inherent dangers of violence, alcohol, drugs, free sexual and, especially in the US, racial mingling to this very day in an effort to *'warn'* concerned parents of the *'devilish temptations'* their kids are supposedly getting themselves into listening to rock 'n' roll, heavy metal, punk, grunge or hip hop, watching science-fiction and horror films, playing video games or admiring a specific celebrity (Barbas 2001; Duffett 2013; Jenson 1992). Once the Elvis Presley and Beatles phenomena of the 1950s and 1960s saw hysterical teenage crowds gathering randomly, cultural critics and media scholars have done so, too.

While nearly all early research appeared to be self-fulfilling prophecies designed to lend similar "scientific support" to popular prejudices as Munsterberg (1916) has previously done for the Christian Temperance Union, later research like Ehrenreich et al.'s (1992) study of Beatlemania has looked at the meaning that such hysterical behaviour may have for teenage girls within the context of their contemporary cultural environments (hysterical fans are always portrayed as 'female'). They concluded that young girls' hysterical fandom had enabled them to open an internal pressure valve and to release the cultural burden of sexual oppression that society had placed upon them without having to face the risk of losing their female *'virtue'* and *'honour'*. Recent studies into teenage girls' hysterical fan behaviour with boybands or young film actors have come to similar conclusions and view fandom among young girls as an expressed emotional transition into sexuality and womanhood (Karniol 2001), which should only be understood as a temporary state that requires parents to provide their daughters with *'proper'* guidance and moral support (Giles & Maltby 2004).

While the research of fan pathology has looked at hysterical female teenagers with benign pity (Jenson 1992), it is especially the image of the weird, alienated, obsessive and fanatical loner (they are often portrayed as 'male'), who has *'lost his marbles'* and threatens to go to extreme lengths to satisfy his delusional belief of having a romantic, sexual or just a *'friendly'* relationship with a (female) celebrity, that has always caught the imagination and interest of the tabloid media and social psychology scholars (Leets et al. 1995; McCutcheon et al. 2006). Yet, because of their strong philosophical grounding in (neo-)behaviourism and the scarcity of pre-existing academic literature, most of their hypotheses and research designs are drawn from the stereotypes generated by the popular media and the (unproven) ideology-driven theories of cultural critics rather than observations of actual real-living fans in the field. In fact, most social psychological studies have simply ignored the insights gained from any prior ethnographic research (i.e. Jenkins 1992; Jindra 1994; Kozinets 2001; O'Guinn 1991; Stacey 1994), which they view as 'inferior' and 'of no academic value' (Maltby et al. 2004; McCutcheon et al. 2002, 2003), while popular media and tabloid reports, in contrast, are apparently considered 'trustworthy sources'. This is not to say that there has not been some solid, insightful research in the past, but too many recent studies have quite clearly been conducted on *'pretty shaky'* conceptual and methodological grounds (to say the least) and have often been ideologically motivated – or at least influenced.

In response to the above-mentioned murders of John Lennon, Rebecca Schaeffer or Selena Quintanilla and the hundreds of threatening letters sent to celebrities worldwide every year by apparently mentally unstable individuals, a need for research was recognised in the early-1980s to prevent any potential attacks on famous people in the future by understanding the mind of the obsessive stalker and by identifying the various types of pathological-obsessive fans as well as the nature and extent of their delusion (Dietz et al. 1991). The most comprehensive study, thereby, was the longitudinal research conducted by Dietz et al. (1991) in cooperation with a major specialised Hollywood security consultant agency, which involved an intensive content analysis of 1800 inappropriate and/or threatening letters written to celebrities by 214 individuals[4] in terms of their content and the differences between approach and non-approach risks. Interestingly, despite identifying 16 variables that would describe pathological fandom (though mainly in their most extreme and excessive variation), Dietz et al. (1991) could not really find any typifying differences between *'approachers'* and *'non-approachers'*.

Strongly contradicting the popular stereotype, however, they found evidence that those fans, who are obsessively fantasising about a romantic or sexual relationship with a celebrity, turn out to be actually the least likely candidates for seeking real-life encounters with their subject of desire. Instead, the most extreme and dangerous pathological-obsessive individuals among both approachers and non-approachers seem to be less fixated on a particular celebrity as a person but more on celebrity fame in general by writing simultaneously to various celebrities at any given time (Dietz et al. 1991). Furthermore, their obsession with celebrities is often little more than the mere extension of much broader mental delusions that are primarily expressed in a radical and only too often incoherent religious or political fanaticism. But most importantly, Dietz et al. (1991) always pointed out in no uncertain terms that they were studying only a microscopic minority, who must never be confused at any time with the vast majority of ordinary, mentally *'normal'* everyday media and celebrity fans – and, therefore, strengthened Horton and Wohl's (1956) initial argument. Yet, even though Dietz et al.'s (1991) research was very thorough, detailed and informative, it still fails to determine in what ways the dangerous pathological-obsessive minority exactly differs from the normal everyday celebrity fan in terms of how their fandom is practised and experienced.

Leets et al. (1995), therefore, followed up by comparing the motivations of *'normal'* consumers to write or contact celebrities, which they obtained through both a survey of university students and a content analysis of fan-letters received and provided by an unnamed celebrity, with Dietz et al.'s (1991) earlier findings. In their student sample, Leets et al. (1995) have identified curiosity/information seeking followed by expressing one's admiration (or criticism) for the celebrity and his/her creative work, and the intent to associate oneself or express one's self-identity with the celebrity (often BIRGing) as the primary motivations. These findings were confirmed by the content analysis of the fan-letters as well – with one exception. Requests or asking the celebrity for favours, i.e. appearing at a for the writer important private (birthday, marriage, anniversary) or social event (party, prom night, fan-club meeting or conference), visiting a terminally ill relative, signing a personal autograph, giving donations in money or kind or forwarding the writer's own creative work to the celebrity's agent or producer, has turned out to be the biggest motivator identified from the actual fan mail (Leets et al. 1995).[5] Compared to Dietz et al. (1991), there is nothing out of the ordinary even though some minor similarities could be recognised. Both groups have expressed their admiration and devotion to the celebrity, requested some kind of favour and often enclosed one or more items with the letter as a personal gift (i.e. a poem, tape, photo or a small present).

Where the normal fans have differed from their pathological-obsessive counterparts has been the extent and excessiveness of their devotion as well as in their perception of the relationship they have with the celebrity. Even though normal fans may fantasise about a romantic and/or sexual relationship with a particular celebrity (especially in absence of a real-life relationship), they are always fully aware that this fantasy is exactly that – a fantasy – and have often expressed some embarrassment about their *'foolishness'* in their open responses to Leets et al.'s (1995) survey. Subjects in Dietz et al.'s (1991) study, by contrast, were mostly under the delusion of actually being in a mutual romantic relationship with the celebrity and that their feelings have been undoubtedly reciprocated, which often also meant that they view the celebrity's real-life partners as adulterous intruders. Moreover, they differed significantly in terms of the items they have enclosed in their letters. While normal fans have enclosed mostly Christmas and birthday cards, personal photos, self-written poems, self-mixed tapes, CDs or home-made video films (Leets et al. 1995), the enclosed items from pathological-obsessive individuals have ranged from the innocuous to the extremely bizarre, such as bibles, half-eaten candy bars with lipstick on them, bed pans, excrements, blood syringes, *'fresh sperms for impregnation'*, medical photos of corpses with the celebrity's face pasted on, etc. (Well, you get the picture!).

Leets et al. (1995) have observed that normal fans will not really go to extreme lengths of getting in contact with their favourite celebrities beyond or other than fan mail (or, these days, sending messages on Facebook or Twitter), attending their shows, premieres and public autograph signings or pure chance encounters on the street. As the works of Dietz et al. (1991) and Leets et al. (1995) have provided such good general insights into the psychological distinction and behavioural differences between the very tiny minority of pathological-obsessive, delusional individuals and the vast majority of normal, mentally healthy fans, it is quite inconceivable that a group of social psychologists has since 2001 set out on a deliberate quest to confirm the popular stereotypes of fans with empirical evidence by largely ignoring or, alternatively, by very 'liberally' reinterpreting ALL previous findings from earlier studies in order to advance their own rather dodgy agenda of painting a very different theoretical picture of celebrity fans (McCutcheon et al. 2002, 2003).

In their research of *'celebrity worshippers'*, McCutcheon, Ashe, Houran, Maltby and their fellow co-authors have argued that every person, who admires a particular celebrity and his/her creative work or celebrities in general, would clearly suffer from a serious inherent mental illness, which they named the *'Celebrity Worship Syndrome (CWS)'* and which may even be hereditary (Maltby et al. 2004). In fact, they even propose that celebrity fandom, as a form of parasocial interaction, represents a psychologically abnormal behaviour that could apparently be categorised as a type of erotomanic delusional disorder. They, therefore, believe that fans are not only obsessive and pathological-delusional in their adoration of celebrities, but must also be expected to *'exhibit verbal, visuospatial, intellectual and cognitive deficits related to flexibility and associative learning'* (McCutcheon et al. 2003).

In other words, Maltby et al. (2004) argue that the admiration and adoration of their favourite celebrities is in itself clear evidence that celebrity fans, in sharp contrast to *'normal'* people, are generally less intelligent, unimaginative, dull, unable to cope with or even enhance their daily lives and even suffer from a potential learning disability (McCutcheon et al. 2003). The underpinning idea, obviously, derives from Munsterberg's (1916) original theory of the vulnerable audience and feeds into the popular interpretation of fans as deprived (but this time of intellectual abilities rather than cultural capital), gullible and mindless dupes put already forward by social reformers and cultural critics (i.e. Boorstin 1961; Cashmore 2006; Thorp 1939). Thus, every suggestion, notion and even genuine empirical evidence from the field that fandom is actually providing lonely and socially isolated, but otherwise normal individuals with a platform to interact with other like-minded people and an outlet for creative self-expression – be it subversive (Jenkins 1992) or co-creative (Kozinets 2001) – has been wilfully ignored or rejected out-of-hand.

Although the theory that McCutcheon, Maltby and their colleagues have put forward is highly questionable, it might have warranted further examination if they had actually provided some valid scientific evidence in at least one of their published papers so far. Unfortunately, the data they have presented in support of their hypotheses actually proves the exact opposite and supports not a single one of their propositions, never mind claimed findings (for example in Maltby et al. 2004; McCutcheon et al. 2003, 2006). It is therefore quite a scary thought that researchers, who supposedly subscribe to logical empiricism and scientific inquiry, not only reject any data as (sic) *'unreliable'* and *'unscientific'*, which is obtained in ethnographic research and through verbal statements of actual celebrity fans, but also seem to lack the necessary experience in properly interpreting the statistical results generated in a multivariate data analysis. The only alternative explanation would be that McCutcheon, Maltby and Co. have been so eager to find empirical support for their hypotheses that they misinterpreted the real findings of their data. Since this may sound harsh, I will now discuss some of the most serious flaws with their work and urge you, the reader, to have a closer look for yourself to make up your own mind – especially as some of their findings have already unquestioningly been adopted in the popular media (Cashmore 2006; www.irishhealth.ie).

First of all, as devoted neo-behaviourists, McCutcheon et al. (2002, 2003) believe that verbal statements of subjects are generally unreliable and cannot be trusted. Consequently, they reject all previous literature based on ethnography or content analysis for the development of their own hypotheses and measurement instruments. Surprisingly, though, the unsupported claims by Munsterberg (1916), other critical theorists or popular media reports have not been questioned in a similar way. But McCutcheon et al. (2002) did challenge earlier celebrity appeal scales (i.e. Stever 1991) as *'unsuitable'* measurements for identifying and measuring the extent of celebrity worshipping, despite their proven high construct validity and reliability ratings. In their opinion (McCutcheon et al. 2002), these scales would be either too *'specialised'* for specific types of celebrities like TV personalities and newscasters (Rubin et al. 1985; Rubin & Hugh 1987) or would supposedly focus *'too much on emotional'* rather than *'rational'* dimensions by including *'irrelevant and distracting'* items related to liking, sexual attraction or romantic appeal (Stever 1991).

Using a Rasch scaling approach, McCutcheon et al. (2002) have instead proposed the Celebrity Attitude Scale (CAS) as a superior and universally applicable alternative. But due to rejecting out-of-hand any knowledge of fandom obtained by previous research and having little other literature to build on, McCutcheon et al. (2002) drew the original 32 items for the scale from popular stereotypes and selected by the researchers based on 'common-sense', before being reduced to 17 items with the deliberate purpose of covering three theorised levels of fandom. At the basic level, celebrity worship has an *'entertainment-social'* value for the individual, who has been attracted by the celebrity's ability to capture attention and entertain. The intermediate level of celebrity worship is characterised by *'intense-personal'* values, where fans develop and are driven by intense and compulsive feelings towards the celebrity. And, finally, *'borderline-pathological'* behaviour is the most extreme expression of celebrity worship, where the individual is so obsessed with one's favourite celebrity that s/he would be willing to spend one's entire fortune on items that have been owned or used by the celebrity, to commit a crime if asked by the celebrity and to engage in anti-social behaviour (McCutcheon et al. 2002).

McCutcheon et al. (2002, 2003), thereby, imply that the more an individual worships the admired celebrity, the more would s/he experience a decline in his/her psychological well-being, cognitive flexibility and intellectual functioning. But despite the reported internal validity and reliability, the very nature of the CAS scale means that applying it to any sample automatically results in a self-fulfilling prophecy. Furthermore, they also argue that celebrity worship would under no circumstances be related to an individual's feelings of loneliness, isolation and shyness[6] (Maltby et al. 2004; McCutcheon et al. 2003), which contradicts all the findings generated by virtually all ethnographic research to-date (see earlier sections in this chapter). Yet, although the CAS scale was set up in this way, as outlined by McCutcheon et al. (2002), the authors insist in each of their other papers that these three factors would emerge from the data during the factor analysis rather than from the very design of the scale (Maltby et al. 2004; McCutcheon et al. 2003, 2006). This *'minor'* issue might have been acceptable, if the CAS actually delivers consistent results across a wider sample range, as the researchers claim in each publication. But, curiously, that has *not* been the case. While the CAS has held up with data drawn from the main student samples at their own university in Florida (McCutcheon et al. 2002, 2003, 2006), data collected from working-class samples in the UK have presented very different factor constellations or been all over the place (Maltby et al. 2004). Curiously, each time the authors have praised the universal applicability of their CAS scale, they have conveniently failed to mention those irregularities. However, it is when the CAS has been applied and the findings are discussed that a flawed research design turns into a highly questionable exercise.

McCutcheon et al. (2003) provides us with a perfect example, since the authors claim to have presented strong empirical evidence that celebrity worshippers' inherent cognitive deficits result from erotomania. The CAS is thereby said to correlate strongly with the six cognitive measures reflecting verbal creativity, crystallised intelligence, spatial abilities, creative thinking and need for cognition (i.e. enjoyment of solving intellectual problems) adopted from various relevant psychological studies. The problem is that the provided table (McCutcheon et al. 2003: 317) clearly shows that the arithmetic skills and need for cognition are *not* statistically significant[7] ($p > 0.05$) in the bivariate regression analyses! Thus, although McCutcheon et al. (2003) clearly state that fans are less intelligent and creative than *'normal'* people and have serious difficulties in associative learning, it is quite interesting to learn from the provided data that they are actually no different to other people in terms of *'relishing the opportunity to solve complicated puzzles and enjoying challenges posed by intellectual problems'* (McCutcheon et al. 2003: 314), which are essential characteristics for the need of cognition or arithmetic/mathematical abilities. And although the other four dimensions may have been statistically significant, as each of them explains merely between 9.6% and 17.6% of the variance in 'celebrity worship, their practical significance[8] has turned out to be of little to no relevance at all'.

Furthermore, while the multiple regression analysis correlated with an adjusted $R^2 = 0.25$, which explains just 25% of the variance, it is even more curious that not a single one of the six measures scored a statistical (never mind a practical) significance in their β values. Multiple regression analyses also show similar results in predicting the three factors as independent subscales, which achieve statistically significant $(p < 0.1)$ adjusted $R^2 = 0.17$, 0.23 and 0.16 respectively, and once again with no statistically significant β values. The only exception is the mildly significant $(p < 0.05)$ verbal creativity measure with regard to the borderline-pathological subscale $(\beta = -0.34)$, which would actually suggest that borderline-pathological celebrity worshippers are slightly more verbally creative than normal people, not less. Nonetheless, despite being clearly contradicted by their own data, McCutcheon et al. (2003) have had no hesitation to interpret these findings as *'strong evidence'* in support of their hypotheses and theory – a trend repeated in each of their publications. And their official explanation for the complete absence of any statistically *and* practically significant ß values is that *'the six cognitive measures only contribute to the CAS and its subscales 'collectively' rather than individually'* (McCutcheon et al. 2003: 319), which conflicts with any standard textbook on statistical analysis.

The need for an alternative conceptualisation of fans

The presented truly interdisciplinary taxonomy offers the first detailed overview of how fans and fandom have been conceptualised across the contemporary literature of various academic disciplines. Considering these different and sometimes even devastating views of fans, it may seem that admitting in this book to my own personal infatuation with the film actress Jena Malone and risking to be branded with one of the above-mentioned stereotypes in the academic and popular discourse would indeed be an unwise move (Wohlfeil & Whelan 2012). Nevertheless, the taxonomy also highlights a number of conceptual limitations and deficits within every single one of the seven fan conceptualisations that often have their origins in the respective scholars' own agendas and prejudices (Smith et al. 2007). Indeed, if you take individual instances, consumption experiences and practices (i.e. the enthusiastic appreciation of the media text or the celebrity and his/her creative work, the admired subject's elevated role in the fan's private life or the dedicated collection and treasured possession of associated items) out of their holistic context and look at them in isolation and through an ideological-theoretical lens, then you may find some empirical support for each of the seven fan conceptualisations in the autoethnographic consumer story of my own fan relationship with Jena Malone in Chapter 4.

At the same time, however, my autoethnographic research data appear simultaneously to confirm *and* to contradict the preconceptions within each of these conceptualisations of fans and fandom in the interdisciplinary literature – to the extent that each of them leaves most of my personal emotional attachment to

Jena Malone unexplained. And as none of these conceptualisations of fans either fully captures or explains many facets of my own everyday fan consumption experiences, I cannot stop wondering whether there is maybe much more to a consumer's fan relationship with a celebrity (or any other media texts) than what previous studies have uncovered and discussed so far. The suspicion is further strengthened by the fact that all previous studies underpinning the conceptual foundation for each of the taxonomy's seven conceptualisations of fans share essentially three major commonalities. As already pointed out earlier, previous research has investigated fans and fandom nearly exclusively from an outsider-looking-in perspective by imposing the researcher's own preconceived abstract ideas and ideologies onto the phenomenon (Smith et al. 2007), which often evolved from sharing and building on the same original sources such as Munsterberg's (1916) theory of the vulnerable audience. As much of the current body of the fan studies literature, except for some ethnographic studies, has often been developed without the scholars actually engaging directly with the subjects of their investigation, many preconceived conceptual ideas and theories have been passed on without ever being challenged or confronted with the reality.

Second, previous research, which has focused on actual fans, has exclusively studied certain, more *'extreme'* subgroups of fans often under very special, extraordinary circumstances like Star Trek conventions, fan-blocks, football or celebrity fan-club meetings or on dedicated fan-sites/-blogs (Jenkins 1992; Richardson & Turley 2008; O'Guinn 1991) for two obvious reasons: (a) they are easily identifiable and *'readily available'* for scholarly observation, and (b) their *'extreme'*, out-of-the-ordinary behaviour makes it easier for researchers to portray them as the *'deviant other'* in society. However, this also means that fan scholars have paid virtually no attention to the ordinary everyday lived experiences of the *'normal'* fan in one's daily life. Third, all earlier studies have focused on the meaning and nature of the social dynamics and symbolic relationships that consumers experience with other fans within the context of their respective consumption subcultures (Henry & Caldwell 2007; Hills 2002; Lanier & Schau 2007) or the psychological well-being and mental states of fans (Jenson 1992; Leets et al. 1995). Thus, neither a single of the seven conceptualisations of fans nor any single previous study has actually explored the nature of fans' emotional attachments to their admired subjects in the first place. In fact, the subjects of their admiration have always been treated as an interchangeable and exchangeable commodity of no further relevance throughout the entire body of fan literature.

This also explains why I was told by academic scholars on several occasions that, despite my obvious strong emotional attachment to Jena Malone, I could not be a fan simply because I do not participate in any fan community. Therefore, I feel that an alternative conceptualisation of fans is needed, which puts the emphasis back on what is normally the most important factor in any consumer's fandom and, subsequently, should matter the most – the special, emotional bond that fans form, experience and seek to maintain with the subject of their admiration. Hence, my own research journey into the phenomenon of celebrity fandom takes an autoethnographic turn in order to address the conceptual and methodological limitations that restricted previous studies of fans and fandom. My aim, thereby, is to obtain truly holistic insights from a genuine fan's point of view into a consumer's personal everyday lived fan relationship with a celebrity and how it manifests itself in everyday consumption practices and experiences. This enables us to capture and explain the many facets of a fan's emotional attachment to a film star, athlete or any other celebrity (and even to a sports team or media text) in their holistic complexity – and, subsequently, to gain a deeper and more honest understanding of what meaning(s) such a fan relationship may have in an ordinary consumer's daily life. Hence, the time has come to take a closer look at the very subjects of fandom that are at the heart of this book – film stars and celebrities. However, since the fan studies literature has paid scant attention to the emotional attachment that consumers develop, foster and cherish towards their favourite film stars or celebrities, it is necessary to review in more detail the stardom and celebrity literatures in the next chapter.

Notes

1 The very early years of cinema – the so-called *cinema of attractions* – revolved exclusively around a consumer interest in what visual possibilities the film technology offered in representing *'reality'* on the silver screen rather than on the films' actual content. While approximately thousands of new films were produced every month to meet the growing demand, the first films until 1897 were actually very short (approx. 1–2 min. long), non-narrative depictions of vaudeville performers, ordinary people and re-enactments of newsworthy events.
2 Up to 1920, films catered mostly to audiences from the society's lower social classes, such as the working-classes and the new immigrants in the cities along the US East Coast (Kochberg 2007). In fact, the early films were shown as special attractions in travelling vaudeville shows before moving by 1896/7 into more fixed locations – the nickelodeons that were mostly found in the poorer working-class areas of town (Kerrigan 2010). For the middle- and upper classes, films and cinema only became an attractive and acceptable leisure activity with the rise of Hollywood cinema (and the UFA studios) since 1919 and the subsequent growth of theatre-like film palaces (Barbas, 2001).
3 But since the Bowery Boys also were one of the leading gangs in 19th century New York and deeply involved in organised criminality, it would be unfair to equate their behaviour with fandom.
4 107 of the subjects were deemed a *'non-approach risk'*, while 107 had actually approached their *'target'*.
5 The findings also highlight once more the qualitative difference between data reflecting hypothetical intentions (i.e. student samples) and actual real-life observations obtained in the field (i.e. fan mail) in accurately reflecting or describing a phenomenon under investigation.
6 The lack of correlation is hardly surprising, since the CAS scale fails to measure or account for those or any other emotional variables in the first place.
7 Statistical significance is merely a "confidence measure" expressed in the p value. To be 'mildly' statistically significant, p has to be less than 0.05 – meaning the researcher is to 95% confident that a correlation between two variables is not random.
8 Practical significance states the strength of a correlation between two variables and is measured in *R* value. An *R* value of 0.6 and higher would indicate a strong practical

significance, while an R value between 0.3 and 0.6 is considered to be mildly significant. An R^2 value indicates to what extent a change in a dependent variable (= variance) was caused by a change in the independent variable. An $R=0.6$ would therefore translate into an $R^2=0.36$ or 36%. Any R^2 lower than 0.09 (aka $R=0.3$) is deemed to be practically insignificant.

3 The Book of Stars

Consuming human brands

For love of the movies

For more than a century, the film industry has continuously been one of the world's commercially biggest and most successful industries (De Vany 2004; Eliashberg & Sawhney 1994; Ravid 1999) and also spawned a number of major sub-industries from glossy tabloid magazines to merchandising and theme parks that satisfy consumers' relentless fascination with the glamour of film stars, starlets and even minor celebrities (Gabler 1998; McDonald 2003; Turner 2004). For better or worse, the film industry has therefore been engaged in a symbiotic relationship with film audiences since its very early days in the 1890s (Barbas 2001). Especially during the Hollywood studio era from 1919 to 1950, the essential role of film stars in the process has thereby been to encourage consumers to participate actively in this relationship with the film industry as film-goers, enthusiastic film fans and/or loyal followers of particular film stars (McDonald 2000; Stacey 1994). This would suggest that the film industry and film consumption present a *'fruitful research domain for scholars in marketing and other fields'* (Eliashberg et al. 2006).

Hence, it is pretty disappointing that the marketing and consumer research literature, when I started my research back in 2005, has paid very little attention to the marketing and consumption of films or film actors as arts or brands in themselves. This only began to change slightly since 2006/7 following a few select special issues in leading journals. While marketing academics have only recently become at least aware of the economic potential offered by films, film stars and film audiences, however, film scholars have traditionally examined through a sociological-theoretical lens how film viewers perceive and respond as individuals or collective audiences to films and the cinematic experience (Jenkins 2000; Mulvey 1975; Phillips 2007). As film stars are in essence a product of the film industry as much as the films in which they perform (Luo et al. 2010; Watson 2007a), they have over the past 30 years received the sociological-theoretical attention of film scholars. And since they have applied the same methodological approaches that dominate the study of films to the study of film stars, we need to have first a look at how film consumption is studied before we can move on to the stardom literature.

The study of film in marketing

Although the consumption and enjoyment of movies has worldwide never been so popular as in the last three decades (Eliashberg et al. 2006; Kerrigan 2010), neither the marketing nor the consumer research literature has paid much attention to the marketing and consumption of films and film stars as arts brands (Batat & Wohlfeil 2009; Wohlfeil & Whelan 2008), at least until very recently. And even when marketing scholars have actually directed their research interest towards films, they have seen them merely as a medium to promote and sell other products within the marketing communications framework (Wiles & Danielova 2009) rather than as products in themselves. One possible explanation for this blunt neglect might be that films, in contrast to conventional consumer product or service brands, are essentially composite arts brands that represent a complex tapestry of various other arts or human brands (O'Reilly & Kerrigan 2013; Wohlfeil & Whelan 2008).

Indeed, the participating actors, director, producer(s), cinematographer(s), editor(s), scriptwriter(s) and composer(s) are individual human brands (Thomson 2006) that, together, create the film as an arts brand in its own right and, in the process, impact on each other's brand image and value in the public and media either positively or negatively (Albert 1998; Luo et al. 2010). And if the film is the screen adaption of a novel, a comic or the spin-off of another film, then this arts brand is even a sub-brand of another arts brand (Basuroy & Chatterjee 2008; Brown 2002, 2005). The difficulty in dealing with the complexity and unpredictability of film brands accurately may have scared many marketing and consumer researchers away, who rather prefer to remain in the safe comfort zone of the simpler, much more *'straightforward'* traditional, mass-manufactured consumer goods, industrial products or services. The few marketing and consumer researchers that do study film consumption and film audiences tend to take different points of departure with marketing scholars favouring an economic or managerial perspective while consumer researchers look at the different motivations and forms of consuming and enjoying films.

As I have just said, until as recent as the late-1990s, marketing and business scholars' primary interest in film consumption has been concerned with the question of how the popular appeal of films can be exploited to position a specific brand favourably in the minds of consumers. Product placement, in particular, has temporarily captured the interest of marketing academics as the *'latest thing'* in the marketing communications mix (Russell & Stern 2006; Wiles & Danielova 2009). The only problem is that product placement is not exactly new! In fact, a strong cooperative business relationship between the major Hollywood studios and the producers of consumer brands from fashion and cars over beverages to electronic equipment already existed during the Hollywood studio era and can be traced back to as early as 1918 (Barbas 2001; Epstein 2005; Gabler 1998). And although the present blockbuster age (Elberse 2014) has raised it to the extremes, Hollywood studio executives have since the early-1980s considered product placement as a welcome opportunity to raise additional funding for ever more expensive film productions (De Vany 2004; Obst 2013; Wasko 2008). But despite product placement being common practice in the Hollywood film industry ever since, marketing scholars are still keen to investigate (a) whether consumers are able to memorise and recall brands placed in films, (b) how consumers evaluate products placed into a film's art decoration, and (c) what forms of product placement would be most beneficial for a brand (Marchand et al. 2015). The films themselves are thereby often treated as irrelevant and interchangeable, because many marketing scholars and practitioners even today find it impossible to see more in films than mere media vehicles for the marketing of traditional consumer products.

Following Eliashberg and Sawhney's (1994) pioneering study, the *'fruitful research domain'* of film marketing and business (Eliashberg et al. 2006) has only since the late-1990s begun to capture the attention of a small handful of marketing and economics scholars, who have identified a great research potential within the field of media management in general and the film industry in particular beyond their mere usefulness as product placement media (i.e. Basuroy & Chatterjee 2008; Eliashberg et al. 2007; Kerrigan 2010; Swami et al. 1999). Obviously, the limited marketing research that has been and is still conducted so far in relation to films (and to an even lesser extent in relation to film stars) is primarily interested in the economic dimensions of film consumption. Hence, these studies usually focus on measuring and evaluating the profitability of films in terms of their box office performances (Basuroy & Chatterjee 2008; De Vany 2004; Hennig-Thurau et al. 2004) and the sales or rentals of VHS, DVD or media files (Hennig-Thurau et al. 2007; Lehmann & Weinberg 2000).

Particular emphasis is thereby paid to how a film's profitability could be enhanced through managing an efficient film production process (De Vany & Walls 2002; Eliashberg et al. 2007; Ferguson 2009) and an efficient distribution channel in domestic and global markets (Hennig-Thurau et al. 2004; Ravid 1999; Swami et al. 1999). Research that is dedicated to understanding the impact of critical reviews (Basuroy et al. 2003; Eliashberg & Shugan 1997) and word-of-mouth (Liu 2006) on a film's short- and long-term profitability also enjoys growing popularity. While most research has looked only at Hollywood and the US film industry, a few selected studies also explore opportunities for European (and other non-US) film industries to position themselves on domestic and global markets without sacrificing their artistic value (Jansen 2005; Kerrigan & Özbilgin 2004).

In either case, film consumption is thereby reduced to the mere purchase of individual tangible media formats like cinema, VHS, DVD or digital download, by specific consumer segments (Basil 2001; Cuadrado & Frasquet 1999; Lehmann & Weinberg 2000) rather than seen as the consumption of the film as an intangible brand in itself (Batat & Wohlfeil 2009; O'Reilly & Kerrigan 2013; Wohlfeil & Whelan 2008). In addition, films are usually treated as identical and interchangeable products that consumers select for a one-off viewing based on some informed, economic-rational decisions (De Vany 2004; Eliashberg & Sawhney 1994; Hennig-Thurau et al. 2007) rather than as unique cultural artworks (Kerrigan 2010;

Wohlfeil & Whelan 2008). This obviously means that virtually all academic studies measure the success of films based on purely economic criteria such as their box office performances, while ignoring criteria like cultural value, artistic merits and entertainment value. The recent move towards big data only increases rather than alleviates the problem.

The logical consequence is that many of these studies suggest some, for film fans and industry insiders (Obst 2013), quite dubious, dodgy and highly questionable managerial recommendations (De Vany 2004; Elberse 2014). Sadly, considering the major Hollywood studios' output for the last 10 years, it seems that some of those – sometimes quite ridiculous (i.e. Elberse 2014) – recommendations must actually have fallen on some quite attentive ears recently. After all, the times when the film studios were headed by senior executives and managers with an enthusiasm for and/or practical experience in filmmaking – as it was generally the case before, during and shortly after the Hollywood studio era (Epstein 2005, 2012) or with the UFA studios prior to the takeover by the Nazis (Kreimeier 1996) – have now become a thing of the past (Obst 2013). Instead, many of today's senior film studio executives are often accountants, economists or lawyers brought in from outside the film industry by hedge funds holding substantial shares in the studio, although they tend to have little prior personal experience and interest in the film business and/or film production.

For instance, De Vany and Walls (2002) have found in their economic analysis of box office data that the typical family-friendly PG-rated film would apparently generate three times more revenues than R-rated films. Hence, they conclude quite forcefully that it would be *'economically and managerially irresponsible'* for film studio executives to continue green-lightning a four times higher output of R-rated film titles.[1] Now, to the ignorant economic analyst, this conclusion might seem sound. But if the major film studios (continue to) heed De Vany and Walls's (2002) advice, then this would essentially mean in practice that science-fiction, thrillers, horror films and the vast majority of dramatic, intellectually stimulating and much more challenging films, including most Academy Awards winners and nominations of the last 50+ years, are no longer produced (Obst 2013). What film audiences would instead be left with is the popcorn-cinema diet consisting entirely of Disney family-films a la *Highschool Musical*, stereotyped family-friendly romantic comedies and, of course, CGI-animated family-friendly blockbuster-franchises like the countless superhero-movies of late, which Elberse (2014) advocates and celebrates as the 'future'. In other words, cinema as dull, unimaginative and boring as never before in its history!

However, what just seems to be a nightmare vision for now has the potential to become reality very soon, if the film business continues to be left in the hands of economists and hedge fund managers. A case in point relevant to my research is the badly mismanaged European cinema release of Jena Malone's film *Sucker Punch* (US 2011). The film is an exciting audio-visual tour de force with a challenging narrative, whose complexity is clearly unsuited to any audiences under aged 15. But instead of targeting the proper audiences, Warner Bothers made some last minute cuts to get a PG-rating for the film and, due to featuring

Vanessa Hudgens in a support role, to target the prepubescent female audience of her *Highschool Musical* fame. The predictable results were alienated audiences, shocked parents and a relatively poor box office performance. And if you still believe that I may exaggerate a little bit, then have a look at another suggestion by business consultants, which is one of many that appear to have already found the listening ears of today's studio executives. As producing a film is an investment-intensive business that promises high returns on investment, if the film succeeds at the box office, but also holds a high risk of failure (Eliashberg et al. 2007; Wasko 2008), it is hardly surprising that studio executives would like to reduce the financial risks of their film projects.

The truth is that only three out of 10 film releases manage to recoup their investment directly at the domestic box office, while most films' profitability depends on the auxiliary incomes from DVD sales, rentals and legal downloads (Epstein 2012; Kerrigan 2010). Thus, in an attempt to reduce this risk of box office failures, several academic studies have drawn on the old concept of brand extensions from the mass-manufactured FMCG industries and, subsequently, recommend urgently a much stronger reliance on familiar stories, faces, titles and the strategic development of film brand franchises that we have increasingly witnessed over the last 10 years (Basuroy & Chatterjee 2008; Sood & Dreze 2006). The brand extension concept implies that consumers are always faced with the internal fear of making a wrong decision, when having to choose a particular film for consumption, and, thus, seek to reduce the level of uncertainty as much as possible (Eliashberg & Sawhney 1994). The application of the brand extension concept, therefore, would supposedly reassure film audiences that the film's quality meets their expectations and reduce their risk and anxiety of making a bad decision (De Vany 2004; Sood & Dreze 2006).

The problem is that the concept implies two underlying assumptions: (a) consumers make film choices based on purely rational cost-benefit criteria by seeking the familiar and avoiding the novel and surprising, and (b) consumers always watch a film only once and never twice. Both are highly unlikely to occur in real-life consumer behaviour, as the excitement and enjoyment of films derives from their novelty, uniqueness and surprising twists. Films made according to standard formula are received as dull and boring (Batat & Wohlfeil 2009). Yet, the contemporary obsession with releasing an ever-growing number of sequels and prequels to previously successful blockbusters, the increasing number of remakes of foreign films or film classics and the growing trend to producing film franchises would clearly suggest some senior executives at the major Hollywood studios heed the advice. Fortunately, some executives at the bigger independent film studios like Harvey Weinstein or the late Bernd Eichinger still tend to buck the trend with commercial success.

The study of film in consumer research

Taking a humanistic perspective, a small number of consumer researchers discovered in the mid-1980s the value of studying films as a means of enhancing our understanding of consumer behaviour in general (Holbrook & Hirschman 1993). Inspired by Mick's (1986) work on how semiotics could provide insights into the understanding of advertising, films are thereby examined as carriers of consumer symbolism (Hirschman 1987, 1988; Holbrook 1988) rather than as consumption objects in themselves. In their seminal paper, Holbrook and Grayson (1986) have examined how the depicted forms of consumption in the film *Out of Africa* are used to describe the development of individual characters in the film and to carry the film narrative visually. While accepting that works of art represent a cultural mirror to our society and, thus, can teach us something about consumption, the authors make instead a case for using consumption symbolism to understand the meaning of artworks in general and films in particular. In fact, Holbrook, Bell and Grayson (1989) have repeated the exercise shortly after in relation to the theatre play *Coastal Disturbances* in order to demonstrate how such a semiological approach could offer much deeper insights into aesthetic consumption experiences than any traditional quantitative methodology would ever allow.

Hirschman (1988, 1992, 1993; Hirschman & Stern 1994) has taken the opposite point of view and made it part of her life's work to learn from films more about the meaning of consumption in our societies – especially in relation to gender roles, materialism, addiction or prostitution. In the process, Hirschman (1987, 2000a, b) has also sought to uncover how the semiotics of film narratives reflect and disseminate a society's underlying myths and culture. Similarly, Holbrook (2011) shows how the depiction and use of jazz music in films mirrors the existential values and questions in contemporary consumer culture. In either case, expert viewers trained in literary criticism or critical theory watch and deconstruct films in order to analyse their semiotic content from a specific ideology-informed lens (i.e. Marxism, feminism or queer theory) with the aim of deriving critical insights into their underlying meanings for society and the human condition (Hirschman 1988, 1999).

However, the questions that consumer researchers were not addressing, when I started my research journey, were how consumers actually enjoy the consumption of films as experiential products and what subjective contribution they make to an individual's quality of life. A few studies have looked at how consumers make purchase decisions when selecting an experiential product like a film (Cooper-Martin 1991) and their preferences for certain types of film (Cuadrado & Frasquet 1999; Gazley et al. 2010), while others focused on comparing whether one media format would be more attractive for the consumption of films than others (Basil 2001; Hennig-Thurau et al. 2007). Moreover, Holbrook (1999) has explored how ordinary consumers judge the quality and popular appeal of a film in comparison to the judgements of film critics. Hence, I felt the need to take a very different approach by observing my own lived consumption experiences with the film *Pride & Prejudice* (Wohlfeil & Whelan 2008).

While the autoethnographic data clearly show that a complex tapestry of interconnected factors contributes holistically to a consumer's film enjoyment, my research also finds that one's mental immersion into the film narrative and personal engagement with its characters is of particular importance. This personal engagement not only allows for a momentary escape from everyday reality into the imaginary world of the film, but is even further enhanced through out-of-text intertextuality (Hirschman 2000b; Wohlfeil & Whelan 2008), by which the consumer connects the film to one's own private life experiences. In a follow-up study, in which my friend Wided Batat and I compared our personal consumption experiences with the film *Into the Wild* (US 2007), we were not only able to confirm the earlier findings, but have also found that the nature and degree of a consumer's experienced immersion into the film narrative is determined by one's very own personal motives and desires (Batat & Wohlfeil 2009). And in case you might wonder about the findings' transferability, an unrelated recent study (Hart et al. 2016) has come to similar conclusions.

Although some quantitative studies have in the meantime also looked at how consumers' immersion and identification experiences lead to film enjoyment (i.e. Fornerino et al. 2008), due to the methodological shortcomings discussed by Holbrook et al. (1989), they tend to be rather superficial. The positive exception is the detailed research by Addis and Holbrook (2010) that, coincidentally, also shares and confirms a number of my own earlier findings.

The study of film in film studies

If the critical theory approach employed by consumer researchers to examine, analyse and interpret films for the meaning(s) of their semiotic contents sounds familiar, then it is because Hirschman, Holbrook and others have adopted this approach from the scholarly discipline of film studies. Following its humble origins within the film fan discourse during the film industry's early years (Barbas 2001; Gabler 1998), film studies emerged as an academic discipline in the 1930s out of the scholarly tradition of both literature and art studies, which also meant that literary criticism has become well-established as their primary mode of inquiry. Literary criticism or discourse analysis represents a linguistic approach from the humanities, which sets out to explore the triangular dynamics between the author, the text and the reader(s) and examines how the various textual elements are likely to reflect and affect audiences (Stern 1989). Since any text also acts as a mirror of the society's contemporary social and cultural structures from where it originates (Dyer 2000; Sandvoss 2007), the researcher examines the text from a specific ideological viewpoint in order to uncover and identify the hidden power relationships within the cultural contexts that it presents (Duffett 2013; Hirschman 1988, 1999). The most popular ideologies, which are of particular interest to critical film and media scholars as well as cultural critics, are a Marxist theory informed by the philosophers of the Frankfurt School (i.e. Adorno, Horkheimer, Marcuse, Lowenthal, Boorstin, Foucault, Baudrillard, Habermas or Bourdieu), a feminist theory that incorporates some elements of Freudian psychoanalysis and, increasingly, a queer theory that adapts and transfers feminist theory towards homosexual contexts.

But the 1930s also were the heydays of the vertically integrated Hollywood studio system, which was characterised by the industrialised mass production of films through a strong division of labour that resembled more the assembly line in a factory (Epstein 2005; Kochberg 2007) rather than a haven for artistic creativity (Cousins 2011; Jaeckel 2003; Kreimeier 1996). Thus, while film scholars regard *'films as art and appreciate its artistic value, which is an expression of artistic creativity that needs to be consumed by ordinary individuals for their own merit'* (Dyer 2000: 7), film is at the same time also seen as an art form that is endlessly reproducible through factory-like mass production and, hence, caters for a supposedly passive mass audience (Adorno & Horkheimer 2006; Benjamin 2006). But even though the film industry itself has in the meantime gone through several significant structural changes (Kerrigan 2010; Obst 2013), this early heritage and legacy in film studies has nonetheless continued to have a major influence on how film scholars examine, analyse and interpret films and film consumption to this very day (Dyer 2000; Phillips 2007).

This heritage of film studies has also had another outcome that could be considered *'strange'* from an outsider position. Although film studies as a scholarly discipline aim to cover a broad spectrum from film as an expressive art form to its impact on audiences, I find it quite curious that film scholars pay by far less attention to the actual process of film production (Jaeckel 2003; McDonald 2000) than to identifying and examining through ideology-informed critical theory the underlying cultural meanings of films as works of art (Dyer 2000; Nowell-Smith 2000). As a result, critical approaches in film studies, quite similar to literary criticism, can thereby be divided into three major schools of thought depending on whether the primary focus lies either on the film text, the auteur (= creative author) or the audience (Watson 2007b).

The study of films as film texts

Ever since the birth of their discipline in the 1930s, film scholars have continuously focused on the educated criticism of *'film texts'*, which also provides the foundation for the critical reviews of new film releases in the press and the expert judgements on the films' quality (Dyer 2000; Holbrook 1999; Perkins 2000). Particular attention is hereby paid to the films' inherent and formal qualities such as acting performances, narrative flow, mise-en-scene (= props and art decoration), cinematographic framing of the film picture, lighting, sound, editing, etc. by deconstructing and examining through explication or close *'reading'* (actually watching!) how the film, for example, adheres to – or, alternatively, violates – audio-visual conventions and cultural expectations in the narrative developments (Nowell-Smith 2000; Speidel 2007). However, because of widespread public convictions in popular discourse that films would have a powerful effect on the viewers' social beliefs, values and consumer behaviour (Adorno & Horkheimer 2006; Munsterberg 1916; Thorp 1939), which has been heavily promoted by social reformers, cultural critics and the media (Barbas 2001) alike, critical theory in film studies has been informed and even driven by different ideologies (Dyer 2000; Perkins 2000; Speidel 2007).

In light of the highly industrialised nature of the Hollywood studio system and its close association to a capitalist consumer culture (Gabler 1998; Nichols 2000), it should therefore come as no surprise that many film studies (especially those until the 1970s) have followed a neo-Marxist ideology inspired by the writings of Adorno, Horkheimer, Marcuse, Althusser, Lowenthal, Boorstin, Baudrillard, Habermas or Bourdieu. Due to not unjustified concerns that Hollywood cinema seems to advocate a white male-dominated society, feminist ideology has since the 1980s/90s become a much more prominent lens for analysing film. Either way, the aim is to uncover how the narrative and character depictions in specific films reflect or even justify a society's cultural norms, values and underlying power structures as a means of maintaining the status quo (Hirschman 1988; Nichols 2000; Perkins 2000).

The study of creative authorship in films

While the focus on film texts remains relatively popular within film studies and has also been introduced to consumer research through the works of Holbrook and Hirschman (1993), the emphasis on the *'auteur'* (= *'creative author'*) has already proven to be a rather delicate and difficult issue for film scholars and, hence, receives less academic attention. The main reason for it is the problem of identifying the *auteur* in the first place. Indeed, creative authorship in art, literature or music can easily be credited to the respective artist, writer, composer or musician (Schroeder 2005; Winston 1995). But due to the earlier outlined complexities of films and film production as a cooperative artwork that combines creative inputs from various contributing sources, film scholars are faced with a number of complications when trying to associate a film's creative authorship with any one particular individual (Watson 2007b). Indeed, who can honestly claim authorship for a film?

During the old Hollywood studio system from 1918/9 to 1950 (and probably also prior to that by the film companies belonging to the MPPC[2]), all creative decisions regarding a film project were exclusively made by the studio executives, which is also the reason the Academy Award for Best Film is awarded to the film's producer(s) to this very day (Epstein 2005; Puttnam 2006). After all, the producer is responsible for getting the film green-lit and made in the first place by selecting the appropriate script and getting it financed while controlling the budget (Eliashberg et al. 2007; Wasko 2008). But does this qualify for creative authorship? The idea, plot and script are essentially the brainchild of the scriptwriter(s) (Ferguson 2009). Yet, scriptwriters have very little influence on the audio-visual realisation of their scripts once the film is green-lit and goes into production (unless the scriptwriter is also the film's director), and on the final product. The cinematographer(s) is usually the one responsible for the visual element of the film by capturing and framing the scene and performance of the actors with the camera in the *'best aesthetic light'* (Speidel 2007). However, in so doing, s/he is essentially implementing the director's vision and ideas by following the given instructions in the very same way as the actors and actresses also bring their portrayed characters to life under the guidance of the director (Pollack 2006).

Hence, it is no coincidence that most of the auteur theory in film studies has focused on the director as the film's creative author by deconstructing and examining especially the works of famous directors like Sergei Eisenstein, Fritz Lang, John Ford, Billy Wilder, Alfred Hitchcock, Bernardo Bertolucci, Claude Chabrol, Sergio Leone, Martin Scorsese, Steven Spielberg or Quentin Tarantino for some kind of *'creative fingerprint'* as evidence of their artistic genius (Staiger 2003; Watson 2007b). The problem with this approach is that during the Hollywood studio era directors were just another division of labour within the industrial film production process, who were assigned to individual projects by their studio executives (Kochberg 2007). And although a number of directors have, since the 1950s, become well-known or even famous for their creative works, most directors today are still hired by film producers via talent agencies as creative labour for a specific film project rather than being the initiators and creators of their own films (Kerrigan 2010; Pollack 2006). The only exceptions to the rule appear to be the increasing number of low-budget independent art-house and world cinema films that enjoy in recent years both critical acclaim and a growing popularity among film festival audiences and ordinary film-goers (Batat & Wohlfeil 2009; Unwin, Kerrigan, Waite & Grant 2007). Young film-makers (*'first-timers'*) or art film directors, thereby, often try to realise a film project dear to their own heart and creative vision (Kerrigan 2010; Watson 2007b). However, the paradigmatic reading of singling out the director as the creative author of film text has also posed some serious questions to be asked within film studies.

First, identifying only the director as the film's sole creative author devalues the artistic work and contribution of all those other individuals that are involved in the film production process (Watson 2007b). For example, to what extent can the impressive and beautiful landscape shots in *Lord of the Rings* be attributed to Peter Jackson or the ones in <u>*Into the Wild*</u> (US 2007) to Sean Penn rather than to their respective cinematographers? Second, the research of film scholars on creative authorship has been limited to the selected work of a few rather exceptional directors. Not surprisingly, this has often led to the charge that much of the auteur theory is biased, because the respective film scholars are kind of star struck (Lovell 2003; Watson 2007b). For example, while many film scholars tend to accredit the creative authorship of the famous court room scene in *A Few Good Men* to the acting performances of the two lead actors Jack Nicholson and Tom Cruise rather than to director Rob Reiner, it is quite curious that not a single one of them has ever doubted Martin Scorsese's creative authorship of *Goodfellas*; even though the film features a cast of exceptional method actors like Robert De Niro, Ray Liotta and Joe Pesci. Why exactly do film scholars now find Martin Scorsese more worthy of being considered an auteur than someone like Rob Reiner? As a result of these and similar questions, film scholars largely tend to side-step the issue of creative authorship by turning away from the practice of filmmaking towards the critical-theoretical analysis of film text described earlier or towards the critical-theoretical examination of spectatorship and audience responses (Phillips 2007).

The study of audience responses to films

Ever since the first pictures began to move and since the first films were shown in vaudeville shows in 1895 or later in the nickelodeons, there has always been an academic interest in understanding how films affect their audiences (Barbas 2001). Having initially drawn on Munsterberg's (1916) idea of the passive and vulnerable audience, a genuine consideration for the film audience's role in co-creating meaning in films through a personal dialogue with the film text has only developed slowly in conjunction with similar developments in literary criticism since the early-1980s (Phillips 2007; Stern 1989). Hence, film scholars seek to explain the effects of films on viewers critically through the conceptual approach of *'audience-response theory'* (Hirschman 1999). But before reviewing the academic film studies literature on *'audience-response theory'*, I need to point out that film scholars seem to have the habit of equating film consumption exclusively with the cinematic experience, while completely ignoring the basic fact that consumers also watch the same films on TV, DVD or even as downloads on their tablets and smartphones.

Due to its focus on how film viewers interact in theory with film texts, audience-response theory would seem to be a critical theory approach that may also be of particular interest to consumer researchers to obtain insights into the phenomenon of film consumption. Incidentally, Scott (1994) has already introduced reader-response theory to marketing as a conceptual approach to examine, analyse and interpret the effects of advertising on consumers from a cultural-critical perspective. Hirschman (1999) has followed up on this introduction by applying audience-response theory in its original meaning to examine how consumers may interpret TV shows as consumption objects in themselves. Thus, instead of the ordinary film audience member like you and me, whom Hirschman (1999) calls *'common-culture readers/viewers'*, a selected group of *'expert readers/viewers'* formally trained in Marxist and/or feminist critical theory have thereby been asked to examine critically how a pilot TV show would be read/ watched by its audiences.

However, despite the interesting theoretical insights that this critical approach may generate, I have some serious doubts regarding the practical value of audience-response theory in providing a genuine understanding of how real consumers, as *'common-culture viewers'*, respond and interact with films as part of their everyday lived consumption experiences (Batat & Wohlfeil 2009). Indeed, audience-response theory only reflects the views of expert viewers trained in ideology-informed critical theory, who seek to demonstrate in theory how an imagined, idealised viewer would respond as an individual audience member to the film text and the overall cinematic experience (Jenkins 2000; Phillips 2007). Based on their own underlying ideology-informed critical agenda, these trained expert viewers, thereby, assume what prior knowledge, motives and probable expectations their imagined audience member[3] supposedly has (Hirschman 1999; Mulvey 1975; Stern et al. 2005). A synthesis of ideas from linguistics, semiotics, Marxism, feminism and, in particular, psychoanalysis has thereby created and often (re-)confirmed the image of the passive, gullible viewer, who tends to be vulnerable to the manipulative qualities of the cinematic experience and adopts the ideological *'look of the camera'* without questioning (Munsterberg 1916; Stern et al. 2005; Thorp 1939).

On the other hand, the ideological *'look of the camera'* is also said to allow the passive (usually male) audience member to satisfy one's personal *'voyeuristic sexual pleasures and desires'* (Hansen 1986; Jenkins 2000; Mulvey 1975). Due to its development primarily in times of social unrest in the USA, the problem with audience-response theory is that, in the process, it has essentially become a study of ideology through the medium of film (Lovell 2003), where expert viewers often discuss assumed audience responses purely as a means of advancing their own personal political-ideological agenda (Hirschman & Stern 1994; Phillips 2007). Influenced in the early-1970s by the US women's liberation movement, feminism in strong connection with psychoanalytical criticism has thereby become the predominant mode of critical inquiry for film and media scholars in relation to today's audience-response theory.

For instance, Mulvey's (1975) famous paper on the supposed role of the *'male gaze'* in the pleasure of the cinematic experience is primarily aimed at supporting her personal ultra-feminist ideological views rather than exploring film enjoyment itself. By drawing quite *'liberally'* on Freudian psychoanalysis, Mulvey (1975) argued that cinematic film viewing pleasure derives exclusively from the *(male) viewer's* sexual exploitation of the female figure on screen. Not only is the female figure, according to Mulvey (1975), supposedly subject to *'his'* voyeuristic desires by being solely displayed in her exhibitionist role as a *'decorative sexual (lust) object'*, but she is then further sexually consummated through *'his'* identification with the male lead protagonist as *'his'* screen surrogate.

But apart from the complete absence of any supporting qualitative or quantitative evidence based on responses or observations of real film audiences, the major problem with Mulvey's (1975) theory is that more than half of the global cinema audiences since the birth of the movies have been ... female. By simply ignoring the existence of female film audiences in their entirety (Hansen 1986), Mulvey fails to explain why and how female film viewers would actually experience cinematic viewing pleasure themselves. Thus, if Mulvey's (1975) theory is true, would that not mean that all those female film viewers must either be lesbians or masochistically disposed? Is it therefore not rather possible that female viewers derive their viewing pleasure from the sexual exploitation of the male figure and his sexual consummation through her identification with the female lead as her screen surrogate? However, while feminist scholars have no problem accepting Mulvey's thesis, they tend to deny the outlined possibility out-of-hand.

Interestingly, Hansen (1986) has found out in interviews with senior citizens that female audiences from the early-1920s onwards have already enjoyed satisfying their very own romantic and sexual fantasies through the visual consummation of male film stars like Rudolph Valentino, Errol Flynn or Clark Gable as sexual objects. In absence of real-life alternatives, male film stars appear to offer female audiences the only culturally acceptable way of living out their sexuality in a morally strict society (Hansen 1986). Stacey (1994) has come to a similar conclusion in her review of female fan-letters from the 1950s. And even though my own autoethnographic data (Wohlfeil & Whelan 2008) suggest that some form of sexual attraction and consummation of the actor, actress or the portrayed character may under certain circumstances occur, it tends to happen after the consumption of the film as temporary romantic, non-exploitative fantasies.

Neon Demon

Following this detailed review of the academic literature on film consumption, we can now finally turn to the very part of the film industry that is the subject of celebrity fandom and, thus, at the heart of the research journey in this book: film actors and actresses. But despite the special focus on film actors, the findings of this research journey also apply to rock/pop stars, athletes or any other celebrities. As already mentioned earlier, film actors and, especially, film stars[4] are not only the one profession that consumers associate most with films, but in essence are also a product of the film industry as much as the films they are featuring in; and which sometimes even make them famous in the first place (De Cordova 1991; Gamson 2006; McDonald 2000). Although, historically, the first film studios and the MPPC in particular initially tried to keep the names of their film actors anonymous as a means of keeping their salaries and costs at a minimum (Barbas 2001; Gabler 1998), the Hollywood studios instead sought since the very early days of the vertically integrated studio system to manage their leading actors as capital investments that attract film audiences in large numbers and, thereby, ensure the profitability of their films at the box office (De Cordova 1991; McDonald 2000).

Thus, from 1918 to the late-1940s, the Hollywood studios employed an entire division of publicists, whose sole responsibility it was to develop attractive images for potential film stars that would meet the demands of the film-viewing public (Barbas 2001; Gamson 2006). And even decades after the enforced break-up of the mighty studio system, it is common practice that film actors and any other celebrities build, develop, position and maintain a recognisable public image for themselves to ensure their own employability within today's entertainment industries – or the *'almighty agencies'* do that for them (McDonald 2000; Tuchinsky 2006). Subsequently, the study of film stars is determined by the same scholarly interests and modes of inquiry as the study of films I have just discussed. But while the stardom literature has emerged within film studies by the 1980s to examine the semiotic symbolism of film stars as textual images in film (Dyer 1998; King 1991), marketing and consumer research have primarily paid attention to the role that these *'human brands'* (Thomson 2006) could play as celebrity endorsers in the marketing of other commercial brands (Erdogan 1999; McCracken 1989).

The study of film stars in marketing and consumer research

When the former independent film companies began to settle between 1912 and 1918 in the Los Angeles region and formed the vertically integrated studio system, they also gave birth to what became known as the Hollywood star system (De Cordova 1991; McDonald 2000). Ever since those early days, film actors have essentially been managed as *'human brands'*, whose on- and off-screen images, personal identities and reflected values are carefully designed and positioned previously by the Hollywood studios and these days by powerful talent agencies to suit market needs (Gamson 2006; Levin et al. 1997; Thomson 2006). Since film stars, rock/pop stars, athletes and even minor celebrities are such big business and have captured consumers' imagination for more than a century (Geraghty 2000), it is quite peculiar that marketing and consumer researchers have until recently paid so little attention to them as *'human consumption objects'*. This scant attention is the more disappointing, as many marketing and consumer researchers still seem to find it extremely difficult to see in film stars and celebrities anything more than their mere potential as endorsers of consumer products (Erdogan 1999; McCracken 1989) or their contribution to the box office (Albert 1998; Elberse 2007; Luo et al. 2010).

Thus, it should come as no surprise that much of marketing's still very limited knowledge of how consumers actually consume and relate to film stars and celebrities is still informed by a quite simplistic celebrity endorsement literature that pays nearly exclusive attention to the positive, but also negative image transfer between the celebrity endorser and the commercial consumer brand (Erdogan 1999; Misra & Beatty 1990; Spry et al. 2011). Celebrities are thereby conceptualised only as static, unidimensional entities with a homogenous image that is not further explored. This allows for a superficial focus on image congruency, similarity and fit (Arsena et al. 2014; Misra & Beatty 1990; Spry et al. 2011) to propagate a straightforward top-down meaning transfer from the celebrity to the endorsed brand (Erdogan 1999). The only exception is McCracken[5] (1989), who defines film and TV stars as *'complex and individualised semiotic sets of culturally constructed meanings'* that they accumulate through their portrayal of virtually identical fictional characters on screen and that they, then, transfer via the endorsed brand to the consumer.

The scant business research that looks since the late-1990s at film stars themselves is mainly interested in measuring either their brand value (Levin et al. 1997; Luo et al. 2010; Wei 2006) or their economic contribution to the commercial success or failure of films at the box office (Albert 1998; Beckwith 2009; Elberse 2007). The studies' overall inconclusive and contradicting findings, however, usually stem from their crucial conceptual failure to clarify who is a film star in the first place – or, more precisely, when exactly is a film actor or actress a film star and when not. While Wallace et al. (1993) have selected the win of an Academy Award as their main criterion, other studies operationalise film stars based on the actors' track records of their previous films' box office performances (Albert 1998; Elberse 2007; Ravid 1999; Wei 2006). Despite being a convenient proxy measure for quantitative modelling, it should be quite obvious that neither of these common criteria is of any practical value to distinguish film stars and their personal contribution to a film's commercial success from that of any other film actors and creative talent.

First, the Academy Awards honour the artistic merits of an actor's performance in portraying a specific character as one's professional achievement rather than the film's commercial success (Wallace et al. 1993). Indeed, most Academy Award winners and nominees are rewarded for their acting performances in films that earn high critical acclaim but often achieve only moderate box office success (McDonald 2000). Moreover, many film actors have received their Academy Awards at a later stage into their career. Does this now mean that those actors are not film stars for most of their professional lives, only to have their *'starhood'* awarded posthumously, so to speak? Furthermore, it is well-known that awards have from time to time been handed out by the Academy of Motion Picture Arts & Sciences for internal political reasons rather than true artist merits.

Second, there are also a number of conceptual flaws with focusing on a film actor's box office track records. First of all, this narrow focus leads us back to the murky waters of creative authorship, as the credit for a film's commercial success is given only to the one or two lead actors, while the contributions of all other cast members and the entire film crew are ignored. And it also fails to acknowledge that many famous film actors choose from time to time to play only a support role in a film rather the lead role. Finally, participating in successful blockbusters does not necessarily earn you stardom. For instance, while the literature generally discusses Will Smith as a film star due to his track record of commercial successes with films like *Independence Day* and *Men in Black* (King 2003), Jeff Goldblum is usually denied the same recognition despite having starred in *Jurassic Park*, *Lost World: Jurassic Park* and *Independence Day*. Furthermore, many blockbusters in recent years, such as *Jurassic Park*, *Harry Potter*, *Spiderman*, *Avatar* or *The Hobbit*, do not really feature any famous film stars in the lead roles at all and still have – or because of it – been commercial successes.

In the last few years, a handful of consumer researchers have become interested in examining the role of celebrities in contemporary consumer culture (Eagar & Lindridge 2014; Hewer & Hamilton 2012b). By deconstructing individual celebrities as iconic brands, they seek to gain deeper insights into the creation of personal identity myths in the capitalist marketplace (Cocker et al. 2015; Hackley & Hackley 2015; Mills et al. 2015). But despite some interest among individual consumer researchers in understanding the nature of consumer-celebrity relationships in recent years, the stranglehold of the celebrity endorsement literature on marketing thought is still so dominant that even those few studies that seek to explore the nature of consumer-celebrity relationships in everyday life (Banister & Cocker 2014; Hewer & Hamilton 2012b; Thomson 2006) tend to feel obliged to look mainly at how celebrities contribute to consumers' personal and cultural identity projects through their direct or indirect (= often unintended) associations with commercial products and brands.

For example, Thomson (2006) focuses on identifying the nature and extent of consumers' emotional attachment to celebrities from the narrow perspective of the consumer-brand relationship literature with the central aim of exploiting them for targeted celebrity endorsements. His findings suggest that consumers feel more strongly attached to a celebrity, when the celebrity does not suppress the consumer's *'feeling of competence'* but enhances *'feelings of relatedness'* and *'autonomy'* instead, and that a consumer's strong attachment indicates a satisfied, trusting and committed relationship with the celebrity (Thomson 2006). However, I cannot say that feelings of 'competence' or 'autonomy' have ever played a role in my own fan relationship with the film actress Jena Malone. Moreover, Thomson (2006) fails to differentiate between very different types of relationships (i.e. professional, social, family, romantic or sexual) and has instead measured consumer-celebrity relationships based on transaction-oriented economic cost-benefit criteria taken from the consumer goods branding literature.

Only a handful of consumer researchers like myself have actually explored how consumers either express their devotion to certain celebrities through the shared meanings and values in like-minded fan communities (Henry & Caldwell 2007; Hewer & Hamilton 2012a; O'Guinn 1991), experience grief after a beloved celebrity's death (Radford & Bloch 2012) or develop a personal, perhaps even *'romantic'* parasocial fan relationship with their adored celebrities by projecting their own dreams and desires onto them (Wohlfeil & Whelan 2011, 2012).

The study of celebrities in media studies

While it is disappointing that the marketing and consumer research literature has, until the last few years, paid such scant attention to the study of film stars and celebrities beyond their potential as celebrity endorsers for consumer brands or their contribution to a film's commercial success at the box office, the audience appeal of film stars and celebrities has, nonetheless, caught the interest of film and media scholars since the 1980s and led to two significant bodies of literature on stardom within film studies and on celebrity culture within media studies. But although the stardom and celebrity literatures often tend to supplement each other, the two academic disciplines have very different conceptual points of departure, because of their very different scholarly agenda. While the stardom literature centres nearly exclusively on the study of film stars as film texts (Dyer 1998), the celebrity literature's focus has traditionally been on the *'bigger question'* of what meaning fame and celebrity have in our contemporary culture (Barron 2015; Redmond 2014).[6]

In incorporating and building directly on the earlier work of cultural critics (i.e. Adorno & Horkheimer 2006; Boorstin 1961; Lowenthal 2006; Weber 2006), who were strongly influenced by a neo-Marxist sociological-ideological agenda or as social reformers like the Christian Temperance Union, media scholars look at *'how the media portrayal and construction of celebrities shape the way in which audiences understand and make sense of the social world'* (Barron 2015). In so doing, the field of media studies investigates celebrities as an abstract concept that supposedly mirrors our quest for fame and the desire to stand out of the crowd (Giles 2006) rather than how consumers really relate to individual celebrities. Media scholars and cultural critics have thereby quarrelled amongst themselves for several decades now whether celebrity culture would really constitute the serious cultural decline predicted in the academic and popular discourse (Boorstin 1961; Giles 2006; Schickel 1985) or whether it would actually represent a genuine democratic process of social levelling (Alberoni 2006; Marshall 1997; Turner 2004).

The proponents of the traditional *'celebrity-as-cultural-decline'* perspective (i.e. Cashmore 2006; Gabler 1998; Giles 2006; Schickel 1985) are influenced by Munsterberg's (1916) idea of the vulnerable audience, which implies that consumers would be passive and defenceless recipients of media texts, who are incapable of differentiating fictional media images from factual reality. Cultural critics like Lowenthal (2006), Thorp (1939) and Baudrillard (1970) have then elaborated on this theory further and theorised that the sole purpose of the creative industries and, by extension, celebrity culture is to divert people's attention away from the important things in life and, instead, direct them towards orchestrated, superficial pseudo-events. But it was Boorstin (1961) in particular, who has informed the current *'celebrity-as-cultural-decline'* discourse (Barron 2015) and inspires contemporary media scholars such as Cashmore (2006), Gabler (1998) or Schickel (1985) to go even a step further.

According to Boorstin (1961), fame was in the past only attributed as a public (usually posthumous) acknowledgement in recognition of a person's special skills and heroic achievements; and, subsequently, had scarcity value. Celebrity, on the other hand, is awarded without the requirement of any talent or heroic achievement. Hence, Boorstin (1961) argued that celebrity stands for a culture that seeks instant gratification and that values *'surface image'*, narcissistic self-obsession and *'fame-for-its-own-sake'* over substance and the personal striving for a *'greater good'*. His subsequent conclusion that celebrities are only *'people who are famous for being famous'* has dominated the celebrity discourse within media studies and the popular media ever since. But although his much-cited, derogatory definition of celebrities may be fitting in some cases like the present reality TV craze (Giles 2006; Redmond 2014), overall it is nonetheless quite unfair, as the respective claim to fame of celebrities can be pretty diverse. Indeed, celebrities can be famous for their artistic-creative talent, their professional achievements, their personal relationships with other famous people (i.e. as a spouse, offspring, relative or love affair) or, well, their notoriety for an *'outrageous'* and *'scandalous'* public life-style, such as an excessive social party-life, having extra-marital love affairs, posing nude for photographs in the tabloids or having a home-made sex video *'leaked'* onto the Internet (McDonald 2003).

While the proponents of the *'celebrity-as-cultural-decline'* perspective view celebrity primarily as the evil manifestation of an excessive capitalist consumer culture that corrupts our hearts, minds and souls (Gabler 1998; Schickel 1985), the proponents of the more recent *'celebrity-as-social-levelling'* perspective (i.e. Hills 2016; Kanai 2015; Levy 1989; Marshall 1997) take a more optimistic point of view by using Alberoni's (2006) work as their conceptual point of departure. In their opinion, celebrity culture represents the natural end-point in a long process of democratisation in capitalist consumer culture (Turner 2004). And while Alberoni (2006) theorised that film stars and celebrities still represent a *'powerless elite'*, who can commend the attention and reverence of their audiences and the media alike but do not have real political power, Levy (1989) and Marshall (1997) argue that, although celebrities may not have the power to make political decisions, they are still in the position to direct the public's attention to certain causes and to mobilise the masses for or against particular policies.

Marshall (1997) also suggests that celebrities are the visual representations of social mobility in democratic societies, where fame is the ultimate reward for one's effort in self-improvement. Celebrities, therefore, express the democratic values and personal freedom that the capitalist consumer culture offers each of us through the widely available access to digital media technologies and consumer products, as epitomised by the growth in reality TV or the bloggers and, especially, vloggers who have become self-made social media celebrities (Marwick 2016; Turner 2004). And even if we, as consumers, do not manage to rise to fame ourselves, we are still empowered as audiences to determine through our consumption preferences which celebrities succeed or fail in a highly competitive marketplace (Marshall 1997); be it through buying or downloading music songs or albums, watching films in the cinema, on DVD or TV or just voting for certain contenders on reality TV shows. Consumers are even given the power to make or break celebrities and to indulge in their private lives through the exchange of gossip in popular media outlets or social media (Hermes 2006; Hermes & Kooijman 2016).

However, while the two dominant perspectives in media studies may differ in their views on the meaning of celebrity in contemporary culture, both their focus is centred on the shared idea that celebrity reflects the human desire for being famous and recognised (Giles 2006; Marwick 2016), but offer no genuine insights into why consumers feel emotionally attached to one celebrity, but not another (Hills 2016).

The study of film stars and actors in film studies

Since marketing and consumer researchers have had very little interest in studying the consumption of film actors, it seems to be a pretty good idea if we take a closer look at the one academic discipline that you would expect to be dedicated to the study of film actors: film studies. However, it is quite surprising to learn that the academic study of film stardom is only a relatively recent development within film studies, even though film (like theatre) is a performing art form that has from its early beginnings relied on the creative work of professional actors (De Cordova 1991; Gamson 2006; McDonald 2000). In fact, without actors there would not be any films at all – if you exclude documentaries and animation films. Yet, film scholars have until the early-1980s shown surprisingly little interest in the art of acting (De Cordova 2006; Thompson 1991) or in the study of film actors themselves (Dyer 1998; King 1991; Staiger 1991).

This initial lack of interest among film scholars in the study of film actors and screen acting can be explained by the discipline's obsessive academic preoccupation with the critical examination of film texts while simultaneously ignoring the actual practice of filmmaking in its entirety. In fact, for most of the time, film studies have treated actors only as a division of labour within the film production process and, thus, as unworthy of any scholarly attention (De Cordova 1991, 2006). Subsequently, the acting performances of film actors have only been examined as another inevitable part of the film text just like the mise-en-scene, the sound, the lighting or the camera frames (Dyer 1998; Thompson 1991). Although there were a few earlier, largely unnoticed studies, this traditional point of view only changed with the publication of Richard Dyer's seminal book *'Stars'* in 1979, which has conceptually and ideologically defined (with very few exceptions) the study and understanding of film stardom within the field of film studies (and beyond) to this very day (King 1991; Lovell 2003). Nevertheless, it still took until the early-1990s, before the study of film stardom could finally establish itself as a scholarly sub-discipline.

Dyer's conceptual understanding of film stardom

You have probably noticed by now that I often try to differentiate between the terms *'film stars'*, *'film actors/actresses'* and *'celebrities'*. My intention, hereby, is to get around some connotative difficulties that arise from the conceptual question as to when exactly a film actor can be called a film star and when not. For me personally, film stars are simply ordinary film actors, who just happen to be famous because of their commercial and/or artistic success as a performer. And I am confident that you and many other consumers would largely agree with my definition. Film scholars, on the other hand, propagate a very different understanding of the term *'film star'* by making very clear conceptual distinctions between *'film stars'*, *'film actors/actresses'* and other *'ordinary celebrities'* (King 1991; Staiger 1991) grounded entirely in Dyer's (1998) original interpretation. First, film scholars have developed the general habit of seeing stardom as an exclusively cinematic phenomenon (Dyer 1998; Haskell 1999; King 1991), which is primarily tied to the glamour of Hollywood. In so doing, the status of stardom is essentially denied to famous performers from other creative industries such as rock/pop musicians, stage actors, TV personalities, athletes and, in particular, those actors, who feature mainly in TV films or soap operas (Lacey 2003; Watson 2007a). Thus, it is hardly surprising that film scholars tend to complain on regular occasions that the term *'star'* is becoming almost meaningless due to its constant *'overuse'* in the public discourse (Dyer 1998; King 1991). The major problem with this argument, however, is that the star system is not really an invention of the film industry in the first place (Barbas 2001; De Cordova 1991; Studlar 2016).

The Italian opera, for instance, had already a century earlier spawned a number of star tenors, who became internationally famous – at least within the culturally educated European societies – for their singing voices and interpretations (Gabler 1998). In the 18th and 19th century, their fame was only outshined by the infamous castrati, whose claim to fame, however, came at a very heavy price that was not really encouraging at all.[7] Furthermore, at the outgoing 18th and early 19th century, a number of British theatre actors earned a popular reputation for their individual acting styles and stage performances and regularly went on sold-out tours throughout the US (Gabler 1998; McDonald 2000; Studlar 2016). This led to the development of a home-grown star system within the US theatre industry long before the arrival of film (Barbas 2001). New York's Broadway should thereby become and remain to this very day the undisputed epicentre of the US theatre industry, while a number of so-called stock companies toured the vast US country-sides (Gabler 1998; Studlar 2016). Interestingly, the first actors in the film industry's early days were usually those stage actors, who were only cast by theatre companies in minor support and chorus roles or were even *'in-between'* jobs – meaning unemployed (Barbas 2001).

Because the promotional emphasis of the MPPC members was still on their patented film technology, the actors in the early narrative films from 1897 to 1913 were not even credited (Barbas 2001; De Cordova 1991). This only changed slowly from 1913 onwards, when the independent film producer Carl Laemmle and his company IMP (now Universal Pictures) began to promote the former Biograph-girl Florence Lawrence as their films' main audience attraction (Barbas 2001). From then on, the independent film companies that should later become the major Hollywood studios started to credit film actors/actresses as a means of differentiating their films from the competition (McDonald 2000; Studlar 2016). However, only after the quasi-monopoly of the MPPC had been dismantled and the independent film companies evolved between 1916 and 1920 into the major global players of today was the foundation laid for the Hollywood star system (Barbas 2001; McDonald 2000).

Second, and more interestingly, Dyer (1998) argues that film stars can *never* be film actors, because they are special! In his opinion, film stars reflect a glamorous artistic elite that by its very nature is different from the *'common film actors'*, who are nothing else but merely the professional labour force within the film industry (De Cordova 1991, 2006). This distinction is firmly grounded in the conceptual idea that film actors are just a division of labour in the industrial filmmaking process, in which film studies as an academic discipline has had little interest in the first place, while film stars are seen as another form of cinematic texts that can be examined through the same critical approaches that are already used in the study of film texts or audience-response theory (King 1991; Krämer 2003; Staiger 1991). Of course, this stardom discourse was helped by the organisational structure of the vertically integrated Hollywood studio system from 1918 to the late-1940s, where employees had their accommodation assigned on the studio grounds according to their hierarchical status. Only the studio's leading directors, producers and film stars were accommodated in their own houses in proximity to the studio. Nonetheless, the interpretation of film stars as texts within film studies shows a strong resemblance to McCracken's (1989) definition of celebrities or Thomson's (2006) concept of celebrities as human brands. In all three cases, film stars are considered to be different from other film actors, because they are *not* humans, who work as professionals in the performing arts, but living semiotic images, whose signification is realised through a diversity of media texts and public discourses (Dyer 1998; Haskell 1999; Hollinger 2006; King 1991).

Despite acknowledging that film stars are real-living human beings, Dyer (1998) argues that we are unlikely ever get to meet and know them in person as the real people they are in private. Instead, we are essentially forced to settle with what we learn about them in various on- and off-screen media texts – in other words, the public image and private identity that they signify to the audience. That is why Dyer (1998) describes film stars generally as systems of semiotic images that personify the capitalist consumer society's cultural ideals of success, glamour, the extraordinary and even the divine. In fact, despite being literally embodied by real human beings through their name, physical appearance, voice and acting skills, Dyer (1998) theorises that film stars are to us only accessible through their semiotic on- and off-screen manifestations in various film and other media texts, in which they portray a firm, stable and recognisable canon of virtually identical characters (cultural archetypes) that personify particular cultural values and desires (Hollinger 2006; Kirkland 2003; Williams 2006).

Moreover, drawing on selected examples from the Hollywood studio era of the 1920s to early-1950s, Dyer (1998) also argues that film stars are always admired as *'flawless, superior'* human beings, who display a consistent mediated public image both on- and off-screen by portraying only those characters on film that mirror their own *'true'* personality and life-style in their private lives (Hollinger 2006; King 1991). He has thereby identified two ideological concerns as the major reasons for studying film stars, which he broadly characterises as the sociological and the semiotic. The former centres on film stars as a social consumer culture phenomenon in a capitalist society, where films are of interest purely because they have film stars starring in them (Dyer 1998; Haskell 1999; Staiger 1991). The latter, on the other hand, views film stars as a representative system of cultural symbols, where film stars and what they signify only exist within the context of film and media texts (Dyer 1998; Hollinger 2006; Krämer 2003). As a result, critical approaches in the study of film stardom have developed broadly into three principle schools of thought that focus on *'stars as commodities'*, *'stars as texts'* or *'stars as objects of desire'* (Watson 2007a). It is only too obvious that the three principle schools essentially mirror the three traditional schools in film studies in relation to the auteur, the film text or the audience.

Film stars as commodities

The first (and oldest) critical school of thought on film stardom essentially views film stars as commodities within the economic contexts of film production and marketing (Watson 2007a); and, thus, shares some commonalities with the recent marketing literature on films and film stars (Albert 1998; Elberse 2007, 2014). Film stars, thereby, represent merely a mechanism for selling films to both exhibitors and audiences by guaranteeing them certain cinematic pleasures and enacting a commercial strategy for the marketing of films (McDonald 2000, 2008). However, this already poorly supported critical school has lost even more significance with the publication of Dyer's (1998) book in 1979; until its revival in the late-1990s with, in particular, the work of McDonald (2000, 2003, 2008).

During the Hollywood studio era from 1918 to the late-1940s, any creative and technical talent were tied through long-term contracts as labour force to a particular film studio, which was holding all the legal rights and sole control over the production, management and commercial exploitation (including celebrity endorsements) of film star identities and images (Barbas 2001; McLeod 2006). Therefore, film star identities were manufactured, promoted and managed by the Hollywood studios according to their specific market needs, while the individual actors and actresses in question had virtually no say in it at all (Barbas 2001; Gamson 2006; McDonald 2000). Basically, the aim of the Hollywood star system was to provide film audiences with *'guarantees of predictability'* in relation to a film's quality by embodying or personifying a clearly-defined set of specific expectations and *'promised pleasures'* (Watson 2007a). And in order to ensure exactly that, the Hollywood studios arranged for film stars to portray continuously a certain, clearly recognisable type of characters in similar, if not even identical film genres (De Cordova 1991; McDonald 2000) – a process that became known as *'typecasting'*. But the film studios went even a step further by attempting to align also the (publicly known) private lives of their film stars with that of their respective on-screen persona (Barbas 2001; McDonald 2000). Thus, the creative authorship of the film star's on- and off-screen persona lay exclusively in the hands of the studio executives and not in the hands of individual actors (Gabler 1998).

Since the enforced break-up of the vertically integrated Hollywood studio system in the early-1950s[8], film actors are nowadays hired as free labour by producers on a project-by-project basis (McDonald 2008). Although their interests in dealing with film producers and studios are represented and managed by talent agencies (McLeod 2006; Tuchinsky 2006), the creative authorship of their public on- and off-screen persona, these days, lies largely with the film actors or, at least, with their personal managers (Epstein 2005; McDonald 2003, 2008). As a vital part of the *'package-unit'* around which films are nowadays produced and that are often put together by the major talent agencies (Kerrigan 2010; Obst 2013), film stars have been upgraded from a former commodity to a capital investment that increases the producers' certainty of return, which is reflected in the high salaries that leading film stars can demand for their films these days

(McDonald 2000, 2008; Wasko 2008). And as producers tend to invest more money into films that feature the latest film star, film stars can attract financial backing for a film that would not be available otherwise and ensure with their involvement and sheer on- and off-screen presence the necessary promotional buzz for the film (Epstein 2012; Kerrigan 2010).

Hence, the industrial role of film stars first as commodities and later as capital investment touches and highlights a number of issues in relation to the power structures within the film industry, which has invited a number of film scholars to study this particular side of film stardom from a mainly neo-Marxist and later feminist ideological perspective. By drawing on the writings of Adorno, Althusser, Marcuse, Gramsci, Lowenthal or Weber, these film scholars seek to uncover how the production, management and consumption of film stars reflect and justify the underlying power structures and struggles within the film industry in relation to creative authorship and, subsequently, ownership of film star texts (Beltran 2006; Geraghty 2003; Krämer 2003; Williams 2006). However, as with contemporary media studies, attention is also paid in recent years to the idea of film stars being a democratic elite (Levy 1989), which addresses the presumed paradox that film stars constitute a social elite, who in contrast to the majority of film actors can both demand high salaries for their creative work and also advance film projects that are dear to their heart, but who nonetheless still lack any real political and social power within society (Dyer 1998; Levy 1989; McDonald 2000).

While interesting to read when you enjoy taking an ideologically-informed view on the industrial side of Hollywood's dream factory, film stardom itself is usually investigated as a rather generalised abstract concept. Individual film stars (mostly from the Hollywood studio era) are only referred to when a fragmented facet of their on- and/or off-screen persona suits a particular study as an example for advancing a specific ideological proposition. Therefore, the question regarding the creative authorship of the film star text is discussed in rather simplistic terms as to who has the power, while ignoring a variety of other factors that may influence a film star's identity and image, i.e. the film scripts, directors, tabloid journalism and private life-styles (Lovell 2003).

Film stars as film texts

As an alternative, the second school of thought has derived from and is strongly influenced by Dyer's (1998) original work on film stardom. His specific blend of semiotics, sociology and critical theory focuses on the film star as a text and seeks to understand film stars as a system of signs, or more precisely as an image, constructed through an intertextual network of various film and media texts (Dyer 1998; Watson 2007a). Central to this critical school is the idea that film stars cannot be viewed as real-living people, because the audience will never meet or get to know them privately in person, but instead must be seen as complex semiotic persona made up of the film texts, in which they feature on-screen, and the off-screen texts that can be found in other media texts (Dyer

1998; King 1991). Although film stars are literally embodied by real human beings through their name, physical appearance, personality, voice and specific acting skills, they are accessible to us only through their manifestation in film appearances and *official* (media interviews, publicity events, press releases, official websites, official Facebook and Twitter accounts, biographies, etc.) or *unofficial* (i.e. tabloid news and gossip media, fanzines, fan-sites or social media chatter) media texts (Hollinger 2006; McDonald 2003). Hence, Dyer (1998) differentiates film stars from all other *'common film actors'*, who exist within film texts but have virtually no further presence in external media texts and remain unnoticed by film audiences because of their subsequent insignificance.

As defined by Dyer (1998) and those other film scholars that followed in his path ever since (i.e. King 1991; King 2003; Kirkland 2003; Krämer 2003; Williams 2006), the aim of the stardom literature, therefore, is

> not to peel away these layers of textuality in order to reveal the true self of the star, but to analyse the explicit and implicit meanings of precisely that mediated image and to read it in the context of wider ideological and social discourses.
>
> (Watson 2007a: 130)

The study of film stars, thereby, investigates in particular the duality between a film star's on-screen and off-screen personas with an emphasis on identifying homogeneities and discontinuities between them (Dyer 1998; Hollinger 2006; Staiger 1991). But despite being the dominant mode of inquiry within stardom research, from the perspective of a film scholarly outsider like me, this critical school exposes a number of major weaknesses in its study of film stars that have also been raised by Lovell (2003) in his critical retrospection on the previous 30 years of academic research in this sub-discipline.

First, this conceptual school of thought suggests that the film star as text is clearly recognisable across a variety of film texts by portraying a canon of virtually identical characters (an archetype), which feature certain individual traits and characteristics that are also representative of the film star's private off-screen persona (Beltran 2006; Dyer 1998; Hollinger 2006; Kirkland 2003). Film scholars, thereby, tend to provide evidence for this view by discussing in particular those selected film stars that match their conceptualisation best. And because this conceptual understanding is a true reflection of the Hollywood star system, many film scholars focus their attention on film stars from this specific era or, at least, from the immediate aftermath of its collapse in the 1950s (i.e. Dyer 1998; Haskell 1999; Staiger 1991).

Yet, faced with the need to discuss contemporary film stardom as well, film scholars seek since the 1980s to substantiate their critical approach and conceptualisation by looking at those selected contemporary film stars for examination that portray in essence the same archetypes as their counterparts during the Hollywood star system (Hollinger 2006; King 2003; Kirkland 2003). For instance, the archetype of the romantic hero personified in the Hollywood studio era by charming film stars like Rudolph Valentino, Errol Flynn or Clark Gable and then taken over by Cary Grant and Rock Hudson in the 1950s is nowadays personified by Warren Beatty, Richard Gere and George Clooney, while Sylvester Stallone and Arnold Schwarzenegger represent the modern versions of John Wayne's asexual action hero (Huffer 2003; King 2003). In addition to the highly selective choice of suitable film stars as texts, film scholars also were and still are highly selective in terms of the film and media texts they discuss in relation to a particular film star (Beltran 2006; Hollinger 2006; Kirkland 2003; Williams 2006). In so doing, they tend to include only those film characters in the discussion that support their ideological argument while they simultaneously exclude all those other film characters that do not (King 2003; Kirkland 2003; Williams 2006).

Hence, the ultimate consequence of this critical school is the implied and often-cited argument that film stars – as opposed to *'ordinary, insignificant character actors'* (Dyer 1998) – cannot really act and, instead, only play themselves (Lovell 2003). As a matter of fact, Dyer (1998) himself argues that it is impossible for a *'real'* film star to play any characters other than oneself, as the film audience, due to their knowledge of the film star's other film texts, will always identify him or her as the film star s/he is. This critical school of thought and argument, however, fails to acknowledge the key realities that (a) most film stars actually have a substantial professional background as experienced theatre and/or film actors before *'becoming'* film stars, and that (b) film audiences may actually enjoy and admire the acting skills and convincing character performances of film stars rather than merely consume their textual presences (Lovell 2003). Furthermore, it also fails to recognise that film actors, whether they are film stars or not, essentially portray their characters by following a pre-written script under the supervision and guidance of a director.

Film stars as objects of desire

The third critical school of thought on film stardom views film stars as objects of desire, which is essentially an offspring of audience-response theory and, hence, entrenched in a feminist-psychoanalytic ideology; though queer theory has also gained some momentum since the mid-1990s (Hansen 1986; Huffer 2003; Weiss 1991). Yet, while being strongly influenced by Mulvey's (1975) theory of the *'male gaze'* and the exploitation of the female figure on screen as a (visual) sex object, this critical school in stardom research is nonetheless associated mostly with the works of Hansen (1986), Haskell (1999) and Stacey (1994). Its stated aim is to look at the film audience's explicit role in (re-)constructing the meaning of the textual star image through the act of reading film and media texts, the politics of spectatorship and the *'pleasures of star-gazing'* (Hansen 1986; Stacey 1994) to theorise on the ideological nature of the film star-spectator relationship (Watson 2007a).

The film star is thereby seen as an *'object of desire'* and studied in relation to how audiences engage with and find meaning in film star texts by interacting with them, identifying with them, obtaining some feeling of fulfilment from their textual images or even experiencing moments of erotic pleasure through them (Dyer 1998; Hansen 1986; Stacey 1994). In relation to my own research journey in this book, this critical school seems at a first glance to be predestined for actually providing some theoretical background on how the relationship between a film actress, her fan and the subsequent lived fan experiences expresses itself in everyday consumer behaviour. Unfortunately, for many of the studies within this critical school of stardom research, advancing the respective scholar's own ideological agenda through the sociological-theoretical examination of film star texts appears to be much more important than providing any genuine insights into the actual relationships that real film audience members form with individual film stars (Beltran 2006; Kirkland 2003; Lacey 2003; Weiss 1991).

Grounded in Mulvey's (1975) feminist-psychoanalytic ideology on gender roles in relation to audience responses, the role of female film stars is thereby presented primarily as sexualised spectacles that are solely designed to *'disrupt film narrative with "moments of erotic exhibitionism"'* (Haskell 1999; Stern et al. 2005; Williams 2006), which have very little to do with the story development – other than being *'eye-candy'*. Male film stars, on the other hand, provide the central mechanism for identification for the film audience by being the heroes in full control of the film narrative (Watson 2007a). To support their ideology-informed argument, film scholars provide theoretical evidence again by discussing a highly selective staple of film stars and highly selective film and media texts, which are mostly from the heydays of the Hollywood studio era and, subsequently, well-suited to advance the underlying feminist agenda of exposing female exploitation rather than allowing for genuine insights into actual spectator-film star relationships (Haskell 1999; Mulvey 1975; Williams 2006).

The rise of critical queer theory in film studies since the mid-1990s has added a new twist to the feminist-psychoanalytic critical approach by examining spectator-film star relationships for an explicit interpretation of the underlying homosexual meanings that they assume to be hidden in film star texts within wider social contexts (Huffer 2003; Weiss 1991). But to be quite frank, as a film scholarly outsider, most of the purely ideology-driven studies and their findings sound to me like being a whole lot of pseudo-elitist nonsense, whereby the respective film scholar's own personal ideological agenda, ideals and assumption are projected onto individual film stars as a general truth; even though there has never been any real-life or empirical evidence to support those ideology-informed conceptualisations. In fact, just as already with Mulvey's (1975) feminist-psychoanalytic theory, I often feel that these film scholars (i.e. King 2003; Kirkland 2003; Williams 2006) must be talking about very different film stars (or films) than the ones I know under those names…

Refreshingly different within stardom research and film studies in general, therefore, is the research by Hansen (1986), Stacey (1994) and Barbas (2001) in terms of both methodology and conceptualisation. While Barbas (2001) has used a historical-structuralist method, Hansen (1986) and Stacey (1994) have followed an ethnographic approach to explore and conceptualise the relationship between film stars, spectatorship and pleasure holistically within the context of real film audiences' everyday lives. For that reason, these are the only studies within film studies that I have come across until the last few years, whose findings are actually based on genuine field observations and empirical data involving in-depth interviews, fan-letters, diaries and footage of news reports. The studies have found that female film audiences, in identifying with the female film star and enjoying the (more direct) sexual objectification of the male film star on screen, actually engage in the very same, but reversed behaviour that feminist-psychoanalytic film scholars, for purely ideological reasons, accredit exclusively to male film audiences (Barbas 2001; Hansen 1986).

Stacey (1994) has managed not only to catalogue the different ways by which female film audiences respond to and identify with textual film star images, but also to distinguish between various modes of identification and the subsequent types of experienced pleasures that derive from them. In addition, both Stacey (1994) and Barbas (2001) have critically examined in detail fan-letters that film audiences have posted from 1898 to the late-1960s either to the film studios or directly to their favourite film stars in person. Their findings confirm not only the ethnographic data and observations in Hansen's (1986) and Stacey's (1994) ethnographic research, but also find very little empirical support in the real world of film actors, film audiences and the actual relationships between them for the assumption and conceptualisations that critical film scholars have espoused in the past. Hence, Barbas (2001) and Lovell (2003) criticise in particular how cultural critics as well as film and media scholars have abused their own elitist powers as influential academics to discriminate against those legitimate interests and relationships that film fans form with film stars merely for the purpose of advancing their own self-serving, political-ideological agenda, their scholarly positions within academia and their cultural perspectives without any empirically and methodologically sound justifications.

Geraghty's alternative understanding of film stardom

After having reviewed the traditional stardom literature within film and media studies in more detail, I am not quite sure to what extent it actually provides any insights that would be really useful in explaining why, for example, I feel so emotionally attached to the film actress Jena Malone, admire her acting talent and enjoy watching her films. If I apply Dyer's (1998) widely accepted distinction between film stars, who are famous as much for their glamorous publicised private lives as for their on-screen persona, and ordinary character actors, who disappear completely in their personified characters, then Jena Malone is definitely *'just'* a character actress and not a film star. And this means that, according to Dyer (1998), I should have never noticed her in films or paid any attention to her; not to mention feeling captivated by her. But it is exactly her flexibility to play a variety of different characters and her ability to make each of them appear to be *'real people'* that I admire in particular about her on-screen performances as an actress.

In fact, as Lovell (2003) brilliantly points out, many film stars like Orson Welles, Marlon Brando, Al Pacino, Robert De Niro, Dustin Hoffman, Sean Penn, Katherine Hepburn, Meryl Streep, Susan Sarandon, Sissy Spacek, Jodie Foster or Jennifer Lawrence are often excellent character actors, who have become famous film stars, first and foremost, because of their acting skills. Furthermore, very little is publicly known about their private lives, which clearly contradicts in particular Dyer's (1998) definition that emphasises the importance of the duality between the on- and off-screen personas for the film stardom concept. On the other hand, several rather mediocre (if not poor) film stars are primarily famous for their well-publicised and mediated off-screen persona rather than any substantial on-screen acting performances (Gabler 1998; Geraghty 2000; McDonald 2003). Does this make them now really film stars? But while, for example, Lindsay Lohan, Katherine Heigl or Megan Fox are more known for their off-screen shenanigans and scandals than for any on-screen acting performances, film actresses like Jena Malone, Ellen Page or Jennifer Lawrence often choose to play character roles in critically-acclaimed, independent low-budget films rather than featuring in mediocre, stereotyped teen comedies and blockbusters that the major film studios produce and market in their dozens.

And since Jena Malone has also largely resisted Hollywood's glamour, party-life and gossip-publicity, understands her acting as art and refuses to become sexualised by meeting any prescribed fashion and beauty ideals (Brink 2008; Lyon 2008; Pachelli 2011), few media texts exist in relation to her private off-screen persona. But although there are many more popular, more publicised, more beautiful (?) and more sexualised film actresses out there, it still is Jena Malone who fascinates and captivates me – and not the Nicole Kidmans, Angelina Jolies, Lindsay Lohans, Sienna Millers or Katherine Heigls of the world. In short, the traditional stardom literature fails to address this important issue as much as to accept that there are many film stars and actors out there, who are famous for portraying a diverse set of film characters that differ significantly from their public image and who do not fit its definition of a film star (McDonald 2008). As Lovell (2003) argues, film stars are first and foremost professional actors, who play both lead *and* support roles by following a pre-written script under the guidance of a director.

As a result, Geraghty (2000) eventually called for a much needed rethinking of film stardom and how it should be studied within the context of the modern age of (digital) media convergence. She, therefore, proposes a new approach that takes Dyer's (1998) original idea of film stars as semiotic texts with an on- and off-screen persona as much into account as the, within film studies largely neglected, profession and art of acting that has gained some momentum among some film scholars. Geraghty (2000), thereby, differentiates between the three categories *'stars-as-celebrities'*, *'stars-as-professionals'* and *'stars-as-performers'* in a way that makes much more practical sense to me and is also much closer to my personal naïve understanding of film stars. In general, all three categories have in common that they represent film stars for the first time as real *'living-and-breathing'* professional actors, so that Geraghty (2000) no longer makes any conceptual distinctions between film stars and film actors, but actually views them as one-and-the-same differing only in their degree of fame. In so doing, the distinction between the three categories reflects less their varying degree of acting talent and abilities, but more the nature of their primary claim to fame and popular success (Geraghty 2000; Lovell 2003).

Film stars as celebrities

While the *'stars-as-celebrities'* category is based on Dyer's (1998) traditional duality between the film stars' on- and off-screen persona, the emphasis is thereby put entirely on the film actor's 'private' biography (Turner 2004; Watson 2007a). However, Geraghty (2000) does not only make no longer the classical distinction between film stars and any other film actors, but also builds a conceptual bridge to the celebrity literature. In her opinion, film stars are professional film actors, who just happen to be more famous and/or successful at a certain moment in time than the majority of their colleagues. Therefore, celebrity is conceptualised as a mode of stardom that has nothing to do with the person's professional excellence, acting talent, critical acclaim and/or commercial success as a film actor (Geraghty 2000; McDonald 2003). Instead, celebrity as a mode of stardom is exclusively sustained by the individual's displayed level of infamy and notoriety in relation to the private sphere that is enough to ensure a regular presence in the tabloid media – especially on the important front pages (Barbas 2001; Barron 2015; Hermes 2006).

Thus, celebrity privileges true and false biographical information about a film actor to the extent that their stardom is entirely rooted in and constructed through gossip, press and TV reports, magazine articles and publicity (Geraghty 2000; Watson 2007a), which means that the professional performance as a film actor is of little to no relevance to the celebrity's fame (Geraghty 2000; Turner 2004). Indeed, even after suffering a series of box office failures and/or negative reviews for their acting performances, many film actors and especially (former) film stars are still able as celebrities to command public and media attention for themselves (Geraghty 2000; McDonald 2003). Often, celebrity – reinforced through reality TV – is the only way left for some film actors like Lindsay Lohan or Corey Feldman to stay in the public eye and to be cast for new film roles.

Film stars as professionals

The second stardom category, *'stars-as-professionals'*, strongly shifts the emphasis towards the film actor's on-screen persona of Dyer's (1998) conceptual film star duality. For Geraghty (2000), the film star as a professional performer makes especially sense, when a particular film star image is intentionally connected with specific film texts, as it was commonly practised within the Hollywood studio system and still appears to be a popular feature in certain film genres (i.e. action, comedy, horror). In practice, this involves the film star's identification with a specific genre as much as consumers' pre-established expectations that an actor's presence in the film actually corresponds with his/her professional role identity and textual image as an actor (Beltran 2006; Geraghty 2000; Huffer 2003). In other words, the respective film actor portrays only a very specific set of virtually identical film characters, whose personality traits and physique seems to match the actor's own private personality, in the same or, at least, similar film narratives within the same genre – though some minor genre variations are thereby possible due to cross-overs (i.e. a modern-day Italo-western like *Desperado, Once Upon a Time in Mexico* or *Kill Bill*, or an action film that plays in the future like *Total Recall* or *The Fifth Element*).

Some of those film stars are actually talented actors like Clint Eastwood, Sylvester Stallone, Harrison Ford, Bruce Willis, Audrey Hepburn, Melissa Gilbert, Jessica Alba or Vanessa Hudgens, who just tend to be typecast by producers, the media and casting agents (Geraghty 2000; Huffer 2003; Lacey 2003). But the majority of male and female film actors in the stars-as-professionals category have come to film from a different field of popular interest (i.e. music, sports, modelling or family relations) with very little acting talent and/or virtually no formal acting training, i.e. John Weissmuller, Chuck Norris, Arnold Schwarzenegger, Dwayne Johnson, Zsa Zsa Gabor, Pamela Anderson, Milla Jovovich or Miley Cyrus.

Despite having been the common form of film stardom during the Hollywood studio system, the film star-as-professional stardom category has regained significance within the contemporary film industry for three main reasons. First, the emergence of video rental stores in the early-1980s brought about a major change in film distribution and promotion, whereby particular attention is paid to the film's genre as a means of product identification rather than product differentiation, since video/DVD rental stores and, nowadays, video-on-demand providers like Netflix or LoveFilm tend(ed) to display films according to broad genre categories (Geraghty 2000). The film star-as-professional stardom category is strongly supporting this categorisation by providing simple clues to sellers and customers (Watson 2007a). Second, although they are not film stars in Dyer's (1998) traditional sense, several film actors have gained a substantial following within the B-movies markets for action, horror or science-fiction films (Huffer 2003) as well as the TV movie sector (Lacey 2003). And, third, the blockbusters of the 1980s, 1990s and since 2006/7 have brought about a wave of film stars, who have become associated with specific genres – mainly action, adventure and fantasy, but also erotic thrillers – and, thus, have guaranteed the film studios some box office successes by essentially playing a fictionalised representation of themselves (Elberse 2014; Watson 2007a). The commonly cited examples include Arnold Schwarzenegger, Steven Seagal, Sylvester Stallone, Will Smith, Demi Moore, Sharon Stone, Jennifer Lopez or Miley Cyrus (Beltran 2006; Huffer 2003; King 2003).

Thus, a consistent, homogeneous film star image is of vital importance for the film star-as-professional category (Geraghty 2000). Nevertheless, the consistent image also carries with it the serious problem that their audiences rarely allow for any change or development in their image to happen (Huffer 2003), which means that the shelf-life of these film stars is rather limited and that their star usually falls as quickly as it has risen. And when the film actor loses his/her appeal for a particular genre due to increasing age as well as decreasing beauty and fitness, film star-as-professionals often face a serious decline in their fortunes. Indeed, only a handful of these film stars – usually the ones with actual acting talent – like Jane Fonda, Clint Eastwood or Sean Connery manage to revive their careers with an altered film star image (Geraghty 2000).

Film stars as performers

The third stardom category of *'film stars-as-performers'*, finally, pays particular attention to the actual work of all film actors, which is *'acting'*! The emphasis, thereby, is on the film actors' ability and acting skills to impersonate any given character in a truly realistic and believable way (Geraghty 2000; Hollinger 2006). According to Geraghty (2003), it also is no coincidence that the film star-as-performer stardom category is strongly associated with method acting, which is described as a pre-eminently realistic, natural style of acting that emphasises the significance of the character's inner emotional life and authentic expression by the film actor/actress (Geraghty 2003). Method acting, thereby, highlights and cherishes the craft, talent and art of a film actor or actress in merging one's self with the character (Watson 2007a). Therefore, this stardom category focuses in particular on the film actor's track record in selecting specific film projects that allow the delivery of remarkable and believable character portrayals in both lead and support roles (Geraghty 2000, 2003), which Dyer (1998) has conveniently neglected in his original film stardom conceptualisation.

While the hierarchy between film stars and the rest of the cast was quite clearly and visibly structured within the Hollywood studio system (i.e. in terms of allocated accommodation on the studio grounds), whereby the film star was surrounded by lesser sidekicks, the method actor tends to view oneself much more as an ensemble member and is also willing to play a support role to a lesser known actor (Geraghty 2000), if the respective character is creatively challenging enough. Moreover, in a complete reversal to the *'film star-as-celebrity'* stardom category, the film star's off-screen persona and private life are largely irrelevant for the claim to stardom in the *'film stars-as-performers'* stardom category (Watson 2007a). In fact, it appears that the film actors in the film stars-as-performers category, and the method actors in particular, seek to reclaim a degree of cultural prestige by demonstrating a disdain for the *'trappings of celebrity'* and vulgar commercialisation in favour of artistic integrity and critical acclaim (Geraghty 2000, 2003). Well, although she may not be formally trained as a method actress (Brink 2008; Miller 2006), Jena Malone undoubtedly fits into the film star-as-performer stardom category. But she would probably reject the notion of being a *'star'* and, instead, describe herself as an artist and/or actress (Lyon 2008; Pachelli 2011).

Understanding a consumer's celebrity fandom through narrative transportation

After this detailed review and discussion of the current stardom literature within the context of both the film industry and the academic discipline of film studies, I do not know how you, the reader, feel. But I am still not convinced that it actually offers us really a true understanding at all of how and why consumers often experience such a strong emotional attachment to their favourite film actors (or any other celebrities) and what meaning(s) the consumption of films and film actors has for them in their everyday lives. While I have to admit that Dyer's (1998) work has surely been ground-breaking in the sense that it has at last managed to direct the attention of film scholars towards film stars as exciting subjects for academic investigation and also makes for some interesting reading, the theoretical insights gained from his film stardom theory and its underlying conceptual thoughts are nonetheless flawed, as I have already outlined on pages 81–82.

Due to his and fellow film scholars' narrow ideology-informed theoretical concerns with the sociological and semiological dimension of film stars, the important human dimension of film stars and their relationship with consumers has never been addressed. Not only have film stars been dehumanised to mere semiotic receptacles of cultural meaning, but film audiences have also been reduced to abstract constructs that suit primarily some ominous ideological agenda of a respective cultural critic or film scholar (Dyer 1998; Mulvey 1975). Even when critical film scholars purport to discuss individual film stars and/or viewers, it only serves to generalise on all film stars and audiences (Krämer 2003; Williams 2006). The dehumanisation of film actors, celebrities and their audiences is even more evident in the underpinning assumption that consumers have the same interest in all film stars and, thus, respond to all of them in the same way (Dyer 1998; King 1991).

However, although Geraghty's (2000) alternative understanding of film stardom offers a welcome move towards a more (re)humanised view of film stars, what the stardom literature still fails to explain at all is why a consumer feels emotionally attached to one specific film star or celebrity, but not to another equally attractive and talented one, who represents a similar image or type of person. Thus, as a major contribution of my research journey in this book to the literature on film stardom and celebrity fandom, I propose drawing on narrative transportation theory as an alternative approach to obtain genuine insights into consumers' actual emotional relationships with their admired film actor/actress or celebrity and also into why they may often feel very differently towards other equally talented film stars/celebrities.

Narrative transportation theory was initially developed by the social psychologist Richard Gerrig (1993) in order to offer an explanation for the mental imagery processes that consumers generally experience while reading fictional literature. His aim is to understand in particular the previously unexplained phenomenon of *'getting lost in a book'*, where the reader becomes so absorbed in a story that s/he is even temporarily unaware of his/her surroundings. Gerrig (1993) has thereby paid close attention to how readers immerse themselves mentally in the fictional story and relate emotionally to the individual characters, whose narrative fates they are following. Drawing on the analogy of a journey to a foreign country, whereby the reader is *'transported'* into the fictional world of books, Gerrig (1993) called this mental process of immersion *'narrative transportation'*. In recent years, narrative transportation theory has also presented itself as an exciting alternative to understanding media enjoyment (Green et al. 2004; Rapp & Gerrig 2002) and advertising effectiveness (Escalas 2004; Escalas & Stern 2003) within the context of textual and visual print media. Of particular interest, thereby, is the underlying idea that *'media enjoyment can benefit from the experience of being immersed in a narrative world through cognitive, emotional and imagery involvement, as well as from the consequences of that immersion'* (Green et al. 2004: 311).

But how does narrative transportation actually work? Basically, Gerrig (1993) conceptualises narrative transportation as a psychological process, whereby the reader seeks to be taken away from one's mundane real life and, thus, ventures mentally to a distant narrative world by some means of transportation (i.e. a fictional story in a book) and by actively performing certain cognitive and emotional actions such as imagining the described story, characters and settings in one's mind (Green & Brock 2000). The reader, thereby, *'travels'* some distance away from one's daily life, which even becomes temporarily inaccessible, to experience a different self and to connect empathetically with fictional characters as if they are real friends (Argo et al. 2008; Cohen 2001; Oatley 1999). But as with any other journey to foreign countries, after some time has passed, the reader eventually returns home again; though *'somewhat changed'* by the emotional experience of the journey (Gerrig 1993; Green et al. 2004).

The biggest problem with narrative transportation theory to-date, however, is that it has only been *'tested'* empirically in controlled laboratory experiments by researchers strictly wedded to the behaviourist paradigm (Argo et al. 2008; Green & Brock 2000; Rapp & Gerrig 2002). The artificial setups of their controlled experimental research designs have thereby not only shown very little resemblance with people's real-lived reading experiences, but also been surprisingly similar (if not identical) to the ironic *pseudo-study* that Holbrook et al. (1989) conducted to highlight the general shortcomings of quantitative research methods in studying aesthetic and emotional consumption experiences and the nonsensical findings they generate. For instance, Rapp and Gerrig (2002) have provided two groups of participants with a self-written 8-sentence text, where care was primarily taken with regard to the text's format rather than content. The difference between the groups was that two sentences of the control group text were changed to *'prevent the immersion experience'* by sounding *'more rational'* than the original text.

This research design is particularly strange, as Gerrig (1993) himself argues that the reader must first get to know the characters *'over time'* in order for an immersion experience to occur. But, surely, this is hardly possible in just eight sentences! Green and Brock (2000), on the other hand, have tried to prevent the control group from losing themselves in a short story by giving them a nonsensical task to do like counting certain words. Personally, I find it seriously questionable, if not doubtful, that people can or cannot lose themselves in a story just because some researchers tell them either directly or indirectly to do so. But despite the methodological shortcomings of such earlier research, in my opinion, Gerrig's (1993) narrative transportation theory has actually a lot of conceptual value and potential.

Since Gerrig (1993) developed narrative transportation theory to understand the phenomenon of getting lost in a book, one of the original ideas has been that it can only work in relation to written texts like novels, short stories or poetry, as the immersion experience would be strongly dependent on the personal relationships that the reader develops with the fictional characters (Green et al. 2004; Oatley 1999). According to Cohen (2001), readers' very personal engagement with literary characters and their stories can express itself with a growing level of narrative immersion in broadly three different forms. On the weakest level, the reader merely sympathises with the character(s) (= feels *with* them) as a side-participant who *likes* them. On the next level, the reader feels empathy for the character(s) (= *shares* the character's emotions) because of perceived *similarities* to one's own private life experiences. Finally, the consumer identifies and *'merges'* with the character (= *feels the character's emotions* as one's own) just like a method actor playing a role.

Cohen (2001), thereby, clearly distinguishes between *'identification'* and *'imitation'*. While imitation implies that a person extends one's self-identity by copying a character's behaviour and appearance, Cohen (2001) interprets identification as a temporary mental role-play, where the consumer (just like an actor) imagines being a character in the story. And once the story ends, s/he moves on to experience the next character role. But despite viewing identification as the ultimate goal of losing oneself in a book, Gerrig (1993) and Oatley (1999) categorically deny this level to consumers' enjoyment of films. Both argue that the viewer is always aware of the fact that another actor is already playing the character and, subsequently, can only sympathise with the character/actor as a side-participant.

As part of my own research journey, I have thus not only taken a different conceptual perspective, but also a very different methodological approach to explore the narrative transportation experience in relation to film enjoyment (Batat & Wohlfeil 2009; Wohlfeil & Whelan 2008) and celebrity fandom (Wohlfeil & Whelan 2011). On a conceptual level, I argue that it is indeed highly possible for consumers to lose themselves in a film narrative and enjoy the narrative immersion as a major part of their film consumption experience; just like any other media text. After all, film scholars have always studied films as texts (Phillips 2007). Hence, in order to explore film enjoyment as a narrative transportation experience, I have conducted an introspective autoethnography into my own personal experiential consumption of the film *Pride & Prejudice* (UK 2005) (Wohlfeil & Whelan 2008). While I have thereby identified a complex tapestry of interrelated factors that contribute to an individual's personal film consumption experience, the major finding of the study is that my enjoyment of the film derives in particular from my ability to lose myself fully in the film's audiovisual imagination. The autoethnographic data, therefore, offer indeed strong support for the extension of narrative transportation theory to film narratives.

Although I have to admit that it is difficult to *'become'* the film character, the obtained autoethnographic data still suggest that I strongly empathise and, on some occasions, even identify myself with several characters[9] (Wohlfeil & Whelan 2008). My personal engagement is thereby enhanced further through a perceived out-of-text intertextuality (Hirschman 2000b) by which I connect the film to my own personal life experiences (Wohlfeil & Whelan 2008). The findings are also confirmed in a follow-up study, in which my friend Wided Batat and I compare through interactive introspection our personal consumption experiences with the film *Into the Wild* (US 2007) for similarities and differences (Batat & Wohlfeil 2009). The main finding of this study is that the consumer enjoyment of films results from the latter's potential for allowing consumers to lose themselves in their narrative worlds, where they can experience a different self, engage with fictional characters like *'friends'* and temporarily escape from their mundane everyday lives. And while a consumer's personal engagement with the narrative, its characters and underlying philosophy is of particular importance, we also find that the nature and intensity of the consumer's experienced immersion into the film narrative is determined not by age or gender, as Argo et al. (2008) suggest, but by one's very own personal interests, hopes, dreams and desires (Batat & Wohlfeil 2009).

But while a strong case can be made for drawing on narrative transportation theory to gain some genuinely holistic insights into a consumer's personal engagement with a film, its melodramatic narrative, its lead and support characters and even its underlying philosophy or message, one major question vital to the research journey in this book still remains: how can drawing on narrative transportation theory actually explain a consumer's everyday lived fan relationship with a film actor/actress or celebrity? This is indeed a very good question! After all, a film actor/actress or celebrity is a living person and not a book, film or any other media text. Or is s/he? Well, let us take a look back at the film stardom and celebrity literature that I have just discussed in this chapter. As you may remember, film and media scholars tend to discuss film stars and celebrities essentially as living textual images or human brands, whose on- and off-screen persona, personal identity and reflected values are carefully managed to suit particular market needs (Dyer 1998; Geraghty 2000; Thomson 2006).

In Chapter 1, I have also mentioned that the existential-phenomenological perspective, which underpins this research, holds that, while it is not text per se, *'human existence has some text-like qualities'* that lends to hermeneutic analysis (Thompson 1998). This means that the consumer and his/her life history are analysed as an autonomous text, whereby specific personal experiences, behaviour and life-events are contextualised within the broader self-identity narrative and established cultural meanings (Gadamer 1989). A consumer's admiration for one's favourite film actor/actress or celebrity could therefore be interpreted as a kind of *'immersing'* oneself into the factual melodramatic narrative that is the film star's/celebrity's public and *'private'* life as depicted by various media texts, which may include interviews, magazine articles and gossip. The consumer may thereby sympathise (= feel as an observer with the film star/celebrity), empathise (= share the film star's/celebrity's feelings due to similar personal experiences) or even identify (= feel the film star's/celebrity's feelings as one's own) with the admired film actor/actress as if s/he is a media character (Wohlfeil & Whelan 2012). In a similar way, it is also possible for consumer researchers and fan scholars to immerse themselves into the narrative of a fan's everyday life. The time, therefore, has finally come for us to go in the next chapter onto our 'back-packer' journey into the 'uncharted territory' of a consumer's everyday lived fan experiences with a celebrity.

Notes

1 By 2016, the major Hollywood film studios do indeed produce much more PG-rated than R-rated films and, instead, have settled with obtaining the distribution rights for R-rated films that are produced by or in cooperation with independent production companies (Obst 2013).

2 The Motion Picture Patent Company (MPPC) trust with its headquarters in New York was a quasi-monopoly of the 10 biggest film companies in the USA from 1906–1915, which held all the film technology patents. It sought to control the US film industry and market from production over distribution to exhibition by forcing the nickelodeons to screen only MPPC-produced and -approved film stock while excluding independent filmmakers from access to the distribution and exhibition sector. In an ironic twist, the very same independent film producers that brought down the MPPC in 1914 became within barely five years the major film studios that formed the Hollywood studio system and have largely led the global film industry ever since (Kerrigan 2010).

3 The imagined, fictional audience member is usually the critic's own alter ego and acts as proxy for his/her personal opinion that is often abstracted and generalised as given fact (i.e. Kirkland 2003; Mulvey 1975).

4 According to Dyer (1998), there is huge conceptual difference between film stars, who are *'the objects of desire'*, and film actors, who are *'the film industry's 'faceless' on-screen labour force'*.

5 Although McCracken (1989) never draws on or references the stardom literature in film studies, his view and definition of film stars is, nonetheless, nearly identical to that of Dyer (1998).

6 You may have noticed that some consumer researchers within the consumer culture theory (CCT) paradigm have in the past 5–6 years taken a similar approach, but with a narrower focus on consumption.

7 Castrati started off as talented choir boys, whose testicles were violently destroyed when they were barely 7–9 years old, to *'preserve'* their beautiful soprano voices forever.

8 In a twist, the five major Hollywood studios, which as former independent film companies brought down the quasi-monopoly of the MPPC in 1914, were in 1947 brought to court for anti-competitive behaviour of their own. As vertically integrated corporations, they controlled not only the film industry's three industrial sectors (production, distribution and exhibition), but also ensured through the practice of *'blockbooking'* (in order to show a particular film, an independent cinema had also to book and screen between 12–20 other films of the studio for a certain time) that independent film

production companies were denied access to the exhibition sector (Epstein 2005). The Paramount Act of 1948 ordered the major Hollywood studios to divest of one of the three sectors, while the long-term employment contracts with creative talent were banned. But as many Hollywood studios have since the 1980s been taken over by bigger conglomerates, which also hold substantial interests in the various multiplex chains and media retailers, the big studios have gained control of the mainstream exhibition sector again (Epstein 2012).

9 See Chapter 4.

4   Confessions of a Jena Malone Fan

A journey into the life of a fan

Following the detailed reviews of the interdisciplinary fan studies literature with its predominant focus on media and sports fandom in Chapter 2 and the stardom and celebrity literature in Chapter 3, this chapter presents the extensive auto-ethnographic narrative of my own personal fan relationship with the film actress Jena Malone, and how it has developed, evolved and manifested itself in my everyday life over a period of nearly two years. In so doing, the chapter takes you on a narrative journey into the 'uncharted territory' of an actual consumer's everyday lived fan experiences with his favourite celebrity. And as the reader, you are thereby invited to immerse yourself, through narrative transportation, into the following case study of my personal lived experience of a fan relationship with Jena Malone and, through this, experience the life of a fan from the perspective of a side-participant.

As already discussed in Chapter 1, this case study is essentially a narrative summary of the collected retrospective and contemporaneous autoethnographic data from my daily Jena Malone fan experiences from April 2005 to December 2006. These have been recorded in their raw form as a large number of small, independently experienced emotional incidences in the exact non-narrative, temporal order in which they occurred. Such an approach permits an overview of the overall data set and to identify key statements and potential themes, but also allows us to obtain deeper insights into how a consumer's fan relationship expresses itself from day to day and evolves over time. This would not be accessible using any traditional research methodologies. Moreover, by trying to keep the felt experiences alive by staying faithful to the original wordings and expressions, this approach should also help you to get a better feel for and under-standing of the experiential nature of a consumer's actual fan relationship with an admired celebrity. However, I would also like to remind you, the reader, that the focus of the autoethnographic narrative presented here is less on the factual recollection of events and observable consumption practices, but much more on how my lived consumption experiences (i.e. inner feelings, thoughts, fantasies and daydreams) both derived from and/or translated into my fan relationship with the actress Jena Malone in my everyday life.

How I met Jena Malone for the first time...

When Jena Malone caught my eyes for the very first time, her beautiful eyes and lovely smile instantly captivated me to such an extent that my entire body filled up with the same prickling warmth that I tend to feel each time I (start to) fancy a particular woman. It wasn't only her natural beauty that caught my attention. Instead, there was something else, something special, about her entire persona that fascinated me straightaway and, in my eyes, made her stand out from the crowd. And although I didn't know anything about her at the time, I had this strong but inexplicable feeling that she, somehow, was a very special person and I wanted to learn more about her. The obvious next step would normally have been to gather all my courage together and somehow try to talk to her. Unfortunately, because I have always been very shy, this is something I have never been good at, and far too many opportunities to meet girls in the past have already slipped away because of it. But, in this case, the simple truth is that I have never actually met or even seen Jena Malone in person (and most likely never will). This is because she is a talented, young US film actress, whom I saw on screen for the first time when I watched a movie she was in called *Saved!* (US 2004). So my closest social and personal encounters with her have been (and most likely will ever be) those where I watch her acting performances on screen, read her interviews and articles about her in magazines, and download her TV interviews from the Internet. Yet, while it is obvious to me that Jena Malone will probably never even know that I exist, my parasocial encounters with her have nonetheless had a profound effect on me. They have changed my life (at least a little), even though it may be hard to tell whether it's for better or worse.

Like many other people, I have enjoyed watching movies since my early childhood for the sheer pleasure value and imagination they offer. But movies mean much more to me than just being another form of entertainment. The experiential consumption of films has always provided me with an exciting way to escape the reality of my lonely, boring and routinised life by giving me the opportunity to live out my hopes, dreams and fantasies in the realm of my imagination and offering me a source of inspiration. As a consequence, I have collected films enthusiastically since I was 10-years old. First in the old Super 8-format for a second-hand projector, which I bought at a flea market, then a few years later on VHS and, after buying my first laptop, on DVD.

From 2003 to 2007, I was living as a postgraduate research student in Waterford, Ireland. And at the end of April 2005, I happened to be in Dublin for a day and used the opportunity as usual to acquire a few new DVDs for my film collection, especially those films that are not so readily available elsewhere. I had recently discovered a shop near Trinity College which was an ideal hunting ground, as it specialised in rare DVDs of arthouse films, cinematic classics and world cinema films. It was here on that particular day when I suddenly found an interesting indie-film called *Saved!* (US 2004) on offer in a special sale. The film uses the narrative framework of a high school comedy to take an ironic-critical look at the hypocrisy underpinning the religious dogmatism promoted by evangelical Christians. I still can't explain exactly why, but I simply felt this sudden urge to buy and own this particular film and I just couldn't leave without it.

To be honest, I didn't know what to expect of the film, as so-called teen comedies usually tend to be squeaky-clean, very dull, uninspired and far removed from any real person's life. But I also remembered that the television critic Jonathan Ross had given the film a glowing review on his film show and that I had actually wanted to see it back then. Unfortunately, _Saved!_ (US 2004) had suffered a backlash from the religious right in the US, and the Catholic Church in Europe for its supposedly 'unchristian' and 'subversive' message. This prevented a wider cinematic release at the time so I had never got the chance to see the film in a local cinema or film club, and eventually I forgot all about it. But being given this second chance, I was intent on not letting it slip out of my hands again and I purchased the DVD together with a few other films. When I arrived back home in Waterford later the same day, I set up my laptop straight away to watch my latest acquisition. I was really intrigued by this unseen gem, and it has since become one of my all-time favourite films.

It may be helpful to tell you a little about the film that began my whole fandom experience. _Saved!_ (US 2004) avoids the typical clichés that usually come with the teen-comedy genre. There are no generic goodies and villains; no ugly duckling who turns into a swan after meeting her handsome, athletic and popular prince; and no geek who enters the realm of the elusive in-crowd just to find out that their own social group was the most suitable one after all. (I've always found this conservative, class-conscious ideology pretty annoying.) Instead, all the characters in the film have their personal strengths and weaknesses, and face the same issues, successes and problems of any other teenagers going through their senior high school years, university or life.

Surprisingly, instead of supposedly poking cheap fun at the Christian faith, as many evangelical Christians in the US and other Christian organisations have claimed, in my opinion, the film actually promotes the true Christian values of love, tolerance and forgiveness. What the film really criticises, is the hypocrisy underpinning the dogmatism of fundamentalist Christians (or fundamentalist members of any other religion), who impose their own beliefs and morals in the form of strict rules without questioning their actual meaning, and self-righteously judge everyone else based on how closely they adhere to them. The film highlights the irony that the self-righteous dogmatism through which they seek to enforce their narrow-minded beliefs, rules and morals often contradicts the very core essence of the faith they proclaim to value and promote. For me, the film discussed those issues in a nice, thoughtful way within the context of an evangelical faith-based US school, the (fictional) American Eagle Christian High School. It does so without resorting to the common stereotypes by depicting ordinary young people (like you and me) who get caught up in everyday situations and have to deal with problems that any of us could face at some point.

Much more importantly for me, from the very first moment I watched the film, I was absolutely blown away by Jena Malone's acting performance. She portrays the lead character, Mary Cummings, who is a devoted, virtuous Christian girl, until her boyfriend confesses that he is gay. In an honest, but ultimately fruitless attempt to 'save' him from his 'gayness', Mary sacrifices her virginity to him and becomes pregnant as a result. Subsequently, she is ostracised by the hypocrites who preach Christian values of love, tolerance and forgiveness, (including her best friend Hilary and the school's headmaster who also happens to be her mother's secret lover) and instead finds support in some real friends, who may not be Christians themselves but still show her what it really means to be truly "Christian".

Although as I've admitted, I was instantly hooked by Jena Malone's beautiful eyes, her charming smile and her natural beauty, I was also totally captivated by her natural and believable acting performance. I simply had to watch the DVD again at once. But this time, I switched the soundtrack off and listened to the commentary track from the two leading actresses instead, Jena Malone and Mandy Moore. While I listened to Jena Malone explaining how she approached and developed her character as well as offering contextual information about the various film shots and scenes, I became even more fascinated by her. Not only did it become obvious to me that she was an extremely talented and attractive actress, but she also appeared to be an exceptionally smart, interesting, articulate and surprisingly mature young woman for her age. In fact, I felt that there was something special about her which really appealed to me, but I couldn't put my finger on it. Many celebrities might be considered to be much more conventionally attractive, (possibly because they are closer to our cultural beauty ideals as promoted in the media) but it was Jena Malone who caught my eye. To me, she was (and is) a naturally beautiful young woman, and the type of girl I always seem to fall for. She is the 'girl next door', pretty just the way she is without lots of make-up or styling, a tomboy with natural charm who would be fun to hang out with. I felt immediately emotionally attracted to her. Jena Malone simply represented the kind of girl I had dreamt of having as a girlfriend to love, marry and 'live happily ever after' with ever since I was a teenager. Actually, it was a bit like being a teenager again, and having a crush on this cute girl you've just seen, but being too shy and insecure to ask her out or even to talk to her – which has essentially been the story of my life.

In addition, although I hadn't really heard of her before, Jena Malone also seemed to be genuinely talented. I felt she wasn't just playing Mary but actually *'became'* her character and portrayed her as the ordinary girl next door without succumbing to the usual extravagant or self-indulgent over-styled portrayal which many other teen actors and actresses tend to do. Of course, there is always a danger of mistaking the film actress with her portrayed character, unless you have seen her in a variety of other roles. For me, a really good actress is one who makes each of her characters appear to be believable and real, and who manages through her acting performances to ensure that you enjoy watching even those films that you would never have watched otherwise. As there are only a few actors and actresses around that would truly fulfil these criteria, I wanted – or rather I needed – to find out more about Jena Malone both as an actress and as a person. I wanted to watch her acting in other films as soon as possible – if only to see whether she really was the exceptional young actress that I believed her to be after watching *Saved!* (US 2004) or whether I had just fallen in love with her character.

So when I arrived at work in Waterford Institute of Technology the next morning, I immediately started browsing the Internet for any piece of information on Jena Malone that I could find. Yet I could hardly find anything at all (which seems unbelievable now that the Internet is flooded with websites and articles dedicated to virtually every single "wannabe" celebrity in the world). In April 2005, hardly anything was available on Jena Malone, and the little that existed had not been updated for years. Nonetheless, I found out on the film database, IMDb, that Jena Malone, despite being merely 20 years old at that time, had already featured in 20 films, three guest appearances in TV soap operas, and voiced the lead character in an audio recording of a theatre play, as well as a support character in the Japanese animation film *Howl's Moving Castle* (JPN 2004).[1] I thought this was quite an astonishing achievement for an actress of her age!

But I was particularly surprised to learn that I had actually seen Jena Malone acting in a film before. Back in 1998, I had seen the film *Contact* (US 1997), in which Jena played Jodie Foster's character, Ellie, as a child. Back then, I obviously paid very little attention to her. Anyway, armed with her film list from IMDb, I went the next Saturday, into Waterford's town centre with the aim to buy a few more of her films on DVD. To my big disappointment, after five hours of intensive searching I could only manage to find just three of those 20 films. I bought the DVDs of *Donnie Darko* (US 2001) and *The Dangerous Lives of Altar Boys* (US 2001) and went home with the intention to watch them that very evening. But I had to postpone the plan for a day, as by coincidence, *Contact* (US 1997) was on TV that very evening and now I just had to watch it just because of Jena Malone.

As it transpired, I could empathetically relate to each of her portrayed characters as if they were real people so all three films confirmed to me that Jena Malone is indeed an exceptionally talented young actress and got me even more interested in her and her work. As a consequence, I felt this increasing desire in me not only to watch all of her films, but actually to acquire them for my personal film collection. I had never experienced this feeling in this form before. In a way, I felt *'hungry'* for Jena Malone and her films! However, since I could only find *Stepmom* (US 1998) in the local shops, I quickly purchased on Amazon.co.uk first the DVDs of *Cheaters* (US 2000) and *Life as a House* (US 2001) on 7 May and 10 days later *Hitler: The Rise of Evil* (US 2003). Furthermore, I also felt at the same time this strong desire in me to learn more about Jena Malone as a private person, so I was absolutely delighted when, in mid-June, I came across a well-written, well-researched and detailed article by Nancy Rommelmann (2000) in the LA Weekly.

To explain briefly, even though there have been one or two other film actresses or musicians, who have briefly caught my attention previously, the truth is that I have never been really interested in any celebrity's private life before. But, curiously, in Jena Malone's case I really wanted to know more and more about her as a private person and her personal life. For that reason, I was, and still am, astonished and totally fascinated by what I have learnt about her personal background and life-story. As well as Rommelmann's *LA Weekly* article, which I had uncovered by chance on the Internet, I also discovered other insightful articles and interviews published in other trustworthy magazines that I bought on eBay at the time (i.e. Baltin 2004; Calhoun 2003; Cohen 2002; Hastings 2004; Rems 2004; Rotter 2003, 2004; Sherwin 2004). In fact, the more I learnt about her as a person and her private life from each new article or interview, the more and more my admiration for her increased.

According to Rommelmann's (2000) article, Jena Malone was born on 21 November 1984 in Sparks, Nevada, near Lake Tahoe, where she spent most of her early childhood growing up in the poverty of trailer parks, but – in her own words – enjoyed her *'unconventional'* life-style (Baltin 2004). And because her single-mother Debbie was a struggling actress in an amateur theatre, Jena apparently wanted to be a performer (either as an actress, singer/songwriter, writer or dancer) or a teacher from an early age (Cohen 2002; Miller 2006). The articles described how, a few months after Debbie moved with her then 10-year old daughter to Las Vegas to take a low-paid job in a call centre, Jena responded to an ad for acting school and persuaded her mother to move to Hollywood (Rems 2004; Rommelmann 2000). Several of the articles (Baltin 2004; Cohen 2002) also discuss how, during an audition, Jena Malone eventually caught the eyes of established actress Anjelica Houston, who casted her for the title character 'Bone' in her controversial, award-winning directorial debut *Bastard Out of Carolina* (US 1996). Houston also apparently introduced the 10-year old Jena and her mother Debbie to Toni Howard, an influential talent agent specialising in child actors, who signed her for the leading talent agency International Creative Management.

What really impressed me when reading Rommelmann's (2000) article was that, even when she was just 11 years old, Jena Malone already preferred to feature primarily in those film projects that were dear to her heart rather than in commercially promising blockbusters (apparently much to her manager's frustration). She apparently turned down roles in *Air Force One* and Disney's remake of *The Parent Trap* in order to play the lead characters in the smaller films *Bastard Out of Carolina* (US 1996), *Hope* (US 1997) and *Ellen Foster* (US 1997). For her performance in these three films, she received critical acclaim, some film awards, two Independent Spirit Award nominations and even a Golden Globe nomination for *Hope* (US 1997) – although *Contact* (US 1997) and *Stepmom* (US 1998) are evidence that some of her film choices also had the potential for commercial success. However, life in Hollywood may not have been as glamorous and rosy as people often imagine.

Hollywood industry practices and legal requirements with regard to child actor supervision[2] and financial issues arising from legal requirements for child actor salaries,[3] manager fees and income tax are reported to have caused growing personal strains and frictions in the previously harmonious relationship between mother and daughter, who became increasingly estranged from each other. And when she was 14 years old and eventually faced a bill of $150,000 in back taxes and near bankruptcy in 1999, Jena Malone filed for legal emancipation from her mother so she could work in the film industry like an adult and also access her blocked trusts to pay off her debts. The legal emancipation was granted in November 1999 at her 15th birthday (Cohen 2002; Rommelmann 2000; Rotter 2003; Sherwin 2004). According to those articles and interviews, Jena Malone has since then taken full control of her career and finances and managed them without the approval and interference from anyone else (Calhoun 2003).

I have learnt from other contemporary articles in US magazines obtained from eBay that Jena Malone has since focused as an actress on portraying in particular complex young female characters with realistic problems in creative, stimulating and challenging independent films rather than catering to the usual teenage stereotypes in some typical 'Disney-like' teen comedies (Calhoun 2003; Cohen 2002; Hastings 2004; Rotter 2003, 2004; Sherwin 2004). It also emerged from her interviews that, for the same reasons, she also refuses to do the usual glamour photo shoots for fashion and celebrity gossip magazines that *'only present girls with false beauty ideals that they could hardly fulfil and only make them feel inadequate'* (Rems 2004). What also impressed me while reading these articles is that, in contrast to many other young celebrities, Jena Malone has shunned LA's *'party scene'* by moving back to Lake Tahoe, where she – in her reported words – had "felt happy as a child" (Calhoun 2003; Hastings 2004; Rotter 2003, 2004; Sherwin 2004). In my interpretation, this may also explain why she apparently managed the transition from child actress to a serious young adult actress without losing her integrity along the way, while many other former child actors have struggled or even failed in their careers as widely reported in 'tabloid scandals' (Brink 2008; Lyon 2008; Miller 2006; Pachelli 2011).

How and why my fan relationship with Jena Malone developed further

After reading these articles exploring Jena Malone's biography, I was really impressed by her personal life-story and how she managed to stay true to herself, her dreams and her ideals despite her young age and the personal and financial pressures she experienced. I can't deny that, somehow, I felt in some personal way inspired by her. Furthermore, Jena Malone's life-story was reminiscent of, and even brought back some very specific memories of my own. Back in Germany, I spent most of my childhood in the late 1970s/early 1980s growing up in one of Braunschweig's most 'disadvantaged neighbourhoods', which really means those run-down, poverty-stricken sink-estates with high unemployment rates, very low social mobility, and high crime rates where most people survive mainly on welfare payments. Fortunately, since both my parents were among the very few in steady semi-skilled employment with a small but comparatively decent regular income, we were able to move to a better working-class neighbourhood when I was 12 years old. However, this meant that while my younger siblings stayed with my grandparents until reaching school age, I became a *'latchkey kid'*, spending most of the time on my own and subsequently I had to be quite self-reliant and self-sufficient from early on. From those early years, films always provided me with a means of temporary escape and I became not only fascinated by the presented stories and imaginary worlds, but also by the art of filmmaking itself. I bought a second-hand Super-8 film projector and a Super-8 film camera at a flea market during that time, and used my father's Super-8 film editing kit to try making my own short films. Just like Jena Malone, I made a list of what I wanted to be when I grew up, which included professional athlete (at first soccer, later table tennis that I played at club level), psychologist, musician, filmmaker and, most importantly, an actor – especially as I had already joined the school's drama society.

Because of my interest in films, being an actor was a particular passion of mine from very early on – not so much in terms of becoming famous, as is often the case, but in order to engage intimately with the characters you portray. Hence, when I managed to be surprisingly among the six pupils from my primary school to get into a gymnasium[4] that year, joining the school's drama society was pretty much the best experience of my entire schooldays. In contrast to Jena Malone, however, I lacked the self-esteem and determination to follow my dreams to the end. Moreover, as my parents were quick to blame my participation in the drama society for my poor grades and overall performance at school, they forced me to quit it for good and to focus exclusively on *'practically relevant'* subjects instead. But the real problem was that the gymnasium represented a world that was alien to me, into which I had difficulties adjusting and which I hated. Its day-to-day business (unintentionally) favoured the children from privileged backgrounds and discriminated against the less well-off. Furthermore, I also felt increasingly that my confidence was undermined by others, as school and guidance counsellors tended to tell my parents and me what careers I would *not* be suitable and/or even intelligent enough for, instead of supporting me in my pursuits. Without having anything left that I was really interested in, I started to rebel against the system by withdrawing mentally from everything in school beyond the bare minimum necessary. In the end, I failed my *'Abitur'* because of my English major, but still managed to graduate with a *'Fachhochulreife'* qualification. But by that time I had already lost all my hopes, childhood dreams and ambitions, and started to work in sports retailing instead. Though I was actively involved in table tennis as a player, trainer and voluntary PR manager, I lived most of my time aimlessly from one day to another and regularly sought my mental escape in the fictional world of the movies – when, many years later, the film *Dead Poets Society* touched a nerve and inspired me to go to university, study marketing and, eventually, become a lecturer (or even professor) instead.

To be fair, I wasn't probably talented enough to succeed as an actor anyway. Still, there has always been this nagging feeling inside me that something is missing or that I have lost out on something special along the way. For that reason, I felt the deepest respect and admiration for Jena Malone and how she was at such a young age able to succeed against all the odds in following and realising her dreams, while I have failed to do the same even under less severe circumstances. And she had apparently managed to achieve it without losing her personal integrity, and by resisting all the temptations of fame and the commercial exploitation by the Hollywood machinery. In my opinion, that's quite an astonishing achievement for a young woman from a disadvantaged background! I was also pretty shocked to learn about the not-so-glamorous day-to-day reality of working in the Hollywood film industry and how it had ultimately led to financial and legal problems that apparently damaged and nearly destroyed Jena Malone's relationship with her own mother. Especially, as I felt I could somehow sense in Jena's affectionate words that she still truly adored her mother. I sincerely hope that both have in the meantime been able to forgive each other and leave the pain behind[5]. But what was particularly surprising to me was how much I became emotionally involved in Jena Malone's life-story. I had never shown a similar interest in another person whom I have never personally met before. For some reason I can't explain, Jena Malone touched a particular nerve.

Anyway, due to reading Rommelmann's (2000) uncompromising portrayal of her as a normal teenage girl caught up in extraordinary circumstances, and because of my own personal history, I became increasingly fascinated by Jena Malone. I simply wanted to see, hear, read and learn more about her as a private person, so that I could gain a more intimate understanding of her personal thoughts, feelings and dreams. Somehow, I didn't view her at all as just another attractive female celebrity, but as a normal, intelligent and interesting young woman with her own positive and negative qualities and habits just like any other young woman that I could have seen in the street, in a pub, or at work. As with any other real-living young woman that has caught my eye in the past, I felt the desire to find out what kind of person she really was. It was particularly appealing to me that she neither fitted, nor ever tried to fulfil the typical celebrity image of glamorous life-styles, parties and public scandals that the celebrity media excessively bombard us with. But, unfortunately, this might also be the reason why the media, especially in Europe, seem to ignore her and meaningful interviews and articles are so scarce. Moreover, despite having so many films to her credit, many of them have never been released in Europe and, thus, are unavailable.

A particularly good example of how I relate emotionally to her films and engage with her characters is the film <u>*Cheaters*</u> (US 2000), which I finally managed to watch for the first time in mid-June 2005 in an effort to relieve the stress experienced in the final days leading up to the submission of my MBS thesis for examination. The film itself retells the true story of the cheating scandal in the 1995 Illinois Academic Decathlon for High Schools, whereby the underdogs from Steinmetz High School had surprisingly outperformed the favourites from serial-winner Whitney Young High School, after they had by chance come a few days earlier into possession of a copy of the competition test.

The film, thereby, uses the story for confronting the much-taught moral ideal of *'cheating is wrong'* in a clever and, in my view, engaging way with the social reality in our modern societies, where *'winning is everything'*, on multiple levels that go beyond the initial school competition setting. Steinmetz is a typical poorly-funded public school in a disadvantaged neighbourhood, where the students are branded from day one as no-hopers with little chance of a better future and the disillusioned teachers have resigned themselves to cater only to the most necessary basics. Having experienced something similar myself, I can really empathise with Jena Malone's character Jolie, who is an intelligent girl hungry for knowledge, but who also struggles desperately to fulfil her academic potential in an endless uphill battle – just because she comes from a *'wrong'* social background. Whitney Young, on the other hand, is an excellently resourced fee-paying school in a well-off neighbourhood that, nevertheless, still receives public funding from the Illinois School Board, whose members are mostly Whitney Young graduates. The Decathlon's committee office is even located in Whitney Young, where the tests are stored prior to the competition as well – a fact that has never been questioned. Thus, it's not surprising that, instead of officially contesting the results, Whitney Young's team coach, as a sore loser, simply asks a friend on the school board to investigate the Steinmetz answer sheets thoroughly and to compare them with their past performances.

Since the school board is not only quick to follow up on the request, they are not only *'bending'*, but deliberately violating the rules. Moreover, although they never had any evidence that any irregularities actually occurred, the school board implied straightaway that the increase in performance was due to foul play and demanded that Steinmetz retake the test and, thus indirectly confirm the suspicion. When Steinmetz obviously refuses, they state school board strips them publicly for cheating – despite no evidence – and, fearing a public backlash, now seeks to justify their decision by getting a confession by any means possible, which even included deliberately violating the students' constitutional rights by interrogating them continuously for hours without the presence of a legal or parental guardian and subjecting them to serious threats. In other words, the Steinmetz students, who ironically did not actually cheat at all, are subjected to cheating on a much larger scale by the state school board's and Whitney Young's favouritism, cronyism and deliberate bending of rules. Overall, the film essentially criticises the hypocrisy in Western societies for paying lip-service to the moral value of *'cheating is wrong'*, while in reality they endorse and only too often reward cheating with success. This point is highlighted in the final scene, where the president of the Illinois School Board proudly proclaims that the important lesson for students to be learnt from the scandal is that *'cheating is wrong'* – just to be convicted six months later for major tax evasion! Moreover, following their involvement in the cheating scandal, Jolie and her team members were awarded scholarships and, subsequently, managed the previously impossible by being able to study at Ivy League universities.

It is without saying that I could immediately relate empathetically to the film story, its message, Jena Malone's character Jolie and her Steinmetz Decathlon team members. And just like reading Jena Malone's personal life-story in Rommelmann's article earlier, the film also triggered some long-forgotten memories from my own schooldays and life experiences, where I encountered or was subjected to various forms of *'institutionalised cheating'* within the German school system and society that readily supported the film's message. On one hand, feelings of anger, frustration, helplessness and vulnerability wracked me inside in response to the perceived as well as experienced injustice and inequality. On the other, I had a simultaneous sense of pride in what I had achieved so far despite all these odds – and this was something that came across nicely in Jolie's closing voice-over at the end of the film.

While none of Jena Malone's other films had triggered such strongly experienced intertextual linkages between their stories and my personal life experiences so far, I did engage and connect emotionally with each of them – and especially with Jena Malone's characters. Subsequently, I felt really *'hungry'* for watching Jena Malone in more of her films and even felt I was somehow in danger of starvation if I couldn't get them! In the meantime, I searched the Internet for any little scrap about Jena that I could find and even created a Jena Malone Info document folder on my laptop, into which I copied all the articles and other information as much as possible into a chronological order. I've never shown this kind of devotion to any celebrity before, but Jena Malone just seemed to be worth it.

Then, during a phone call, my sister suggested that I might look on eBay. After typing in "Jena Malone" into eBay, I found 386 items listed worldwide and, though the majority of listed items were the *'usual'* films, I registered at the end of June 2005 to use the chance for bidding on the VCD of *The Ballad of Lucy Whipple* (US 2000), a Dutch DVD of *Confessions of an American Girl* (US 2002) and the rare 'Emmy Consideration' VHS tape of *Hope* (US 1997), of which I won all a few days later. Over the next few months, to satisfy my hunger for Jena Malone and her films, I bought a Hong Kong VCD of *The Book of Stars* (US 1999) and US VHS tapes of *Bastard Out of Carolina* (US 1996), *Ellen Foster* (US 1997), *The Badge* (US 2002), *Corn* (US 2002) and *The United States of Leland* (US 2003). While I was clearly shocked by her debut *Bastard Out of Carolina* (US 1996), in which she had proved her acting talent by quite realistically portraying the victim of physical and sexual child abuse, and I was impressed by her portrayal of the neglected lead character in *Ellen Foster* (US 1997), it was *Confessions of an American Girl* (US 2002), which she had also co-produced, that captured my imagination. It seemed to me that the film narrative had a particular private relevance to Jena, as her character Rena seems to personify her deeper fear of how desperate her trailer park life might have turned out, if she hadn't succeeded as an actress. I actually like it because somehow it just feels truly honest.

Since several other films still remained unavailable in European media formats, I still needed another solution. However, I did manage to find and purchase a number of magazines with Jena Malone articles or interviews on eBay that weren't available here. Unfortunately, what all of them had in common was that I paid more than the usual retail price for them. For me though, it was worth it! While some were short and disappointing, others were really brilliant and exciting – especially in terms of the picture of Jena Malone as a private person that emerged from them either directly or between the lines. She came across as an extremely lovable, funny, natural and intelligent young woman, who is also surprisingly mature and independent for her age. Sadly, one thing I learnt from the articles was that Jena Malone was apparently a smoker, which I recalled she had mentioned something about in the commentary on the DVD of *Saved!* (US 2004). (I think I chose not to hear it at the time). Why am I mentioning this? The point is that I find smoking a real turn-off, and simply not attractive. So, in the past, I would normally have lost interest soon after seeing a girl smoking. In the case of Jena Malone, however, I simply 'chose' to ignore the fact, as if it didn't exist. She is therefore the first person I still find highly attractive and am romantically drawn to despite her smoking habit. That's an absolutely new experience for me, and hence worth mentioning.

How *Pride & Prejudice* strengthened my fan relationship with Jena Malone

Since the Irish cinema release for *Pride & Prejudice* (UK 2005) had been announced for 16 September 2005, I was looking forward in excitement to the opportunity of finally being able to watch Jena Malone on the big screen. I must admit that I would probably not have cared about the film *Pride & Prejudice* (UK 2005) at all, if Jena Malone had not played the role of Lydia Bennet in it. In fact, I was never even tempted back then to read Jane Austen's famous novel. One reason was that, a long time ago, I had the misfortune of watching the highly praised and critically acclaimed BBC TV version with Colin Firth. Like most British period dramas (in particular those made for TV by the BBC), I experienced this TV mini-drama as the clichéd glorification of a nostalgic past that, for sure, has never existed in this form. But, who knows, this might be the reason why so many female viewers saw in Colin Firth the ultimate per-sonification of *'their'* Mr. Darcy? In my personal opinion, however, the por-trayed characters were so wooden and one-dimensional that I couldn't care less about any of them. On Sunday, 31 July, I saw that the *Sunday Times* fea-tured an article about the forthcoming *Pride & Prejudice* (UK 2005) film in its *Culture*-supplement, which can be seen in Figures 4.1 and 4.2. In the hope of also finding something written about Jena Malone I bought the paper for the first time ever. But, to my big disappointment, there wasn't one single word about Jena Malone – only about leading actress Keira Knightley and director Joe Wright.

Joanna Briscoe's (2005) article itself, though, was well-written and insightful. Interestingly, she compared the new film version to the literary original by placing Jane Austen's novel in the context of her time and, thus, argued that all previous small and big screen versions have set the novel in the wrong period (and social class) and, subsequently, altered inevitably the understanding of the

Figure 4.1 Articles from the Sunday Times *Culture* magazine.

story as well as its societal background. The forthcoming film, apparently *'bypasses all the previous traditional Regency-lite conventions of a painterly tableau of empire-line dresses, sotto voce ballroom squeals and high-ceilinged elegance'* (Briscoe 2005) of the well-known BBC version of the 80s. In fact, the director placed the new film in the Georgian time of 1797, when Jane Austen

Figure 4.2 Pride & Prejudice memorabilia.

actually wrote the initial draft of the book, rather than in 1813, when the book was published. To ensure realism, the actresses were prohibited from wearing any make-up that wasn't available in the 1790s. I had no doubt in my mind that the actresses would look even more beautiful in their natural appearances than any of the styled glamour girls from the ads of a well-known make-up brand. All in all, the article captured my interest for the film and my inner excitement mounted. As a form of release for this excitement, I went the next day to the local bookstore and brought a newly released copy of Jane Austen's novel that featured the forthcoming film's poster artwork on the cover. As I read the book over the coming weeks, the story and its many characters grabbed me more and more. However, you must note that my personal reading of the novel differed increasingly from the stiff interpretation of the dull BBC TV version I saw before. I couldn't wait for the film's release on 16 September and started to count down the days.

Meanwhile, in early September, something else had happened in my personal life. After several months of struggling, I finally plucked up the courage to ask a particular girl out for a date. Due to many bad experiences in the past, I've always had low self-esteem and been very shy when it comes to making the first move or – in the words of Mr Darcy – *'conversing easily with women'* I'm attracted to. So this had been a very big step for me – especially as I hadn't been on a date for five years. Moreover, as she was due to leave on 20 September for an exchange year in Germany, I planned to make the date as romantic and memorable as possible. And what could be more romantic than sitting next to each other in a dark cinema and watching a romantic film like *Pride & Prejudice* (UK 2005), whose story has been loved by women for centuries? While I was looking forward in excitement to our date the following Saturday, TV ads were announcing the film's Irish and UK wide release for the coming Friday. On Sunday, I even bought the Sunday Times, because its *Culture*-supplement, as shown in Figure 4.1, featured a detailed article by Garth Pearce (2005) about Jena Malone – the first 'full' article about her in an Irish/UK publication that I'm aware of. And on Wednesday, I enthusiastically watched the news to catch glimpses from the Dublin premiere of *Pride & Prejudice* (UK 2005). Jena Malone even appeared for 30 seconds on a short TV3 news report! Strangely, it never occurred to me that I could have gone to the Dublin premiere myself. Overall, the critics for the film were surprisingly good. Not that I cared much about them, but it was reassuring.

But then followed a major disappointment! The Irish-wide release of *Pride & Prejudice* (UK 2005) was for some mysterious reasons restricted to Dublin, Limerick and Cork only. After all the promotional build up, my personal expectations and my excitement, this no-show was a big blow! With the initial plan for my first date in shatters, we both went on to see another film, *Cinderella Man*, instead. The film wasn't really great and no romantic feelings developed from it that might have encouraged me to hold my date in my arm or dry a tear. I was so frustrated that, in my awkwardness, I spent half the film wondering whether there was too much salt in the popcorn or too little popcorn in the salt. After some careful deliberations I came to the conclusion that the latter must have obviously been the case. Although the date was very nice after years of loneliness, unfortunately, it didn't work out the way I was hoping for. Instead, I returned again to my usual, unexciting daily life as an unwilling, lonely single. But I was hoping that *Pride & Prejudice* (UK 2005) would be released the next week in my town as well. After all, it was topping the box office. And at last the film was finally released in all other areas in Ireland – with only one exception, Waterford. When I tried phoning the cinema to enquire their plans for showing *Pride & Prejudice* (UK 2005), however, I experienced first-hand how their *'customer service'* treats their *'valued customers'* these days. The only thing I was connected to on the phone was a recorded message that gave me the current programme I already knew and allowed for automated bookings, but not for human inquiries. The website provided exactly the same information. And when I tried to enquire directly at the cinema, I was just rudely repudiated by a bored, disinterested employee behind safety glass, who couldn't be bothered to make some inquiries. As a result, I felt angry and helpless.

But happily, one week later *Pride & Prejudice* (UK 2005) was finally released in Waterford. I was filled with an exciting kind of happiness mixed with anticipation or even joy to finally see Jena Malone on the big screen. I needed to see the film and couldn't wait any longer. It was worth the wait, as *Pride & Prejudice* (UK 2005) is a magnificent film, in my opinion, that you can watch over and over again. The film never gets boring and is just a joy to watch – beautiful landscape pictures a la *Lord of the Rings* combined with nice camera frames that outline the England of the 1790s. All actors did a great job in making every single character appear to be real and believable. Deep in my heart I can feel the way they feel and know why they do what they do. It doesn't even matter whether you sympathise with them or dislike them. In fact, *Pride & Prejudice* (UK 2005) as a story plays with judgement errors made due to first impressions (the novel's original title). At the end, there aren't any good or bad guys – only human beings.

The only exception is Mr. Wickham, who represents the typical handsome, smooth talking guy girls always seem to fall for. Men like him apparently know how to be the centre of attention and how to charm women. Behind their pretty masks and smooth words, however, these *'mercenaries'* (curiously, Wickham is a lieutenant with a travelling regiment) often turn out to be arrogant, shallow and selfish cowards, who don't care for anyone else but themselves. Yet, because shy, nice and decent men (like me) can easily look through their apparent 'fog of deception', I don't understand why women always appear to be falling for them regardless and even turn a blind eye to the falseness in their cheap words. Obviously, I feel jealous of their constant, undeserved success with the ladies. Every time, when a girl that I fancy ignores me and instead falls for the false charm of just another *'Wickham'* despite all the apparent warning signs, I experience this painful feeling of heartache and helplessness running through my entire body. But it hurts even more, when the same girls then, once *'their Wickham'* has left them in misery again, always tend to blame *all* men for the pain they feel instead of asking themselves why they fall for those shallow guys in the first place – instead of giving the nice but shy and unpopular geek next door a chance. I have witnessed it many, many times in my life so far and I'm still counting. Poor Lydia will soon learn the hard way that she hasn't found her happiness either!

Maybe this is also the reason why I somehow sympathised with, rather than laughed at Mr. Collins? Still, because Tom Hollander has done such an excellent job in portraying Mr. Collins exactly like I have imagined him while reading the novel, that seeing him on screen helped me to feel a bit better about myself. I know that I'm not very handsome and women usually don't tend to notice me, but I'm quite sure that I can never be *that* dull and boring – hopefully! I got a confidence boost just by realising that! Nevertheless, I also felt empathy for him, as I have experienced many times myself how it feels like to find yourself being ignored or even laughed at by the very same women you fancy – and only because you are unable to make *'charming'* conversation.

But I empathised even more with Mr. Darcy, the central male character, because like me he is uncomfortable in *'conversing easily'* with people he doesn't know – and especially with women. Similar to my own personal experiences, his insecurity and introverted behaviour is often (mis)interpreted by the ladies (and other people) as arrogance, pride and incivility, which results in their prejudices and dislike of him. In his excellent portrayal, Matthew Macfadyen lets his Mr. Darcy come across as dislikeable in an involuntary and passive manner, whose real character must be discovered by the audience in the same way as Elizabeth does by looking behind the prejudices that resulted from first impressions. Thus, his interpretation differed significantly from Colin Firth's rather theatrical performance in the BBC TV version. I could especially identify myself with Darcy's internal struggle in trying to talk to Elizabeth and to show his affections to her, which always results in forced mimics and in saying the wrong words at the wrong time. Of course, this only supports and even feeds her initial prejudices against him. The same happens to me all the time and only reinforces my personal insecurities. Hence, I share Mr. Darcy's inner struggle, his disappointments and loneliness, but also his hopes and dreams to be finally seen as the person he really is – at least by the woman he loves. In difference to me, however, Mr. Darcy has three major advantages that seem to attract at least some level of female interest: he is rich, tall and handsome, while I'm unfortunately none of them! Otherwise, however, the similar personalities are striking. I just hope that at one point in time I will finally be rewarded like he was at the end.

As a male consumer, I'm more interested in the female characters and the actresses playing them. The main female characters are Elizabeth (Keira Knightley) and Jane Bennet (Rosamund Pike). Jane is the good-hearted oldest daughter, who always sees the best in people and is said to be the most beautiful girl in the country. But although she surely is attractive, she isn't really my type. Due to her free spirit and wit, Elizabeth would appeal more to me. Keira Knightley delivers probably her best performance to-date in bringing this character to life. I was particularly stunned by how closely Elizabeth resembles many girls and women I have met in the past in terms of how she responded to the different types of men represented by Mr. Darcy, Mr. Collins and Mr. Wickham. She responded to each of them with prejudice based on her first impressions of their physical and social appearances rather than their actual personalities. Based on my personal experiences, I always find it quite ironic that women often complain in the public and the media that men would only judge them on their physical beauty, but then forget that they, despite their claims that women look mainly for the *'inner values'* in men, actually do exactly the same in reverse. At least, Elizabeth recognises her mistakes and tries to change her prior judgements.

As a Jena Malone fan, I obviously paid particular attention to her character of Lydia Bennet, the youngest daughter. Although I've to admit that I'm clearly biased, Jena did an outstanding job in portraying Lydia as a rather wild, over-romantic 15-year old girl with an obsession for fashion, dancing and officers – in short as the typical spoilt teenager of today and back then. Lydia is young, naïve and just romantically *'in love with love'* itself (Pearce 2005) rather than any particular man, which ultimately leads her into serious trouble, when Wickham seduces her to elope and have sex outside marriage with him. Although Wickham is eventually forced to marry her, she is too naïve to see that he only wanted to exploit her youthful beauty and innocence for little more than an one-night stand. I feel really sorry for Lydia when she eventually finds out that Wickham never cared for her, that he will treat her badly and soon betray her with other women. Nevertheless, Jena Malone looks incredibly beautiful in her Georgian-style dresses and is a real natural beauty to fall in love with. But then again, I'm biased!

Perhaps surprisingly, the female character I most empathised with is Mary Bennet (played by Talulah Riley). She is very shy, introvert and lonely – just like me. She is also said to be only *'ordinary'* looking and less beautiful than Jane and Elisabeth. Still, I find her to be much more attractive than her sisters. To find her place, Mary consistently tries to be the perfect daughter to her parents by wanting to fulfil all the cultural expectations that society has held for women in that era. But no matter how hard she tries; all her efforts go unnoticed by her parents, sisters, relatives and men alike. Mary seeks her escape and happiness in playing the pianoforte and singing. Hence, she is very enthusiastic about grasping her chance to shine by singing and playing at the grand ball. Unfortunately, while she is a relatively good player on the pianoforte, Mary's voice can't hold a note and her performance ends in a total disaster. Everybody's laughing at her. I could really feel inside me how hurt and heartbroken she is. Unable to comfort her, I sat lonely in the cinema, watching her left on her own crying and feeling sad and alone too. The next day, it even got even worse for Mary. Because Jane was *'unavailable'* and Elizabeth rejected him, Mary was sure that, as the third daughter and probably the only person in the family who would have settled for marrying Mr. Collins, it would now be her turn. While nothing was said either in the film or in the novel, I could read it in her face (excellent acting by Talulah Riley!). But even Mr. Collins ignores her and marries Elizabeth's friend Charlotte Lucas instead.

All in all, watching *Pride & Prejudice* (UK 2005) was a really great experience, which exceeded my expectations by miles and was surely worth the wait and excitement. I simply knew that I would watch the film again. Because I had been an involuntary single for too many years and had no hope of being in a loving relationship at any time soon, a week later I felt very lonely, sad and unable to concentrate on my work while happy couples seemed to surround me. So I left my desk early and drifted towards the cinema. After reviewing the listings my choice fell once again on *Pride & Prejudice* (UK 2005), because I simply knew that it would be good for rescuing my emotional well-being. While my impressions from the first viewing a few days ago were all confirmed, this time I paid even more attention to Jena Malone, who is so sweet, sexy and really owns the screen with her charm, even when she isn't in the centre of the frame. She simply is Lydia, but also continues to add her own style in portraying this silly girl. Despite her young age, she showed that she is an excellent actress with a great future. It just required her smile, her eyes and her presence to raise my spirits and to make me feel warm and happy. The film also made me feel much better about myself and much more relaxed. I think I was even smiling for the first time that day! But my experiential consumption of the film didn't stop with the two visits to the cinema.

As shown in Figures 4.2 and 4.3, I started over the next moths to acquire a number of collectibles on eBay in an effort to transfer my intangible film experience into tangible objects that I can hold on to. Obviously, I focused in particular on those items that involved Jena Malone. In early September, I had already obtained two mini-film posters, but now I acquired two promotional US lobby cards, the original CD-Rom press kit, a film cell plaque to decorate my desk at WIT with and a photo poster of Jena Malone at the film's London premiere.

Figure 4.3 My *Pride & Prejudice* collection.

However, these acquisitions merely represented an extension of my growing effort to possess any Jena Malone-related collectibles I could find, the more personal the better (possibly because they were so hard to obtain). I had recently discovered a new and up-to-date fan-site called *Jena Malone Fan* (no longer functional) and had been continuously downloading digital photos of Jena Malone and saving them into my designated photo-folder on my laptop.

More importantly, the walls in my room, which were previously too white, cold and impersonal for my taste, were increasingly covered with the original film posters of <u>*Saved!*</u> (US 2004), <u>*Life as a House*</u> (US 2001) and <u>*The United States of Leland*</u> (US 2003), which I obtained via eBay over the summer and with Jena Malone's photo poster from the <u>*Pride & Prejudice*</u> (UK 2005) London premiere. As Figure 4.4 shows, the posters not only added some much needed colour to the room, but also symbolised somehow Jena Malone's growing virtual presence in my personal everyday life – especially as I found that looking at them and my collection of digital photos would fill me with a kind of inner warmth and calm. I also managed to acquire two film posters of <u>*Life as a House*</u> (US 2001) and <u>*Donnie Darko*</u> (US 2001), which have both been hand-signed by the respective casts (including Jena Malone!) and, thus, were much too valuable to risk damage by *'just pinning them to the wall'*. But although the material possession of Jena Malone's films and collectibles had become quite important to me, they were no longer the only means through which I experienced my

Figure 4.4 Jena Malone and film posters.

growing emotional attachment to her. Indeed, the night after I watched *Pride &
Prejudice* (UK 2005) in the cinema for the first time, something else happened
that changed the nature of Jena Malone's presence in my life.

How a dream sparked my romantic emotional attachment to Jena Malone…

While I honestly believe that I have managed against the odds to be quite successful in my professional career, especially since entering academia, my private
life, nonetheless, feels more like a total failure to me. Since my early teenage
years, I was imagining (probably like anybody else, I suspect) what it would be
like to go out with a girl, to be in love with your girlfriend, what it feels like to
share the first kiss and the first time with each other. But the years passed by and
nothing even remotely happened in this regard. While everyone else around me
seemed to be happily falling in and out of love with their special ones (and loved
talking about it), I suffered one rejection after another, as no woman found me
attractive and interesting enough even to contemplate going on a date with me.
Hence, in my entire life I have barely been in five relationships so far, none of
which lasted longer than five months and the last one ended over 10 years ago. It
wasn't really for the lack of trying, but I believe that my social skills are somewhat … *'underdeveloped'*.

At school and later work, I felt being excluded most of the time, so that my
social network has been rather limited. A strong contributing factor is surely that
I'm privately very shy, have an increasingly low self-esteem in private matters
and, like Mr. Darcy, *'don't converse easily'* with attractive women I don't know.
And when I finally have the courage to talk to someone I'm attracted to, my
pulse rises, my hands become sweaty, my nerves run amok and I end up merely
mumbling something idiotic through my dry mouth, usually the wrong thing at
the wrong time. Previously, I have compensated the feeling of loneliness by
active participation in sports, even to the extent of taking up voluntary admini-
strative positions, just to learn later that those social networks were just superficial rather than based on friendship. With every year that I'm getting older, this
feeling of loneliness, emotional starvation and the lack of experience of romantic
love turns increasingly into frustration, desperation and helplessness. Due to
these unfulfilled emotional and social needs, I've inevitably started to question
seriously my purpose and value in life. You might ask: What has my personal
emotional misery to do with Jena Malone? At the beginning: nothing…

While I certainly felt attracted to her as a person, my initial interest and admiration for Jena Malone was still based mainly on her work and achievements as
an actress. But the nature of my emotional attachment to her changed in October
2005 following another major disappointment in my emotional life. As mentioned previously, when, to my surprise a nice girl finally agreed to go out with me
in September, I was filled with enjoyable feelings of excitement, anticipation,
happiness and nervousness mixed together. I hadn't been on a date for such a
long time, so I was also very insecure, scared that I would lack the necessary

social skills and experience in knowing how to behave appropriately in this kind of situation. But although the woman was really nice and I enjoyed being with her, the date didn't really work out, because I was never sure whether she was really interested in me. If she was, then I failed to interpret her signals correctly.

So frustrated with having to continue living my lonely life as an involuntary singleton, I started to seek romance and love from a very different source – Jena Malone. I'm aware that this may sound quite weird at this point. But I can assure you, that it's actually an innocent manifestation of the parasocial relationship concept. As Horton and Wohl (1956: 223) have argued, *'nothing could be more reasonable or natural than that people, who are isolated and lonely, should seek sociability and love wherever they can find it'*. This could be by forming a compensatory emotional attachment to a particular celebrity, who is *'readily available as an object of love'*. Parasocial relationships with celebrities can provide lonely individuals with a cathartic experience that helps to restore their emotional well-being. This clearly seems to reflect my own situation. Horton and Wohl (1956) do not consider a parasocial relationship as pathological and dangerous, unless the behaviour proceeds into fanatical obsession and an absolute defiance of reality – which is obviously not the case in my situation. My case of parasocial relationship started approximately two weeks after my previous date had ended in failure, when I finally managed to watch *Pride & Prejudice* (UK 2005) in the cinema on 30 September.

That very night I dreamt that I was of Prussian decent and just moved to the English countryside of the late-18th century. Apparently inspired by the ideals of the Romantic Movement, I had run away from a family committed to the Prussian values of authority, diligence, loyalty and militarism. I went to a ball of the local gentry and witnessed the doomed singing performance of a pretty girl, who turned out to be Mary Bennet (as played by Talulah Riley). As she ran out crying, I followed her down a narrow stairway to the garden, where I sat down beside her, gave her my handkerchief to dry her tears and started to comfort her, and we talked for a bit longer. The next day, I paid a visit to the Bennets to ask for permission to start courting Mary according to the local customs at that time. Most of her sisters were present (except Lydia unfortunately), as were some of the other characters from *Pride and Prejudice*. Initially, Mrs. Bennet was a bit suspicious regarding my income, but I was apparently a successful publisher of books and had earned £7000 the previous year which would be considered a great deal.

However, before I could get any further, I was rudely awakened by the alarm clock. I have to admit that this was a very strange dream. But while I would normally forget most of my dreams in the very moments I woke up, this dream kept spinning through my head the whole day. Moreover, the dream came back the following night – but this time with some significant changes. Again, due to my fortune obtained through my publishing business, I'd just moved from London to the English countryside of the late-18th century. Now, I was paying my obligatory visit to my new neighbours the Bennet family. I was sitting in a drawing room playing a boring card game with them. But this time, the girl I was courting was gorgeous and looked like Jena Malone. The whole time I kept a secret eye on the Jena Malone-like girl, who turned out to be Lydia Bennet. I noticed that she was seated in the background corner of the room and soon learnt that she had been *'ruined'* by Mr. Wickham. After a short, passionate affair, Wickham, instead of marrying her, ran off to seduce another, much richer girl. However, in my dream I didn't seem to care about Lydia's past and viewed her, though foolish, as a lovely person. I asked her whether she might like to accompany me for a walk. We talked a lot while drifting through a park of trees. Eventually, she asked me why I would *'waste my time'* on her, as her reputation was ruined in society after having lost her *'honour'*. My reply was that I simply didn't care about what people thought as I believed her to be a good person, which is the only thing that counts to me. I also pointed out that everyone could make mistakes and if I dared to criticise somebody's virtue and honour, then I would have to be impeccable myself, which I wasn't. Then, I pulled a small knife out of my pocket and scribbled a heart-shape into a nearby tree and asked her to marry me. She was about to answer me with her charming smile ... when the alarm clock rudely intervened again.

This dream repeated itself in various forms over the next few nights, with the fictional relationship/courtship between the Lydia/Jena Malone-like girl and I taking an increasingly central role in the dream and the *Pride & Prejudice*-theme receded. I really began to enjoy these dreams; they filled me with inner warmth, happiness and calm, and they also made me feel better about myself. My feelings of loneliness and my negative self-image, even my growing unhappiness with my personality[6], virtually vanished. So I was devastated when a week later, without warning, the dreams suddenly stopped. To compensate for this loss, I started to imagine what it would be like meeting Jena Malone in person – talking to her, going out with her and even dating and kissing her. Imagining these kind of things is something I've done in the past (often secretly) when I feel attracted to any woman I see regularly (such as a waitress, barmaid, or colleague), but whom I'm just too shy and too scared of rejection to even talk to. So each time I was feeling lonely, unattractive and ignored by women around me, or when I was sitting alone in a café, in a pub or just walking through the town, I began to imagine what it might be or feel like to go shopping with Jena Malone, or to have a coffee or a drink in a bar together or to go to the cinema together. Given that I felt lonely pretty often, you could genuinely say that Jena Malone was *'always on my mind'*.

But since an actress like Jena Malone is unlikely to meet an ordinary guy like me on the street and fall in love with him (I'm not Hugh Grant in *Notting Hill* after all), I also developed fantasies in which I had become a film actor by chance. While I was reading Stephen King's psychological thriller *Rage*, I ima-gined the story as a film directed by Wolfgang Petersen, in which Jena Malone and I, as actors, were each playing a character in it. In this self-created day-dream, I imagined that we met on set, got along fine, started dating, fell in love and eventually became a loving couple. Once I'd perfected this fantasy, I could switch it on and off whenever I wished – just like opening, reading and closing a book. Over the next months, I also imagined other novels I was reading as if they were film productions in which Jena Malone and I had been cast as actors playing certain characters and, in the process, spent some time together.

This escapist behaviour strengthened temporarily after attending the postgraduate business ball in October, an event which turned into another total disappointment for me, if not to say emotional disaster. I had officially received my MBS at the graduation ceremony the day before, and initially I thought it would be a good idea to go along to see friends. However, everywhere I looked I was surrounded by couples, while the single girls didn't even bother to hide that they couldn't care less about me and seemed to look for the quickest way out each time I tried talking to them. As the evening progressed I felt increasingly pointless, uncomfortable and extremely lonely. At the end, it was just all just a waste of time and money! And when I finally got home, I was too upset to fall asleep and felt like crying for hours. In search of comfort, I browsed through my photo collection of Jena Malone, watched _Saved!_ (US 2004) on my laptop and finally went for a long walk – just to get out and away.

Two days later, I still felt sad, hurt and depressed from my disastrous experience at the ball. I really felt like crying, but a serious aspect of bipolar-2 depression is that you hide all your emotional feelings deep inside to the point where it eats you up from within. Suffering such massive rejections by numerous women, who wouldn't even talk to me, only added to my very long list of disappointments, failures and bad experiences. Was it any wonder that my self-esteem and confidence was virtually non-existent?! From that moment, any time when I was sitting in a café or had a couple of pints in my local pub at the weekend, went to the cinema or theatre, or just took a walk in the park on a Sunday afternoon and was feeling lonely, unattractive and consequently ignored by every woman around me, I just began to fantasise about being together with Jena Malone, right there and then. I imagined walking hand-in-hand with her through the park, having a cappuccino and a lovely chat in a café together, having a good time in a pub, cuddling on the couch in front of the TV, having a romantic dinner in a restaurant, going to the movies etc. all to make the feeling of overwhelming loneliness more bearable. I know that this will sound very weird to many readers, especially those are fortunate enough to have never been in a similar position, or like fulfilling all the stereotypical, pathological media descriptions of fans. Yet, in practice, it was no different to reading a book or watching a film, where you also enjoy the immersive experience of losing yourself in the narrative. The only difference was that I was mentally writing the script for my very own fictional narrative about a romantic relationship between Jena Malone and me – a kind of ongoing personal romance novel or soap opera.

In other words, whenever I felt emotionally starved of romance and love in real life, I could mentally lose myself for a while in my fictional narrative and, to some degree, fulfil my emotional and romantic desires in my imagination at least. In this regard, I was behaving no differently to the teenage girls adoring their teen idols in Karniol's (2001) study. And just as you can close a book after a few chapters, I could drop out of my mental role-play at any time and go back to the daily business of my everyday life. Over the coming weeks and months, I even printed out a few photo images of Jena Malone and displayed them framed in my room (see Figure 4.5) to enhance the overall experience of my imagined relationship. Of course, should anyone enter my room while visiting me, I felt I could mask it as the 'usual' strongly expressed fandom they would expect and nobody would ask any questions ... However, this wasn't really a problem, as nobody dropped by anyway.

In the meantime, I noticed that I hadn't bought any films since the summer that didn't feature Jena Malone. Furthermore, my interest in the cinema also changed, as I no longer bothered going to the multiplex and became much more interested in arthouse, indie- and world cinema films like the ones Jena Malone featured in. I also continued to think about different ways to obtain and watch those films that weren't easily available on the European market. As recommended by a friend, my first attempt involved downloading DVD Ghost, a software that is supposed to trick the hardware into believing that the DVD is region free, and DVD Shrink, a software with which you can make a Region 0 copy of any DVD. To test my theory, I purchased the Region 1 DVDs of *Hidden in America* (US 1996), *Ellen Foster* (US 1997), *The Book of Stars* (US 1999) and *Corn* (US 2002) on eBay. (Actually when they arrived, it turned out that DVD Ghost wasn't compatible with my laptop's DVD drive. Luckily, though labelled as Region 1, two of the DVDs actually turned out to be Region 0 DVDs and ran without a problem.) Finally, I had another idea and in November bought an external DVD drive, which I locked into Region 1 to watch all those US DVDs of Jena Malone films that are unavailable in Europe. By using DVD Shrink, I was also able to make a back-up copy of each film in Region 0, so that I could watch them everywhere on my regular DVD drive. Fortunately, by the end of November 2005, I had finally managed to acquire all of Jena's films to-date on DVD for my collection – with the exception of *The Ballad of Lucy Whipple* (US 2000), which was only available on VCD, and *The Ballad of Jack & Rose* (US 2005), which I was working on obtaining as a US DVD.

November also brought a memorable experience of a different kind. Until now, nobody seemed to have ever heard of Jena Malone before, and most of her films were never screened in the cinema – except of *Pride & Prejudice* (UK 2005) – or on TV. And then, suddenly they showed *Stepmom* (US 1998), *The Ballad of Lucy Whipple* (US 2000), *For Love of the Game* (US 1999) and *Bastard Out of Carolina* (US 1996) all in the space of two weeks. Obviously, I didn't miss any one of them – I just had to watch them! At the same time, I also learnt by browsing IMDb and the *Jena Malone Fan* fan-site that she was involved in the production of three more films *Lying* (US 2006), *Four Last Songs* (US 2006) and *The Go-Getter* (US 2007). To be honest, I couldn't wait for their release.[7]

How my romantic emotional attachment to Jena Malone evolved further...

With Christmas approaching, I increasingly felt utterly lonely again. As the only one in my family who is single, I knew I'd be the fifth wheel again. As a result,

Figure 4.5 Evidence of Jena Malone entering my private space.

my imagined parasocial relationship with Jena Malone intensified as a form of emotional comfort to myself. The way I sustained it varied in many ways. The most obvious form was daydreaming about Jena Malone and me being lovers, which was aided by looking regularly at her photos and films in my collection. I even set my screensaver up to depict the Jena Malone photos in my folder and used her photos also as background images. But while I continued to download photo images of Jena Malone into the designated photo collection folder on my laptop and to look on eBay for interesting Jena Malone-related items, my frantic hunt for her films, articles, posters, and any other collectibles that had dominated the previous months decreased suddenly and substantially from mid-November 2005 onwards. One reason might have been that I had already obtained all of Jena Malone's available films to-date – except of *The Ballad of Jack & Rose* (US 2005) and *Pride & Prejudice* (UK 2005) – for my personal film collection and any relevant article that was written about her, which I knew of, so that nothing was left to obtain anyway. As a result, my emphasis shifted towards looking for new information and developments in her career and for new photos or articles. Sadly, those remained extremely scarce. Still, I was very proud when I actually managed to get possession of four original hand-signed Jena Malone photos – though they were already a few years old. But my emotional attachment to Jena Malone remained very strong, as my material consumption of Jena Malone-related items was by no means the only way I experienced her increasing presence in my life.

The Christmas break in Germany was basically as I expected. Apart from seeing my one-year old nephew, I felt isolated most of the time among all the couples around me. This was made even worse by *'well-meaning'* relatives constantly reminding me of my singlehood with the usual insensitive questions like: *'When are you (thinking about) settling down with a nice girl?'*, *'At your age, shouldn't you be married already?'* or *'Why haven't you got yourself a nice woman and got married by now?'* You can't imagine how painful that is and how it makes you feel even more like a failure than you already feel you are anyway! Equally bad are the typical well-meaning comments like *'Every pot has its lid!'* or *'There's someone for everyone, you just have to go out to find her!'* Yeah, right! When I finally arrived back in Waterford in early January 2006, I comforted myself with a present to myself: I finally managed to obtain the DVD of *The Ballad of Jack & Rose* (US 2005) for my personal collection. While browsing the Internet for new Jena Malone-related news, I also learnt that she would be performing as Sister James in the Off-Broadway play *Doubt* from January to June 2006. I would have loved to see her live on stage – if only I had the money to afford such a trip. But unfortunately my PhD scholarship didn't allow me to consider such expenditures. Instead, I impatiently looked forward to the forthcoming official DVD release of *Pride & Prejudice* (UK 2005) that was scheduled for 6 February 2006.

Actually, the supermarket Tesco put the DVD on sale early on the Sunday before and I was one of the first to buy it! The advantage of DVDs for me is not only the great picture and sound quality, but all the bonus features on the disc. In addition to the obligatory subtitles and director Joe Wright's audio commentary, there were a number of exciting bonus features on the *Pride & Prejudice* DVD ranging from an alternative US ending, and galleries of the 19th century to a number of short behind-the-scenes documentaries. Obviously, I was primarily interested in those documentaries that featured Jena Malone in front of and, especially, behind the camera. I loved to watch the bonus features on *The Politics of Dating in 18th Century England*, and *The Bennets*, which include not only film scenes with Jena Malone as Lydia Bennet, but also show her in her own clothes during the rehearsals and include short interviews with her. I also enjoyed watching the *On Set Diaries*, where Jena Malone, Carey Mulligan, Keira Knightley, Talulah Riley, Rosamund Pike, Brenda Blethyn, Matthew Macfadyen, Tom Hollander and Donald Sutherland talk in private about their personal experiences while filming the film and the close *'family'* bonds they have developed before and behind the camera. It's heart-warming to see how they become the *'Bennet family'* even off the screen, which made me really wish to be included in this perfect family bond. Another aspect I particularly enjoyed is that the actors and actresses are shown in private, when they are not playing their characters, as natural, lovely people like you and me. The documentary increased my admiration for Jena Malone even further, and I loved to watch this film as one of my favourites.

As a devoted Jena Malone fan, I increasingly wanted to refresh the daydreams of my imagined relationship with her. I started to look for *'personalised'* items that would in some way also symbolise her physical presence in my life. I particularly began to concentrate my limited financial resources on acquiring original hand-signed photos of her. The more up-to-date both the photo and the signature were the better! Sadly, apart from two autographed agency photos from 1999 and 2001 respectively, three (identical) movie stills of *Cheaters* (US 2000) which had also been signed around 2001, and a 2002 photo that seems to have been signed recently, I couldn't really find anything. However, this changed drastically when Jena Malone finally made her Off-Broadway debut in *Doubt* in early 2006. By mid-/late-February 2006, a number of (semi-)professional autograph hunters and traders were offering autographed photos of Jena Malone on eBay with prices ranging between $45 and $85. All of these traders claimed that they had obtained Jena's autographs personally in front of the theatre. While it soon became apparent that several of the autographs were clearly fakes, a few genuine autograph traders differentiated themselves by accompanying their autographed photos with a "proof candid", which is a photograph that shows Jena Malone signing the respective photo in front of the theatre. Immediately, there was no doubt in my mind that I needed to have as many of these in my possession as I could afford to obtain – or, alternatively, at least one! My pulse started to rise, my hands became sweaty and my mouth turned dry for desire to have them in my possession. But $65 is a lot of money when you are living on a scholarship. Not knowing what I should do, I was fighting with myself for the next two weeks – until I finally gave in and bought the first one, a signed *Saved!* movie still, from a seller nicknamed 'Aplusgraphs'. As it turned out, this was just the start of a second, much more intense and targeted buying frenzy.

Between March and June 2006, I acquired approximately 40 original hand-signed photos of Jena Malone from four trustworthy autograph traders in New York. Contemporary signed photos of Jena Malone as private person, like the one shown in Figure 4.6, were particularly high on my personal priority list. As many sellers got the same photos signed by her (usually movie stills from *Contact*, *Ellen Foster*, *Donnie Darko*, *Life as a House*, *Saved!* and, eventually,

Pride & Prejudice), I increasingly demanded a free bonus "proof candid" of Jena Malone signing the autographed photo as an important selection criterion. For one thing, it was the only way to obtain recent pictures of Jena after the only two recent and up-to-date fan-sites had been shut down. But my main reason for this approach was that these photos were taken privately and, thus, would be unique possessions, and second they provided a true authentic reflection of Jena Malone by showing how she actually is in private. These private and natural candids of Jena Malone, thereby, served as a further legitimate means through which I could manifest and experience her *'personal presence'* in my own personal everyday life.

Figure 4.6 Original hand-signed photo of Jena Malone.

During those weeks I had developed a closer contact to the professional auto-graph trader I knew as "Aplusgraphs" (aka Anthony). In April 2006, Anthony asked me if I would like to get any specific photo images of Jena Malone perso-nally signed by her, and if so, I should just email them to him and he would get the job done for me (for a fee obviously). Tempted by this offer, I emailed him four of my most precious Jena Malone photo images the very next day. Only a few days after emailing him these very precious Jena Malone photo images, he asked me whether I would like to have Jena dedicating them to me personally. Was he kidding me? What kind of a question was that?! If that was really pos-sible, I would obviously love it!!! So spurred on by this exciting experience, I emailed him five more photo images of Jena Malone and a few more after that … In the end, I had emailed him 25 photo images in total. Most of them were taken within the previous two years at the film premieres of *The United States of Leland*, *Saved!* and *Pride & Prejudice*, but some were also 'private' photos that were shot for more detailed articles in the *Nylon* and *Venice* magazines. On 30 May 2006, I sent the final batch of recent pictures of Jena Malone that were taken just three days earlier at the Cannes Film Festival while attending the pre-miere of *Babel* and promoting her own new film *Lying* (US 2006). I had only obtained them from *WireImage.com* the previous day. Anthony actually did manage to get Jena Malone to dedicate 21 of the 25 photos to me personally with her hand-written signature. Figure 4.7 shows the final 10 hand-signed and

Figure 4.7 Collection of autographs.

personally dedicated photos, which I received in mid-June after days of nervous waiting. As you can surely imagine, these photos that Jena Malone had personally hand-signed and addressed to me have become some of my most precious and valuable possessions, my absolute treasures, my crown jewels! I don't really care what other people might think about them, because for me they are absolutely priceless.

Unfortunately, for these three months from March to May 2006, buying original hand-signed autographs became a kind of an addiction. My expenditures exceeded my monthly income not only for the first time in my entire life, but also for two consecutive months, and just barely equalled it for the third month. I have to admit that this was a shocking experience, which even manifested itself in physical stress-related symptoms, headaches and stomach aches, for two weeks in mid-June. It took a while to come consciously to terms with the experience of losing control and to get the expenditures back under control by late-July.

How my emotional relationship with Jena Malone actually '*Saved!*' me ...

Despite being short of money due to both living on a scholarship and the excessive acquisitions of Jena Malone original hand-signed photos during those months, I was still very tempted to fly to New York, so that I could watch Jena Malone performing live on stage in front of my eyes and maybe even meet her afterwards in front of the theatre with all the other fans, visitors and autograph hunters. As I only knew her from films, photos, articles etc., I was always wondering what she would look and be like as a real person face to face. Going to New York and watching her perform on stage might be a good chance to find out. Naturally, I imagined what it would be like to meet her finally in person backstage, to be able to talk to her and to get to know her in real life. But I'm only too aware that I'm just not the kind of guy who gets to experience a *Notting Hill*-storyline (i.e. bookstore-owner Hugh Grant bumps accidentally into Julia Roberts's Hollywood film star and both fall happily in love with each other). To me, these things only happen to other men. After all, if I couldn't even attract the interest of a nice girl in my daily life, why should then someone like Jena Malone even notice – never mind be interested in – me in a brief chance encounter?! Ultimately, I was simply too afraid of bursting my imaginary romantic Jena Malone bubble with yet another real-life personal disappointment, so I used a number of excuses like lack of time and money (not exactly untrue) for convincing myself not to go ahead with it. (Looking back on it, I've regretted that decision ever since!)

Instead, I started to consider writing her a letter, in which I could use my research as an '*ice-breaker*' – and this might also be a good means to stand out from other fans and, maybe even get me noticed in her eyes. Although between April and July a number of friends and colleagues encouraged me to do this, I was still much too afraid of the consequences that a personal response – or even more likely a non-response from her would potentially have for my emotional well-being. As long as I had this imaginary relationship to fall back on during the times I felt lonely and unattractive due to another (perceived) rejection by women around me, everything was fine. But what would happen if even my imaginary parasocial relationship with Jena Malone resulted in rejection and disappointment? Surely, it would be much better to keep this parasocial imaginary relationship with her safe in my mind and to hold on to it for as long as it would last! But there was also the small chance that I might actually get a nice personal response from her, which would just be too good to miss. But I kept on thinking, how likely is it really that it's going to happen?

During the months from May to early-July, I often consoled myself by browsing regularly through my collected treasures – especially those most recent autographed photos in Figure 4.7 that Jena Malone had personally dedicated to me – or her photos that I had sorted into a special photo album. I especially loved those private "candids" that I received as proof with the autographs and even framed three of them to decorate my room. As the summer months that year were also extremely sunny and warm ones, I used the opportunity to wear all my Jena Malone print T-shirts, which I had purchased the previous autumn, to express my fandom openly in public. In some way, I think I also enjoyed answering the many questions I was asked about who Jena was and what films had she been in. But I also began to notice that I hadn't actually watched any of her films for months now. Though I still had a strong desire to, I just never really got round to it. Since October 2005 I had planned on several occasions to have a personal "Jena Malone film festival" at the weekend. However, it never actually happened, because I often just couldn't decide what films to watch and in what order – somehow, I just didn't want to *'offend'* any one of them by favouring one over the other ... even though I definitely had my favourites.

Soon I didn't need to worry about the potential consequences of my imaginary relationship with Jena Malone being dashed by a disappointing response. Some of my extraordinary expenditures in May 2006 originated not in my excessive acquisition of Jena Malone's autographs, but in a certain development within my private life that occurred at that time and which should have a major impact on how my (parasocial) fan experiences with Jena Malone progressed further. Back in June the previous year, I had met a very nice, intelligent and beautiful young woman from a French university at a conference. Since that time, we had stayed in regular contact with each other via email. At first, our email exchanges were just professional networking between two PhD students in consumer research. But over time we got to know each other more personally and, by spring 2006, we had become close friends. Actually, I'd really liked this girl right from the very first moment we met and, secretly, I was hoping that I might have finally found "the one" I'd always been looking for. So I was absolutely delighted when in late April she finally invited me to visit her for a week in the summer. It felt like I had just been given a belated birthday present that I had been wishing for all my life. During the following weeks, we arranged my visit for mid-August and, despite my hugely overstretched budget, I booked the flight in May. I was so excited and enthusiastic that, from June onwards, I just couldn't stop imagining what this visit and my time with this girl would be like. But while I was looking forward to visiting her with ever growing anticipation and inner excitement, something unexpected happened. In late-June, I suddenly stopped dreaming about having a relationship with Jena Malone. I still enjoyed watching her films, admired her acting talent and performances, and cherished her hand-signed photos, but the daydreams of an imaginary relationship with her were completely wiped from my mind.

When my highly anticipated visit to France eventually arrived in August, I became increasingly nervous and afraid that I would unintentionally scare my friend away, because I simply wouldn't know how to express my feelings to her in a proper and socially competent manner. After all, I hadn't really had any practical experiences besides my romantic fantasies to draw on. Fortunately, my worries evaporated quickly after she picked me up at the airport. I felt really happy, as everything during the first days was nearly perfect and we had a lot of fun together. But unforeseen circumstances drastically interfered with our plans in the second half of the week and my visit turned steadily into another major disaster. Perhaps I was too overenthusiastic, or I just misread the signals once again. It also is quite possible that my poor, untrained social skills let me down once again without me even being aware of it and contributed to this further romantic disappointment. In the end, we separated on such bad terms that it ate me up inside. I returned home, sad, frustrated and totally heartbroken, and immediately turned to the only *'person'* that promised me unconditional comfort, love and warmth: Jena Malone.

For the following days, until I was ready to face the cruel world again, I watched her films nearly endlessly – some of them like *Cheaters* (US 2000), *Life as a House* (US 2001), *Saved!* (US 2004) and *Pride & Prejudice* (UK 2005) I watched more than once – and spent hours watching Jena Malone's video interviews that I had downloaded from the Internet. And as I also read the magazine interviews and articles I had collected and browsed endlessly through her photos and autographed photos, I began to store them in a special corner on my desk (see Figure 4.8) to have them close to hand. By doing this, I was also hoping to gather some internal strength, as I desperately hoped to be given the opportunity to make up with this young woman. She was coming to a forthcoming Irish conference in early September, where I would be seeing her. In fact, back in May, while we were arranging my trip to France, we had also planned to use this conference for her to visit me in return.

Although I hadn't heard anything from her since the nasty argument we'd had due to my underdeveloped social skills, I was looking forward to seeing her again in order to apologise for my stupidity in the hope of restoring our friendship, and maybe even more. But, once again, random bad luck interfered in the person of a B&B proprietor, who had managed to overbook his B&B and, then, told my friend at her arrival that I had supposedly cancelled her booking – which was simply not true. Unfortunately, she believed him and, as you can imagine, was so upset that she didn't want to talk with me at all. Although not my fault,

Figure 4.8 Albums of Jena Malone.

these circumstances made all my efforts for reconciliation and the renewal of our friendship virtually impossible.

These events pushed me back into an extreme psychological turmoil. I was filled with inner darkness and the intense emotional pain of desperation, hopelessness, sadness, isolation, loneliness and above all the perceived absence of any hope of future personal happiness. During the following two months, on the outside I appeared to be functioning quite well going about my daily business, but internally I was locking myself in and shutting everything out. Of course, I turned to Jena Malone as the only person who – at least in my created imaginary form – promised me love, comfort and emotional warmth by letting me join her through her films, photos and in particular through the original hand-signed photos that she had personally dedicated to me, which more than ever symbolised her *'physical presence'* in my life. During the weeks until the end of November 2006, I must have watched *Saved!* (US 2004) at least a dozen times, but I visited her many other times through my laptop screen in *Pride & Prejudice* (UK 2005), *The Book of Stars* (US 1999), *Cheaters* (US 2000), *The United States of Leland* (US 2003) and *Life as a House* (US 2001). Instead of going to the pub in the evenings, I would spend hours flipping through her photos and hand-signed autographs to look into her pretty eyes and embrace her lovely smile and to adore and internalise her natural beauty. Somehow, it felt like she was there with me, taking me in her tender arms and comforting me through her personal presence in my private space.

As weird as it may sound, her imagined love and support actually helped to put me back on track and finally in late November, my mood began to brighten up again. At that time, I had also discovered that Jena had put some home-made video clips on YouTube, which also strengthened the feeling of her personal presence. Of course, I always truly knew that I would never ever be in the position to meet Jena Malone in person, never mind be given the chance of actually dating her. In fact, I was always aware of the simple truth that she would probably never know who I am or that I even exist. I would also never actually be in the position of genuinely knowing what kind of person Jena Malone really is in her private life. In fact, everything I have ever known about Jena Malone is, in reality, my personal impression of her, which I have deduced from a variety of media texts, such as her interviews in magazines, her DVD interviews and commentaries, her self-produced YouTube videos and articles about her in magazines. Nonetheless, her textual persona and creative performances have provided and continue to provide me with meaning, purpose and a source of inspiration for enjoying life despite all the personal disappointments I have suffered so far.

Not only had I watched the film *Saved!* (US 2004) and her performance as Mary Cummings countless times during those weeks, but I honestly believe that, in some way, Jena Malone actually *'saved'* me from my emotional darkness by giving me – at least within the parasocial context of my imagination – the kind of love and romantic relationship with an idealised girlfriend that I had been longing for all those years, but had been denied in real life. In December 2006, I finally wrote the personal fan letter to her that I had planned half a year earlier. I posted it to her last known fan mail address before Christmas, though in all honesty, I don't actually expect to receive a real personal response from her.

Notes

1 By summer 2016, at the age of 31, Jena Malone had already featured in 46 films, 9 short films and 5 TV soap guest roles, voiced 4 animation films, 1 documentary and 1 audio-recorded theatre play, and performed on stage in 2 Off-Broadway plays in spring 2006 and spring 2009 respectively – with further films in production.

2 US Legislation with regard to minors working in the entertainment industries requires that a parent or parental guardian has to be present on set with the minor at all time (Rommelmann 2000).

3 Coogan's Law is a US legislation that, following the 1939 landmark court case in which former child actor Jackie Coogan sued his parents for mismanaging his entire earnings, requires film production companies to pay one third of a child actor's gross salary into a blocked trust that can only be accessed by the child actor at his/her 18th birthday. However, despite the child actor's inability to access his/her full earnings, s/he is still liable to pay both manager fees and income tax on the earned full gross salary (Cohen 2002; Rommelmann 2000).

4 In Germany's 3-tier secondary system, students graduate from the Hauptschule and Realschule after 9th grade or 10th grade respectively to learn a blue- or white-collar trade, while students of the Gymnasium, as the highest secondary school form (similar

to a grammar school), graduate after the 13th grade with the 'Abitur' that enables them access to university.

5 I was actually really glad to hear/read in later interviews and articles (i.e. Brink 2008; Lyon 2008; Miller 2006; Pachelli 2011; Sherwin 2004) that Jena and Debbie have apparently managed to rebuild their relationship as mother and daughter again.

6 The fact that I suffer since birth from bipolar-2 disorder – though I was only diagnosed with the illness when I was 25 – has contributed significantly to the negative self-experience over years.

7 Unfortunately, it actually took more than two years before two of them were eventually released on DVD, while *Lying* (US 2006) was only released as a limited US DVD in 2009 despite its premiere at Cannes in 2006 and a few further screenings at various other film festivals over the next months.

5 Catching Fire

The polysemic allure of celebrities

Time Out of Mind

In the previous chapter, I have taken you, the reader, on a narrative journey into the real life of a celebrity fan by presenting you with the extensive, emotional, honest and self-revelatory autoethnographic case study of my own everyday lived fan experiences with my favourite film actress. To keep the lived fan experiences truly *'alive'*, this consumer narrative has thereby contextualised the collected retrospective and contemporaneous autoethnographic data in a storied format while also staying faithful to my original thoughts, feelings, words and expressions recorded in the diaries. This way, you have been afforded the opportunity to immerse yourself as a side-participant into the presented consumer narrative and to witness through my narrative insider perspective how I have experienced my fan relationship with my favourite film actress developing, evolving and manifesting itself slowly but steadily in my everyday life, thoughts, feelings and daydreams over a period of 21 months. Now, should the intense, personal and emotionally honest nature of the presented autobiographical consumer story narrative have left the one or another reader perhaps wavering with an *'uneasy'* and *'uncomfortable'* feeling, then it might be a good idea for you to reflect for a moment on why you may feel this way. There could be a number of underlying reasons as to why the autoethnographic consumer narrative might have caused such a feeling.

Is it because the emotional nature of the consumer narrative has taken you, the reader, out of your *'safe'* scholarly comfort zone commonly offered by traditional desk or laboratory research and, instead, confronted you with the holistic, subjective, *'messy'* and complex reality of an actual consumer's experienced life as a fan? Then, the underlying issue here is clearly an epistemological-methodological one, where some scholars trained in either the *'scientific'* (aka *'empiricist'*) or the sociological-theoretical (aka *'critical'*) research traditions feel uncomfortable with any research approach that departs from their expectations of being presented with a detached, objective, rational and rather simplistic theoretical representation or model of consumers and their (fan) behaviour based on economic modelling, experimental laboratory research or ideology-driven theories. In such a case, I recommend that you review the discussion of the underlying research philosophy and autoethnographic approach in Chapter 1 again.

Or is it perhaps because the autoethnographic fan narrative has touched a more personal nerve closer to home and, hence, resonated unexpectedly with your own devotion to someone or something? If that is the case, the underlying issue should actually be self-evident, since you have offered a practical example of how we, as human beings, tend to engage with the stories we read, hear or watch and, then, relate to ourselves and our own lives – just as Gerrig's (1993) narrative transportation theory suggests. And this is exactly the kind of reader response that autoethnographic, ethnographic, phenomenological and other storied research approaches seek to achieve in order to demonstrate the transferability of their findings and to provide a deeper understanding of a phenomenon.

Or is it rather because your judgements and feelings about the case study's narrator (me) and his reported fan experiences have been shaped by your selective focus on exactly those individual characteristics and instances in the autoethnographic fan narrative that match popular prejudices and, thus, your own preconceptions of celebrity fans? The underlying issue here relates to how the common prejudices and stereotypes underpinning our popular and academic discourse determine the way consumers' fan stories and experiences have traditionally been represented for over a century. Indeed, if you, the reader, have only taken the usual quick, highly selective and often ideology-informed glance at the autoethnographic fan narrative in Chapter 4 and focused your attention exclusively on those individual, eye-catching characteristics, instances and/or events in isolation that match, confirm or reinforce those commonly-held, popular preconceptions of celebrity fans discussed in Chapter 2, then it is not difficult for you to find some supporting evidence for any one of them. But a closer look at the fan narrative would also reveal that for each supporting evidence you may find, you quickly find either even more evidence that contradict the very same fan conceptualisation or that the broader context of the supposedly *'supporting evidence'* actually contradicts the underpinning ideas of the fan conceptualisation in question.

Nevertheless, whatever feeling the autoethnographic consumer narrative of my fan relationship with the film actress Jena Malone, its meanings and manifestation in everyday life may have invoked in you, the reader, rest assured that I have not presented you with the emotional self-revelation of my personal fan experiences from over 10 years ago for the purpose of some vain and narcissistic self-indulgence. Instead, the central idea behind this detailed, emotional autoethnographic account in Chapter 4 is to examine how an actual consumer's lived fan relationship with a celebrity is experienced in everyday life in order to understand, first, what it is about a celebrity that appeals to the individual consumer and, second, how and why individual consumers may experience and develop over time an emotional attachment to their admired celebrity that could evolve into a parasocial relationship. For that reason, it is now time to take a much closer, holistic look at what we can learn from my own fan relationship with my favourite film actress Jena Malone about how and why a consumer feels attracted to a specific celebrity and, subsequently, develops an emotional attachment to her or him, how this fan relationship evolves and expresses itself in everyday life over time and what personal meaning(s) it has for the individual along the way.

Obviously, this does not mean that every other consumer's fan relationship with his/her favourite celebrity develops, evolves, manifests and expresses itself is an exactly the same way as mine has done in this case study. However, by *'going back to the things themselves'* (Heidegger 1927; Husserl 1986) and understanding the underlying essences of the personal fan experiences, meanings and behaviours in this autoethnographic fan narrative and how I related to other celebrities, we are able to identify and explain the essential constituents of consumers' fan relationships with their admired celebrities that underpin the personal nature of how individual consumers relate emotionally to their own favourite celebrities with varying degrees of intensity. In so doing, we are also able to obtain finally a deeper understanding of why a consumer may experience a deep emotional attachment to one celebrity, but at the same time remains emotionally indifferent to many other celebrities, who are equally talented, attractive, of similar age, type and represent the same personality. To gain such insights, we need to understand how celebrities appeal to consumers in general and how most consumers tend to relate to celebrities in daily life. Hence, we draw now on the autoethnographic consumer narrative to reconceptualise our understanding of celebrities and to provide an alternative explanation of how they actually appeal to consumers first.

Four Last Songs

As I have already discussed in Chapter 3, the stardom literature in film studies (Dyer 1998; Geraghty 2000; Hollinger 2006), celebrity literature in media studies (Marshall 1997; Schickel 1985; Turner 2004) and the recent marketing literature (Eagar & Lindridge 2014; Hackley & Hackley 2015; McCracken 1989) have. to this very day, maintained the traditional habit of conceptualising and discussing film stars and celebrities as *'homogeneous semiotic receptacles of cultural meaning'* (Dyer 1998; McCracken 1989) that, supposedly, personify the capitalist consumer society's cultural ideals of success, glamour, the extraordinary and even the divine. This means that celebrities are not human beings, but essentially semiotic accumulations constructed of all the individual characters they portray on screen or stage and all their other public media appearances. Subsequently, the general view is that each film star or celebrity possesses his/her own universal consumer appeal that resides in a consistent public image, which personifies specific cultural values, desires and archetypes. Their own *'true'* personality and private life-style is thereby mirrored in the firm, recognisable canon of virtually identical characters they portray on film or stage (Hollinger 2006; King 1991).

However, once we take a closer look at the autoethnographic case study in Chapter 4, it becomes pretty clear that Jena Malone has actually appealed to me during the entire time as both a very talented actress and a beautiful young woman, which means as a real-living human being, and never as the personified symbol of some cultural archetype, ideal or value. Furthermore, there is clear evidence that, despite never experiencing even a remotely similar emotional attachment to any of them, I have also related to any other film star and celebrity mentioned in the consumer narrative or in this book as a human being, too, by focusing on their skills as professional performers rather than their public images. Thus, we can conclude from the hermeneutic analysis of the collected autoethnographic data that, in contrast to the above-mentioned discussion in the literature, consumers may not be so much attracted to any particular celebrities for what they, as semiotic symbols or systems of cultural meanings, may represent in society, but instead much more to their actual skills and work as creative performers and who they are as real human beings.

This also means that, contradicting traditional conceptualisation in the literature, each film star/celebrity does not appeal universally to all consumers in the same way, but offers instead a multi-constituted attraction. Thus, each film star and celebrity can be consumed in highly complex, diverse and multi-constituted heteroglossic manners by offering each individual consumer a different personal appeal based on the latter's personal interests and desires (Brown et al. 1999; Scott 1994). In this respect, the consumer – and the fan in particular – relates to the celebrity not only on a human level, but also becomes a co-creator of the polysemic texts encompassing the evolving celebrity narrative and consumer appeal. Indeed, if we look at the autoethnographic case study, the film actress Jena Malone caught my personal attention and interest, first and foremost, as a very talented and creative film actress, who has amazed me through her convincing portrayal of a variety of different characters on film. Hence, I enjoy watching her films irrespective of whether she plays the leading role or just a support character. Moreover, the fact that she features mainly in smaller independent films and, subsequently, is less known to the broader public in Europe provides me also with something of a *'hip'* insider knowledge (Holbrook 1986) that I could share with others or use as a means of differentiation by appreciating something that many other people are unaware of.

However, Jena Malone has also quite clearly appealed to me as the nice, intelligent, interesting and very beautiful young woman that she appears to be in her private life – at least according to my perception of her. Furthermore, the case study also shows how I am strongly interested in collecting her films on DVD, magazine articles about her and, obviously, her original hand-signed autographs. We can therefore infer from the hermeneutic analysis of the autoethnographic consumer narrative that each celebrity's personal consumer appeal is not only polysemic in nature, but also consists of four major constituents that represent (a) the creative performer, (b) the 'private' person, (c) the tangible possession, and (d) the social link to other people (see Figure 5.1). Each constituent of the celebrity's personal appeal, alone or in symbiosis with each other, offers thereby with varying degrees of intensity a personal attraction to the individual consumer, capture his/her personal attention and elicit emotional responses that may range from curiosity, interest or disgust over empathy, envy or sexual attraction

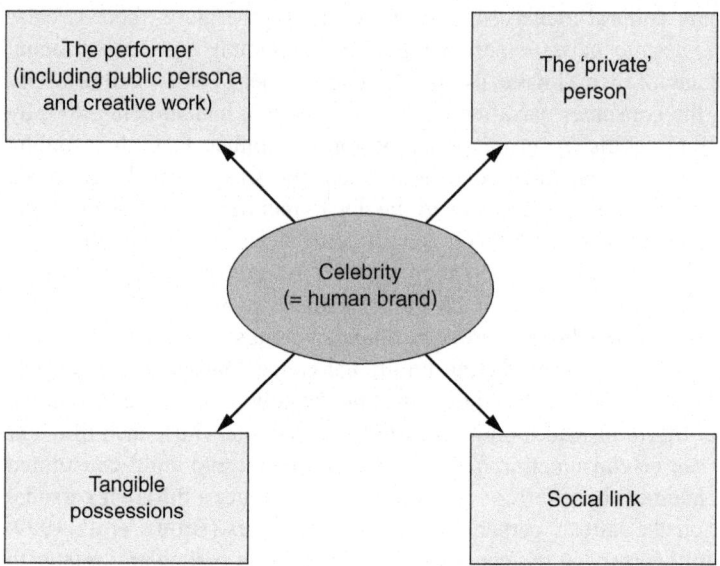

Figure 5.1 Constituents of a celebrity's consumer appeal.

to feelings of friendship or even love. I will now discuss each of the four identified constituents of a film star's/celebrity's polysemic consumer appeal in more detail.

The celebrity as a performer

The first (and perhaps strongest) constituent of a celebrity's attraction to a consumer is that of *'the performer'*, which refers to what the celebrity actually does, what s/he is known and famous for as well as the public media image and gossip surrounding him or her (Geragthy 2000; Mills et al. 2015; Turner 2004). Due to the nature of the creative industries, every celebrity – irrespective of his/her claim to fame – is first and foremost a performer of some sorts and, therefore, appeals to consumers through the (perceived) quality of his/her artistic performances and creative work. In other words, film actors are usually admired for the quality of their acting talent and performances in films or theatre plays (De Cordova 2006; Wohlfeil & Whelan 2011) – or critically derided for the lack thereof. Musicians and rock/pop stars are celebrated for the (perceived) quality of their recorded songs and live performances (Eagar & Lindridge 2014; O'Guinn 1991). And even those much derided socialites and reality TV celebrities are performers in the sense that they perform a certain representative image of themselves for the public and the tabloid media; irrespective of whether this portrayed media persona is a true or a staged reflection of their real personality (Turner 2004).

Therefore, it usually is either a creative performance (i.e. a film or stage character, a song or album, a TV appearance or a live performance) or a news media report by which a consumer becomes first aware of the celebrity. Indeed, the autoethnographic consumer narrative in Chapter 4 shows that it was due to her screen presence and her convincing portrayal of the lead character Mary Cummings in the film *Saved!* that Jena Malone caught my eye and I became aware of her existence. But depending on the intensity and the nature of the individual consumer's situational and, in particular, enduring interest in the celebrity, much of the latter's continued attraction to the individual consumer lies in the personal enjoyment gained from engaging with the celebrity's creative performances (Batat & Wohlfeil 2009) and/or from following his/her media appearances (Redmond 2014). As I have already pointed out on several occasions, my own interest in the actress Jena Malone revolves around admiring her convincing acting performances and watching her films regularly in the cinema, on TV, on DVD and as digital iTunes downloads on my iPod Touch, while also searching continuously for relevant news about both her forthcoming film projects and personal information, as the following original extract from my autoethnographic diary proves:

> My interest in this movie (*Into the Wild* (US 2007)) actually started already as early as October 2006, when I read in an interview with Jena Malone in Mean magazine that it was just being filmed ... As it so happened, in this article she talks not only about her then recent release *The Go-Getter* (US 2007) and her increasing interest in expressing herself in self-produced music and short films, but also that she would soon starting to film *Into the Wild* (US 2007) with Sean Penn.
>
> (Introspection, 30 December 2006)

Thus, the celebrity's consumer appeal constituent of the *'the performer'* seems at first sight to have much in common with what the stardom literature (Dyer 1998; Geraghty 2000; King 1991) and also some of the recent marketing literature (Hackley & Hackley 2015; McCracken 1989; Mills et al. 2015) have already discussed in more detail as the film star's *'on-screen'* (= film character) and *'off-screen'* (= other media appearances) persona. The findings in this study, however, differ substantially from the traditional view in the way a film star/celebrity has been conceptualised.

As already mentioned earlier on a few occasions, Dyer (1998), McCracken (1989) and the complete body of the stardom, celebrity and recent marketing literatures have essentially *'dehumanised'* film stars and celebrities by turning them into *'semiotic receptacles of cultural meanings'*, whose consistent public images would derive from playing only those characters on screen or stage that mirror their actual personalities and private life-styles and, thereby, personify specific cultural archetypes (Hollinger 2006; Eagar & Lindridge 2014). In other words, the traditional discourse has viewed and discussed film stars like Mary Pickford, Rudolph Valentino, John Wayne, Marilyn Monroe, Doris Day, James

Dean, Clint Eastwood, Sylvester Stallone, Jennifer Lopez or Kate Winslet as playing essentially themselves in their films. For that reason, much of the recent media frenzy in the UK regarding, for example, Miley Cyrus's *'wild, sexualised behaviour'* or Kristen Stewart's supposed *'sexual indiscretion'* apparently stems from the fact that some people (such as the tabloid press and self-appointed *'concerned parents'*) just seem to be unable to separate the performer Miley Cyrus from her fictional Disney character Hanna Montana or the film actress Kristen Stewart from her fictional *Twilight* character Bella Swan.

The autoethnographic data in this study, however, strongly suggest that consumers may actually consume and *'value'* film stars and other celebrities as creative artists and performers – and, therefore, as real-living human beings rather than as personified cultural archetypes. One of Jena Malone's personal attractions as a performer to me is her ability and versatility as an actress to portray a very diverse range of female characters that all differ significantly from each other and, especially, from her public and/or perceived private persona. In fact, my own consumer narrative shows unambiguously that I separate the actress Jena Malone from her creative performances, which are all the different characters that she has portrayed on film or on stage. And it is not just Jena Malone, since the case study and this book in general clearly prove that I also separate any other actress like Winona Ryder, Claire Danes, Natalie Portman, Ellen Page or Jennifer Lawrence from the different characters they have portrayed on screen or stage. In a similar way, Eagar and Linbridge (2014) also distinguish between the singer David Bowie and his famous 1970s on-stage persona Ziggy Stardust. We can therefore suggest that the celebrity's personal appeal as *'the performer'* to the individual consumer depends on how the latter perceives:

(a) the quality of the celebrity's creative work and performances, i.e. an actor's films, theatre plays and portrayed characters or a musician's records and live shows;
(b) the quality of the celebrity's talent and performance skills, i.e. an actor's acting skills or a musician's songwriting, singing voice and/or virtuosity with a musical instrument;
(c) the personality and behaviour that the celebrity shows during media appearances and/or that are reported in the media, i.e. TV appearances, interviews, news reports and gossip.

A closer look at the autoethnographic consumer narrative in Chapter 4 presents many instances, such as my consumption of <u>Cheaters</u> (US 2000) and <u>Pride & Prejudice</u> (UK 2005), where I have judged the quality of a film by how well I am able to lose myself in its story and to what extent I can relate to the characters through sympathy, empathy, and even identification (Cohen 2001; Wohlfeil & Whelan 2008) or, alternatively, through dislike and repulsion by connecting them in some way to my personal life experiences. Thus, a particular attraction of the mainly independent films, in which Jena Malone usually features, for me, is that I can relate emotionally to the storylines and characters – especially to those played by Jena Malone, even when her character is a less likeable one.

> Lydia is portrayed like a spoiled and 'entitled' middle-class teenager today ... Pretty much like I actually imagined Lydia while reading the book! Lydia only cares for officers, ribbons and balls – just like today's teenagers only care for boys (primarily athletes and artists), fashion and parties – with no sense for taking responsibility for one's actions, the consequences, etc. Yet, the Bennets are still an ideal family to be intrigued by and to be jealous of.
>
> (Introspection, 15 February 2006)

A consumer's attraction to a celebrity is therefore maintained by the perceived quality of the latter's performances – or output of those performances – and their consumption. In case of actors, the output of those performances would obviously be films, TV shows or theatre plays. In case of musicians, they would be live shows and/or recordings on vinyl, CD or digital download. In case of models, they would be extravagant fashion photographs in glamour magazines. And in case of athletes, the output of those performances would be matches, games, scores or races. Nonetheless, an important factor that the stardom and celebrity literature, due to their *'dehumanisation'* and reduction of the film star or celebrity to a semiotic system, has usually ignored is the simple, but *'essential'* fact that the film star or celebrity has to have the necessary talent and skills to deliver those performances in the first place. For that reason, McCracken (1989) famously experienced major difficulties to explain the consumer appeal of Meryl Streep, while Dyer (1998) simply denied *'character actors'* the status of *'film stars'* out-of-hand.

However, the autoethnographic data in this study show that the consumer's admiration of those performance skills and talent, in particular, strengthens in return the attractiveness of the celebrity as a performer. Indeed, while I enjoy immersing myself into her films and engaging emotionally with the lead and support characters she plays, *'the performer'* Jena Malone appeals to me in particular through the quality of her acting talent by which *"she makes all of her portrayed characters appear to be real and believable"*. And, as already mentioned, the same is true for other film actors/actresses like Winona Ryder, Natalie Portman, Ellen Page or Jennifer Lawrence, who have caught my attention in a similar manner and appealed to me based on how (much) their acting performances captivate and engage me emotionally through their believable portrayal of their characters. The same also applies to how bands and musicians like Stiff Little Fingers, The Clash, Buzzcocks, The Pogues, Heinz Rudolf Kunze, Bruce Springsteen, R.E.M., Warpaint, The Adverts or The Damned appeal to me in terms of how their albums and live gigs speak to me personally, touch the right nerves and, subsequently, have a certain relevance to me.

Obviously, a consumer's assessment of the quality of a celebrity's performance skills and talent is very subjective and based on his/her personal taste, interest, background knowledge and the expertise to make such *'educated'* judgement calls (Holbrook 1999). But it is hereby important to reiterate once more that I clearly distinguish between the actresses Jena Malone, Winona Ryder, Claire Danes, Natalie Portman, Ellen Page, Jennifer Lawrence, etc. and their various on-screen characters as opposed to reading them in each case as one-and-the-same, as suggested by the stardom literature. In fact, the presented fan narrative in Chapter 4 also makes it abundantly clear that I actually go through great lengths to avoid assigning any archetypical image to Jena Malone or any of the other actresses other than that they are very beautiful, intelligent, and confident, but otherwise ordinary down-to-earth young women, who also happen to be very talented and creative artists. Hence, besides the physical appearance and style, the consumer seems to define the public image of the film star or celebrity, just like that of any other person on the street, by his/her status and profession as an artist rather than the personification of a certain cultural archetype.

Nonetheless, their media appearances at film premieres, at film festivals, on TV talk shows or in magazine articles also tend to offer a certain attraction to me. And since the primary purpose of many of those media appearances for a film star or celebrity is to promote a forthcoming film or music album release, a new TV show, a theatre premiere or a book launch, his/her consumer appeal as *the performer*'s public persona for the consumer would usually stem from three areas of personal interest:

(a) as a source of information for the celebrity's forthcoming creative perform-ances, projects and outputs;
(b) as a means of staying up-to-date with the latest news surrounding the celeb-rity, such as how s/he looks like in everyday life when s/he does not perform a character, her relationship status and any personal news;
(c) as a means of catching glimpses of the celebrity's *'true'* personality and 'private' person by paying attention to how s/he moves, speaks, argues, interacts with others, responds in various situations and behaves in general.

But although it is evident from the autoethnographic consumer narrative that I enjoy watching and reading news stories and articles about Jena Malone, the autoethnographic data analysis also reveals my sheer contempt for the kind of gossip about celebrities that the tabloid press and fashion magazines are feeding to their audiences with their obsession for what celebrities wear or (according to self-appointed or proclaimed 'style experts') should not wear, whom they sup-posedly date, what parties they attend, how much they have supposedly earned and, of course, with their alleged affairs and scandals. A principal reason for my contempt throughout the entire collected autoethnographic data set is quite simply that, in my opinion, most of those articles are extremely superficial and contain very little (well, virtually no) truth value whatsoever. Most of their content consists either of small re-edited bits of information that are taken out of context from other sources or is completely made-up to tell some fictitious stories to underline some paparazzi or red carpet photos. For example, the sums and amounts reported as facts in tabloid stories, but also increasingly in academic publications (Elberse 2014), about how much money a film star or a celebrity has earned in relation to a certain film, a music album or over a year are generally just plucked out of thin air by the tabloid media.

Obviously, for the talent agencies, these fictional media stories are a welcome gift when it comes to negotiating the next real salaries for their clients in future film productions (Epstein 2012), media appearances or concert tours. Rumours have it that talent agencies, in the past, may have sometimes even planted such stories in the gossip media in order to boost the salaries of their clients (and, of course, their own commission fees in the process) (Epstein 2005; McDonald 2000). For me, however, it is the paparazzi that are a particularly annoying, *'borderline-criminal'* nuisance, as they not only make it their business to invade illegally the privacy of celebrities with the sole intention to catch them out for some *'exposing, scandalous'* photos that provide the material for just another fictitious and pointless story, but also ensure that many celebrities become increasingly reluctant to appear in public, to go out like *'normal people'* and/or to meet their fans on the streets.

Nevertheless, the enormous global popularity of the gossip magazines and tabloids for more than a century (Barbas 2001; Gabler 1998; Hermes 2006) suggests that many consumers take a different view. Indeed, it seems obvious that much of the media fuzz surrounding Miley Cyrus, her raunchy MTV performance, her risky music video and shocked parents that are apparently unable to separate her from the fictional Disney-character Hannah Montana has actually been created by the tabloid media themselves in an effort to sell copies. Furthermore, while fans like me may have a specific vested interest in the public persona and the celebrity as a performer in general, the truth is that to many other consumers the celebrity appeals mainly as a subject they can gossip about with friends, colleagues and neighbours. As Hermes and Kooijman (2016) argue, celebrities often serve the purpose of providing many consumers with a safe target they can talk about behind their back without the risk of suffering any potential repercussions.

In fact, while most of the discussion in this book looks at how consumers relate to a celebrity in a positive manner by forming even an emotional attachment, we also need to acknowledge that, on some occasions, consumers tend to relate to celebrities instead in a more negative manner by enjoying their poor performances, mistakes, failures, bad reviews and comments with Schadenfreude (Hermes 2006). In these cases, consumers tend to harbour either feelings of jealousy, dislike or even disgust or, alternatively, feelings of personal, moral superiority towards the celebrity. Sometimes, it might just be the case that they perceive it as unfair that certain celebrities get all the public attention, critical acclaims and credits, while the celebrity they personally champion tends to be overlooked – just I have done a few times in the consumer narrative, when I felt that *'less talented and less skilled'* celebrities receive more public attention than Jena Malone. But in other cases, consumers just tend to be really jealous of the celebrity's talent, success and popularity, which they perceive to be unfair and undeserved. Hence, celebrities offer a canvas, on which those consumers can project their inherent dissatisfaction with their own professional lives. Sharing, thereby, the gossip about celebrities' failures, misfortunes and bad reviews enables them to forget about their own situation by being able to look with Schadenfreude down on those celebrities' humiliations and public *'fall from grace'* (King 2011; Redmond 2014).

The celebrity as a 'private' person

The second (and perhaps second-strongest, but most under-researched) constituent of a celebrity's attraction to a consumer is that of *'the 'private' person'*, which refers to what kind of person the celebrity in his/her private life really is – or, more accurately, is perceived to be – when s/he is not portraying a character either on stage or on screen or when not appearing publicly in the media. In other words, the consumer is often not only attracted to the celebrity as a creative performer and his/her creative output, but also to the celebrity as a real-living human being with a unique face, physical appearance, beauty, intellect, personal interests, values, beliefs, political views and, of course, sex appeal. Hence, a male or female consumer can be attracted to the celebrity in the same way that s/he would also be attracted in everyday life to any other person at school, university, work, on public transport, on the street, at a retailer or in a bar (Wohlfeil & Whelan 2012). And as with any other person that we have never met before, it is obviously the film star's, rock/pop star's or any other celebrity's unique personal look, face, figure, beauty, appearance and sex appeal by which s/he, at least in the eyes of the individual consumer, stands out of the crowd of all the other talented, attractive, intelligent and (sometimes even more) popular celebrities and, subsequently, can capture a consumer's attention and personal interest.

Indeed, as the autoethnographic consumer narrative clearly shows, what awoke right from the start my interest in Jena Malone while watching the film *Saved!* (US 2004) was not only her incredible acting performances, but also, if not even more so, that she – unlike many other talented, beautiful and interesting young film actresses and celebrities – as a young woman actually personifies my personal 'ideal of female beauty' and looks like *'the girl I am always dreaming of'*, as underlined in the following retrospective autoethnographic recall of my first time seeing her on screen:

> I really got hooked by Jena Malone's beautiful eyes and her charming smile. Although there are many actresses who may be much more attractive than her, for me, Jena Malone is a gorgeous young woman – a natural beauty the way she is. She simply is the type of girl I'm always looking and falling for – the girl next door who is fun to hang out with and to spend your life with …

> (Retrospective Essay, September 2005)

Although Dyer (1998) acknowledges that any film star or celebrity is embodied by the physical presence of a real-living person, who provides the film star or celebrity with a unique face, body, voice and personality that differentiate him or her from other film stars/celebrities, the stardom and celebrity literatures have not only ignored, but fully *'erased'* the human side of the film star or celebrity from the academic discourse by conceptualising them as *'semiotic receptacles of cultural meaning'* (Dyer 1998; McCracken 1989). This is quite unfortunate, as the film star's/celebrity's physical presence provides the consumer with the clear proof that s/he is not just an artificial *'personified cultural archetype'*, but actually a real human being with a private life, personality, personal political opinions and social relationships, who experiences joy and sorrow or success and failure just like any other person (Cocker et al. 2015).

Nevertheless, apart from the odd psychological study (Giles & Maltby 2004; Karniol 2001), which has looked in particular at how certain celebrities like teen pop stars, young male actors or athletes serve teenage girls as *'safe objects of affection'* that enable them to explore their own sexual awakening in a playful manner[1], very little is actually known about how a film star or celebrity appeals to individual consumers and is *'consumed'* as a real-living human being. Opening therefore the door to a new territory, the hermeneutic analysis of the collected autoethnographic data reveals that consumers, indeed, may value and consume the celebrity not only as *'the performer'* or for their physical beauty and attractiveness, but also as the real *'private person'* underneath the public media persona. In fact, it is not only the fans, as one might suspect, but consumers across all walks of life who, often out of curiosity, crave for getting a closer look behind the *'performer's'* curtain to learn more about what the admired film star or celebrity is really like as a private human being in everyday life (Cocker et al. 2015; King 2011), when s/he is neither portraying a character on stage or on screen nor standing in the public spotlight of the media.

Underpinning this curiosity or even desire to discover the *'true person'* underneath the film star's/celebrity's public persona is the consumer's search for the *'authentic'* and the real in everyday life (Beeton 2015; MacCannell 1973). Since most consumers (often not unjustified) tend to perceive the usually mediated representation of a film star's/celebrity's personality, life-style and relationships in the (gossip) media only as just another part of the latter's public performances and, therefore, as a sanitised, inauthentic simulation (Schickel 1985), being in some way given *'backstage access'* (MacCannell 1973) into his/her real private life would promise the consumer to get to know the film star or celebrity as the unvarnished, authentic person s/he really is in everyday life. The process of *'getting to know'* the real *'private person'* also makes it possible for the individual consumer to bring the admired or even adored, but at the same time distant, unreachable celebrity down to an equal social level and, hence, for him/her to become more *'accessible'* on a human level. Depending on the individual consumer's personal needs, the film star or celebrity can subsequently appeal to him/her as a role model, as an acquaintance, as an ideal *'friend'* or even as a potential love-interest within a parasocial context (Horton & Wohl 1956; Wohlfeil

& Whelan 2012), as has been the case in my autoethnographic fan narrative. However, while many consumers, and fans in particular, tend to seek genuine insights into the private person and life of the film star or celebrity in order to get mentally and emotionally closer to him or her on a human level, the film star or any other celebrity can also appeal in a similar way to other consumers as a figure of pity or even sheer contempt (Redmond 2014).

The film star/celebrity, thereby, serves as a canvas, on which these consumers are able to project their inherent dissatisfaction and frustrations with their own personal lives and social relationships. In some cases, these consumers have a very critical opinion of celebrities in general and tend to view them mostly as narcissistic, self-absorbed, overrated, fake and inauthentic individuals. Thus, they gleefully indulge themselves in precisely those *'news stories'* in the gossip magazines and tabloids that promise with the help of paparazzi photos to *'expose'* the film stars', celebrities' and, especially, reality TV stars' *'hidden truths'*, such as their unvarnished real appearances when they are caught out unaware, their *'indiscretions'*, their *'scandals'* and *'affairs'* or any other weak-nesses and wrongdoings (Hermes 2006). Reading and sharing such gossip enables those consumers to take up a *'morally superior'* position from where they can look down with Schadenfreude on a film star's or any other celebrity's public *'fall from grace'* and, in the process, forget about their own private lives and personal situation (Turner 2004).

In other cases, consumers just seek to gain a cathartic experience from feeling good about themselves after learning from such *'exposed hidden truths'* that the successful and popular film star, celebrity or reality TV star may in his/her private life either be worse off than they are or, in contrast to the public image, be a rather nasty, spoilt or otherwise disappointing individual. It, therefore, is quite a paradox that the most avid readers that the tabloids, gossip magazines and paparazzi cater to are often those consumers, who claim to have no interest in celebrities or even look down on *'today's celebrity culture'* with contempt. Nevertheless, the main problem with the celebrity's consumer appeal constituent of *'the 'private' person'* is that consumers, with very few exceptions, are highly unlikely to ever meet their favourite film stars and celebrities in person – never mind to get to know their real, genuine private selves in their private lives. Sub-sequently, the constituent of the celebrity's attraction as a *'private person'* is another paradox, where the individual consumer, instead of really getting to know the film star or any other celebrity in his/her private life, constructs one's personal image of what s/he thinks or believes the film star or celebrity to be like as a *'private person'* in his/her everyday life outside the media spotlight based on a continuous process of introjection and projection (Gould 1993; Wohlfeil & Whelan 2012) that I will discuss in more detail later in the next chapter.

The celebrity as a tangible possession

The third constituent of a celebrity's attraction to a consumer is that of *'the tan-gible possession'*, which refers to how the elusive film star or celebrity actually becomes accessible and tangible to the individual consumer either as a commodity or as a treasure. Because film stars and celebrities are only human beings and cannot be everywhere at any time, consumers are normally only able to consume and admire the film star's/celebrity's creative performances and works as *'the performer'* in person, if they manage to be at the right place at the right time and with one of those often limited tickets. The frustrations experienced by consumers, when they are unable to attend a celebrity's performances because they either could not get a ticket or, more often, do not live even remotely close enough to the locations of those events, are reflected in the autoethnographic consumer narrative in Chapter 4 as well. On several occasions, I have voiced my frustrations that some of Jena Malone's independent films (especially some of her better ones) are never released in European cinemas at all and, hence, are inaccessible to me, or that I has been unable to see her performing live on stage in a Broadway play, since a weekend trip from Ireland to New York was simply not within my budgetary limitations at the time. And because she is also little known in Europe, even some of the well-known global magazines have often replaced in their European editions elaborate articles of her with articles about a local reality TV star or socialite instead – which obviously has frustrated me even further.

The intangible nature of a film star's/celebrity's creative performances, work, public media appearances and, especially, his/her private life, therefore, is for the consumer a constant reminder of the film star's/celebrity's inaccessibility and even illusiveness as both *'the performer'* and *'the "private" person'*. But due to the commercial nature of the creative industries and the need to make a decent living from their art, film stars and celebrities (and only too often the management behind them) also have a vested interest in making their creative performances and works available to as many consumers as possible by offering them their reproductions in the form of vinyl records, CDs, DVDs, digital downloads, photos, posters, books, magazines and/or any other branded merchandising on the marketplace (Thomson 2006).

It is, therefore, only fair to conclude that a film star's/celebrity's attraction to the individual consumer would stem to a certain degree from the possibility for the latter to take indeed physical possession of the film star's/celebrity's creative performances and outputs as *'the performer'* and/or even, to some extent, of *'the private person'* through the acquisition of such products as their tangible manifestation. The attached meaning and consumption of such celebrity branded products is obviously quite diverse, as consumers acquire them for very different personal reasons and purposes. For many consumers, the purchase of a CD, DVD, digital download or a vinyl record is primarily a means of being able to listen to their favourite recorded music or to watch their favourite film whenever, wherever and as often as they like. In other words, the commercially available reproduction of the film star's/celebrity's creative performances allows the consumer to enjoy repeatedly what would otherwise only be a once-off temporary experience; and also to share it with others at one's leisure. A T-shirt obtained at the gig of a rock/pop band or at a musical performance has often the same meaning as a T-shirt obtained at a tourist destination – signalling to others that *'I was there!'* and, therefore, one of the *'chosen ones'*.

In other cases, the purchase of recorded performances also enables consumers to consume and admire even those creative performances of a film star or celebrity that are not available or accessible in their home region, because the celebrity neither lives nor is able to perform in those areas. In fact, it was not even so long ago that even the creative performances of a film star could only be enjoyed if and for as long as the film was actually screened in a local cinema nearby or on local TV (Wohlfeil & Whelan 2008). The autoethnographic consumer narrative in Chapter 4 shows repeatedly that, since Jena Malone primarily features in small, but more artistic independent film productions that have been and still are rarely screened in my local cinemas, I have always been highly dependent on acquiring the films on DVD or digital downloads in order to enjoy both the film and, of course, her acting performances.

What the autoethnographic consumer narrative also reveals is that the difference between fans and 'less dedicated' consumers is primarily the great of lengths that they go to in order to obtain such recorded performances. While the latter may only visit the local shops or Amazon to look for a particular recorded performance (i.e. a music album, a film, a book, etc.) and purchase it, if available at a suitable price, fans tend to be more willing not only to pay a slightly higher price (up to a certain limit), but also to chase up rare or less available items through a greater network of niche retailers, fairs, festivals, etc. across the world. For example, the autoethnographic consumer narrative clearly demonstrates how I even went so far to buy an external DVD drive and locked it into region 1, so that I can purchase, collect and watch the US DVDs of all those independent films with Jena Malone at my leisure that have never been released in Europe to-date. Thus, *'taking possession'* of a film star's films on DVDs or a musician's songs on vinyl, CD or digital download (and, by extension, of the respective celebrity as a *'performer'*) enables consumers to overcome the initial problem of access and availability.

But for some consumers, it is just not enough to possess only the one or other recorded album, film or book that caught their eye at one time. Instead, some of them are collectors, who long to *'possess'* the entire creative works of celebrities in a certain genre of music, film, literature, etc., while others, such as fans or collectors, have the desire to *'possess'* the complete creative work of a specific celebrity. In so doing, the ability to *'take possession'* of a film star's/celebrity's creative works and performances allows the consumer not only to consume them whenever and wherever s/he likes, but also enables them – like a *'museum curator'* – to keep them and the celebrity as a *'performer'* 'alive' even after a music band has split up, a TV show has been cancelled, a theatre venue or show has been closed down, a celebrity has retired from the stage or, sadly, even passed away (Radford & Bloch 2012). For one or another consumer, the attraction of the film star or celebrity as a *'tangible possession'* is that it can give both *'the performer'* and the creative performance or artwork a touch of immortality. Indeed, the creative performances, works and public persona of an ever-growing number of film stars, rock/pop stars and other celebrities, who have passed away some time ago, can still be enjoyed these days by audiences from different generations, some of whom have personally never had the opportunity to see and hear them alive in the flesh, thanks to the recorded performances collected by dedicated individual consumers (Holbrook 1987).

While it therefore seems obvious that I would make Jena Malone's creative work and performances as a film actress tangible through the purchase of her films on DVD or digital download and her public persona through the collection of video clips and articles of her interviews in the media, my autoethnographic consumer narrative also provides us with some very interesting insights into how the physical presence of Jena Malone as *'the private person'* has also manifested herself over time in the posters and photos of her that have been increasingly decorating both my living- and work-space. Hence, we can deduct from the case study that consumers also tend to use certain types of products, such as photos (especially those that show the film star or celebrity in their private life), posters, T-shirts and, in particular, personalised items like hand-signed autographs or personal artefacts, which were once owned or personally used by the celebrity like film props, costumes, a guitar or a jacket (Newman et al. 2011), as proxies in order to make the illusive film star's/celebrity's *'private person'* at least symbolically accessible and a part of one's everyday life.

However, strongly contradicting much of the conventional media discourse, fans are not the only consumers to have a serious interest in a celebrity's original autographs, former personal belongings or the original film/stage props and costumes. In fact, these items have become subject to a highly competitive collectors' and investors' market at reputable auctions, where many celebrity objects – especially those of deceased celebrities – fetch sales prices that, even at the lower end, are way out of the league for the ordinary celebrity, film or music fan (Newman et al. 2011). Even on eBay, a single hand-signed autograph usually retails somewhere between $50 and $500 (depending on the film star or celebrity in question) but, in some cases, can fetch up to $2000, while an autographed film poster signed by the entire cast and director at the premiere usually sells for somewhere between $800 and $8000 a piece – depending on the film and who has signed it. Unfortunately, due to being such a profitable market with such a high level of demand, a growing number of fraudsters try to take advantage of the trade and have been flooding the market – especially on eBay – with fake autographed photos, whereby the quality of the celebrity's faked signature can range from amateurish-obvious to very difficult (even for experts) to distinguish from the original.

The celebrity as a social link

The fourth and final constituent of a celebrity's attraction to a consumer is that of *'the social link'*, which refers to how the film star or other celebrity often serves as a source and site for social interaction or even social relationships between individual consumers. Due to the very nature of the creative entertainment industries, it is only too obvious that a film star or celebrity and his/her creative performances and output are usually known, consumed and admired or, alternatively, disliked by more than just one consumer. In our increasingly anonymous and 'individualised' society, where the individual experiences a growing feeling of social isolation and alienation from community (Cova 1998; McAlexander et al. 2002), a significant appeal of a film star, rock/pop star or any other celebrity (and, especially, a very popular one) to the individual consumer seems to lie in providing the latter with the potential opportunity to link up, meet, interact and even form closer bonds with other like-minded individuals that share the same interests (Henry & Caldwell 2007; Kozinets 2001). Indeed, it seems only natural that many consumers would not only enjoy or, alternatively, dislike a film star's/celebrity's creative work and performances in the social company of other like-minded consumers, but also share together their mutual appreciation for the performance and their mutual admiration or criticism for the film star or celebrity as *'the performer'* and even *'the 'private' person'* with each other – especially, but not exclusively, in so-called fan communities (Hewer & Hamilton 2012a; Kanai 2015).

It therefore comes to no surprise that, as I have already shown back in Chapter 2, the social interaction and dynamics among fan community members in sharing their admiration for a particular celebrity, sports team or any other beloved subject through communal rituals in either online or offline gatherings have already caught the specific research interest of scholars in both CCT (Henry & Caldwell 2007; Hewer & Hamilton 2012a; O'Guinn 1991) and fan studies (Barbas 2001; Duffett 2013; Hills 2002). The fan community – whether offline in the form of traditional fan-clubs or online in the form of fan-sites and fan forums – is thereby presented as the central site where fans negotiate their polysemic meanings of the film star or celebrity and his/her creative outputs with the *'proper meanings'* championed by the fan community's official *'canon'* (Duffett 2013), which they share together in their social discourse, communal rituals and the display or *'worship'* of valued artefacts (Belk et al. 1989; Henry & Caldwell 2007).

But although the autoethnographic case study may not offer any evidence that I have ever joined either a virtual or a local fan community at all, never mind ever intended to meet other like-minded Jena Malone fans, it appears that the main consumer appeal of certain rock/pop stars, film stars, directors or any other celebrities may in some instances lie indeed in the kind(s) of people that the individual consumer associates with being interested in *'the performer'*, his/her creative performances and work and/or the *'tangible possession'* of the relevant recorded performances, photographs, posters and any other material collectibles. In fact, we can witness every year how just another interchangeable pop boygroup or girlgroup based on the same old formula with the same type of stylistic 'character line-ups' among its group members is launched to target just another 'generation' of (pre)adolescent teenagers usually aged between 11 and 15 years with the same, virtually identical musical output of cover versions of the same standard songs that their predecessors had already delivered to the previous 'generation'[2].

Since this young age group is just beginning the process of forming their own self-identity (Karniol 2001), what tends to be in particular on the minds of these young consumers is not so much expressing a 'refined musical or artistic taste' and the appreciation for the actual quality of a celebrity's talent and creative work (Holbrook 1999), but instead the search for belonging and social approval from their peers (Larsen et al. 2010). Hence, the true consumer appeal of many teen pop stars to young consumers may actually lie often in their (perceived) popularity with those popular – or alternative – peers, whose social approval these kids seek (Ehrenreich et al. 1992; Larsen et al. 2010).

Of course, despite the popular media images of hysterically screaming (pre) adolescent girls that have filled the pages of teen, entertainment and gossip magazines since the 1960s (Jenson 1992), it would be unfair to ascribe this kind of behaviour solely to teenage girls' collective adulation of the latest teen pop or film stars. When my own interest in music awoke as a 9-year old, boys in my class and neighbourhood began to listen to either Status Quo, Kiss or AC/DC, because we believed (informed by teen magazines like Bravo) that these are the *'cool bands'* for the *'cool kids'* – although I soon preferred listening to my personal choice of Kraftwerk and the early German punk acts like Ideal, Extrabreit and Joachim Witt instead of just following those bands that happen to be popular with my peers. But let us also not forget that the reason why consumers often pay attention to and share celebrity gossip is to interact socially with other people (Hermes & Kooijman 2016).

The Messenger

So, what does this all mean? Well, based on these findings that have emerged from the hermeneutic analysis of the collected autoethnographic data and the subsequent consumer narrative presented in Chapter 4, we are now able to gain a valuable deeper understanding of how film stars and any other celebrities really appeal on a human level to the individual consumer. Far from being just a personified semiotic receptacle of some cultural archetype with a homogeneous consumer appeal that is universal to all consumers, as the traditional stardom and celebrity literature has argued (Dyer 1998; McCracken 1989; Turner 2004), each individual film star or celebrity offers consumers a very personal polysemic and multi-constituted appeal as a professional and/or private human being that both could be consumed through *'tangible possessions'* or serve as a site and subject for social interaction. Indeed, as the autoethnographic case study demonstrates, rather than as the cultural archetype of the *'troubled, streetwise young girl/woman from society's wrong side of the tracks'*, which would actually ignore a substantial number of different characters she has portrayed in her career so far[3], Jena Malone has in fact appealed to me quite clearly as a film actress, whose talent and acting skills *'make each of her characters come to life'*, as well as a beautiful, intelligent, creative, nice and interesting young woman in everyday life, both of which I have sought to integrate physically into my life through the tangible possession of her films on DVD, articles about her, her photos, her hand-signed autographs and other collectibles.

Because of these findings, we are finally able to explain not only why the same film star, rock/pop star or any other celebrity may have a different attraction to different individual consumers, but also why a consumer may experience a strong emotional attachment to a specific film star or celebrity while feeling complete indifference or even repulsion towards another one who, objectively seen, seems to be equally talented, attractive, intelligent and, at a first glance, even to embody the same type of person and/or cultural archetype. Since each film star's/celebrity's personal polysemic consumer appeal consists of the identified four main constituents, every consumer responds to each of these appeal constituents with varying levels of intensity either positively or negatively in accordance with one's personal needs, desires and aspirations.

To understand clearer how the polysemic, multi-constituted consumer appeal works in practice, let us consider the following example. Since my early teenage years, I have been listening to the music of numerous different rock or punk bands, going to their live gigs and also buying their recorded albums on vinyl, CD and/or digital downloads. In other words, each of those different individual rock and punk bands has appealed to me with varying degrees of intensity as *'performers'* through the *'perceived quality'* of their creative performances, such as their actual songs, albums, live shows and overall public persona, and, obviously, as *'tangible possessions'* through the ownership of their recorded music. At the same time, some of those bands have also been much more important to me and for a longer period of time than others, which means that I purchased a number of the formers' albums over the years versus just one of the latters at a particular time in my life, that I listen to the former bands' albums more often than to those of the latters, and/or that I actually go to see their live gigs in the first place (Hermann 2012), and even more than once, rather than just leave it with listening to the record for a few times. Obviously, those bands, whose relevance to me has been rather weak (i.e. never extended beyond a specific song), quickly stopped catching my attention again. In some cases, however, a particular band may fall in, then out and eventually back into favour again during the course of my life, which indicates that a celebrity's appeal to the consumer is not static but fluctuates. Yet, it must be noted that I have remained at all times completely indifferent to their *'private persons'*.

Moreover, while I enjoy the shared social atmosphere at live punk gigs and also to chat at specialist record stores positively or negatively about particular albums or bands from time to time, the appeal of those bands as a *'social link'* tends to be rather low and in many cases even close to indifference. The reason might be that my musical taste had departed very early from what was popular among my peers and I preferred to listen to the music I liked rather than to follow any band that might be 'popular' but I did not care about. In other words, the strength of a consumer's personal interest, liking or dislike towards any individual celebrity depends on how much s/he is positively or negatively attracted to each of the celebrity's personal consumer appeal constituents. And the stronger the accumulation of the personal attraction to each individual constituent the more the celebrity catches his/her attention. And should a consumer pay no attention to some celebrities at all, it is because s/he is across the board indifferent to their personal appeal.

Notes

1 Interestingly, not a single study, so far, has actually looked at how female teen pop stars or young actresses may also serve teenage boys in a similar way as *'safe objects of affection'* that enable them to explore their awakening sexuality. Instead, the sole focus has been exclusively on teenage girls – but often for quite different ideological reasons.
2 It appears that, in the last 10–15 years, the music industry launches these new boy-groups (but also girlgroups) with increasing pace in ever shorter intervals. While most boy- and girlgroups from the 1960s–1990s, such as Ronettes, Supremes, Jackson 5, Osmonds, Bay City Rollers, Duran Duran, Take That, Backstreet Boys, Westlife or Spice Girls, usually lasted at least 3–5 years before a 'new model' was introduced to target a younger segment, acts during the noughties like All Saints, S-Club 7, Five, Blue, Busted or McFly were given 2–3 years. But, these days, many recent boygroups or girlgroups, such as JLS, One Direction, The Saturdays or Little Mix, have barely lasted a year before facing a potential replacement.
3 A common practice in the scholarly stardom and celebrity discourse.

6 Lovesong

Living everyday celebrity fandom

Five Star Day

Since we are now able to explain why the same film star, rock/pop star or any other celebrity may have a very different personal attraction to each individual consumer that can be positive or negative, it is finally time to take a closer look at how understanding the multi-constituted consumer appeal also provides an explanation why the individual consumer may experience a strong emotional attachment to a specific film star or celebrity and even become a devoted fan but feels very differently towards other ones, who appear to be equally talented, attractive, intelligent and to embody a similar type of person. Therefore, let us take another look at what, beyond my fan relationship with Jena Malone, the autoethnographic case study (and this book in general) reveals about how I have also related to other film stars and celebrities over the years.

As the actress Natalie Portman had caught my eyes only a few years earlier and Kristen Stewart did so shortly after Jena Malone, while in the meantime Ellen Page and Jennifer Lawrence have also caught my attention, it might be a good idea to compare here the individual personal consumer appeal that each of them has had for me in order to explain why I have become a fan of Jena Malone and not of the others. Every one of them is not only a very beautiful, intelligent and interesting young woman, but also a talented character actress, who (with the odd exception[1]) features primarily in independent film productions. What they also have in common is that each of them caught my attention through both their portrayed character and their acting performance in a specific film (Natalie Portman: *Anywhere but here*, Kristen Stewart: *Into the Wild*, Ellen Page: *Hard Candy*, Jennifer Lawrence: *Winter's Bone* and Jena Malone: *Saved!*).

However, following my usual 'quality test' of watching each actress in a few other films, I have had a pretty low opinion of Kristen Stewart's acting skills and performances (influenced by the *Twilight*-films), which only improved slowly with some of her recent films. Furthermore, even though all of them are very beautiful young women, I have never experienced an emotional and/or romantic attraction to Natalie Portman or Jennifer Lawrence so far, while its intensity has varied significantly between the others. In fact, Jena Malone has remained the only one of them, who has appealed to me as a *'private person'* and where I have experienced a strong desire to learn more about her personal life and what she is like in private. Subsequently, I have never really cared for Ellen Page's homosexuality or any of the other actresses' private lives and relationships. Finally, Jena Malone has also been the only one, whose entire films I wanted to own on DVD rather than just a select few individual ones.

In other words, the major difference in their personal consumer appeal to me is that Natalie Portman, Ellen Page and Jennifer Lawrence have all strongly and positively appealed to me as a talented actress (*'the performer'*) through their convincing acting performances and portrayed characters in their films. But the other three constituents have only appealed to me moderately or even very poorly, if at all. In fact, because their *'private person'* constituent largely failed to catch my interest, I have only been marginally attracted to their *'tangible possession'* manifested in the ownership of a select few individual films on DVD. In case of Kristen Stewart, her appeal as a *'performer'* has been much lower or even negative. But since she, similar to Jena Malone, looks like *'the type of girl I am always falling for'*, there has also been some lower-to-moderate level of romantic attraction to her as a young beautiful woman. At the same time, I have felt indifferent to the *'tangible possessions'* of either *'the performer'* with regard to her films or *'the private person'* in the form of photos, articles and collectibles (Newman et al. 2011).

The findings from the hermeneutic analysis, therefore, suggest that the nature of a film star's/celebrity's personal polysemic consumer appeal to a fan differs from that to the *'non-fan'* primarily with regard to the positivity, intensity and multi-constituency of the experienced attraction. A *'non-fan'* consumer tends to experience only a mild-to-moderate positive or negative attraction to one, or maybe two of the film star's/celebrity's personal consumer appeal constituents, which is usually to the *'performer'* with a focus on the creative performances and the public persona – often together with the *'tangible possession'* of the recorded performances and/or the *'social link'* to other people. But only too often, it is primarily the *'social link'* constituent that appeals to many consumers. A fan, on the other hand, tends to experience a strong positive attraction to at least three, if not all four of the film star's/celebrity's polysemic consumer appeal constituents on a relatively consistent and prolonged basis. As a result, the individual consumer as a fan feels much closer and emotionally attached to this specific film star or celebrity rather than to any other celebrity, who only appeals through one consumer appeal constituent moderately to him or her.

Thus, the next step is to understand how the film star's/celebrity's personal polysemic, multi-constituted appeal to the individual consumer determines how s/he experiences his/her fan relationship with the admired film star in everyday life. Based on the insights gained from my own personal fan relationship with Jena Malone, I now examine in more detail how the interplay between the five identified fan relationship constituents shown in Figure 6.1 reflects a consumer's everyday lived fan experiences with the admired film star or celebrity.

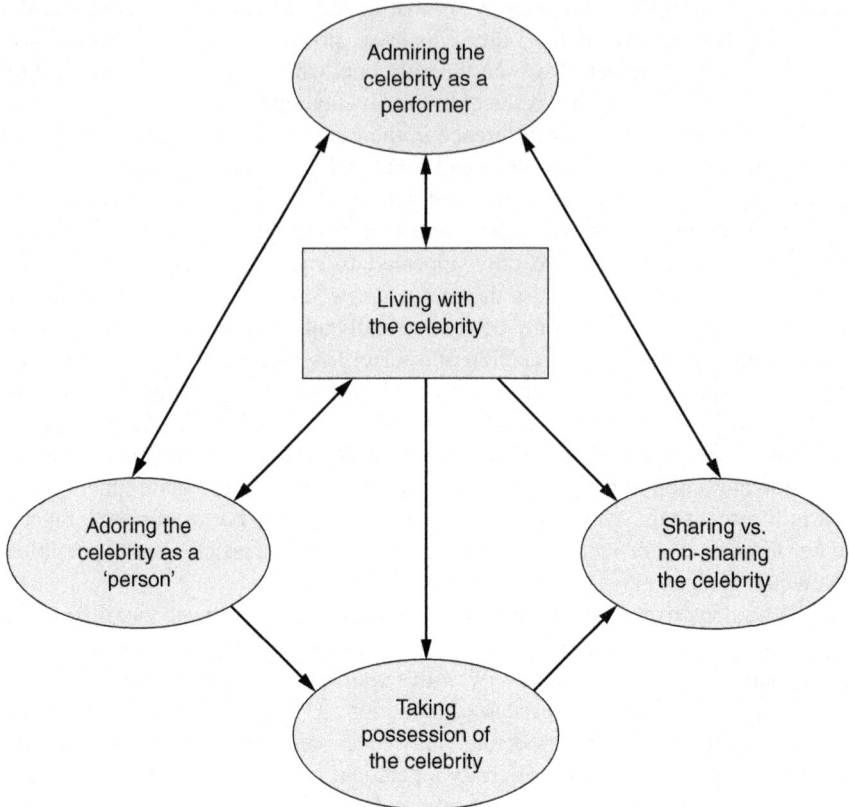

Figure 6.1 Model of a consumer's everyday lived fan relationship with a celebrity.

Admiring the celebrity as a performer

As mentioned earlier, every film star, rock/pop star and any other celebrity is first and foremost a creative performer, who is known for their creative/artistic performances and output, their portrayed characters on screen or stage and their public persona (Geraghty 2000, 2003). Hence, it usually is a specific creative performance in a certain artwork like a specific film, TV show or public appearance by which the fan – just like any other consumer – becomes for the first time aware of the admired film star or celebrity. Thus, it should come as no surprise that Jena Malone, as shown in the autoethnographic case study, first caught my personal attention through her outstanding and convincing portrayal of her character Mary Cummings in the film *Saved!* (US 2004). In this regard, there is no difference between the fan and any other consumers.

However, while the interest of most consumers is usually limited to a moderate, often fleeting or even indifferent appreciation for the film star or celebrity and/or the creative performance, some consumers experience a much stronger and much more enduring admiration for this film star's/celebrity's creative performances and artwork, which encourages them to seek out *'the performer's'* other creative artworks and, if the level of admiration is sustained across a range of creative performances over a longer period of time, become fans. In other words, this particular film star or celebrity provides the fan with a very specific appeal as a *'performer'* that has captured one's personal imagination and is keeping one interested in enjoying the performer's creative performances beyond mere entertainment and in searching for new relevant information. The autoethnographic consumer narrative shows how I, after Jena Malone caught my attention in <u>*Saved!*</u> (US 2004), quickly began to watch other films with her, admired her acting performances and gradually turned into a fan. Since then, I have not only enjoyed watching her films over and over again on DVD, TV or digital download and, if the opportunity arises, in the cinema, but have also admired her acting performances, skills and flexibility in portraying a wide range of very different characters, while also searching for relevant news, articles and other information about forthcoming projects.

Because stardom and celebrity scholars (Dyer 1998; Geraghty 2000; King 1991), as discussed earlier in this book, have reduced and *'dehumanised'* film stars and celebrities to *'semiotic systems of archetypical cultural meanings'*, whose consistent public images would derive from playing only those characters on screen or stage that mirror their actual private lives and personalities (Cocker et al. 2015; Hollinger 2006), they have tended to ignore the essential fact that most film stars or celebrities have to have the necessary talent and skills to deliver those creative performances. The autoethnographic consumer narrative, however, suggests that fans relate to their favourite film star or celebrity as a talented human being by separating not only his/her public and (perceived) private person quite clearly from his/her portrayed characters, but in fact admire especially the (perceived) quality of the displayed professional skills and talent as an actor, musician, writer, athlete, artist or model.

Again, there is little difference in this regard between the fan of this film star or celebrity and any other, more *'detached'* consumers. Instead, the contrast between them may actually lie in the rose-tinted view with which a fan tends to admire the creative performances and artworks of the beloved film star or celebrity much more favourably and less critical than the *'non-fan'* consumer, whose opinions could range from very positive to very negative. Indeed, as the autoethnographic consumer narrative proves, while I enjoy losing myself into the narrative of her films as well as engaging emotionally with the individual lead and support characters she portrays on screen, *'the performer'* Jena Malone appeals to me especially through the quality of her acting talent by which *'she makes each of her portrayed characters appear to be real and believable'*. You, the reader, may have thereby noticed the enthusiastic, adoring language I use to describe her acting performances and screen presence very favourably, as is evident in the following original extract from my autoethnographic diary:

I focus mainly on Jena Malone each time she's on the screen. She's simply fantastic and brings Lydia *(= her character in <u>Pride & Prejudice</u>, UK 2005)* really to life. Even when she's in the background of a frame, she still dominates the screen. She's simply a brilliant actress … and has the ability to bring every character she plays to real life – no matter how different they are. She's so good that you never notice that she is acting at all (no artificial gesticulations, mimicry or pronunciation). Sadly, a lot of less talented actresses still get the bigger roles and higher acclaim.

(Introspection, 5 October 2005)

As with any other consumer, it should be obvious that a fan's personal assessment of one's favourite film star's/celebrity's performance skills and talent is very subjective and based on one's personal interests, background knowledge, expertise and devotion towards this film star or celebrity. But the extract from my autoethnographic diary also demonstrates how my personal attention focus is particularly on Jena Malone each time I watch one of her films and she is on the screen – irrespective of who else is in the scene or where she is placed in the frame. This suggests that a fan's personal attention would often be occupied especially by the admired film star's/celebrity's on-screen or stage presence. As a result, the fan is also more likely to pay a closer attention to each single detail in the latter's creative performance and displayed skills that, in return, strengthens the admiration for the beloved film star or celebrity as a performer.

The autoethnographic case study also provides evidence that I have not only separated the actress Jena Malone quite clearly from the many different characters she portrays on screen (or stage) instead of perceiving them as being one-and-the-same, as proposed by the traditional stardom literature, but also go actually through great lengths to avoid assigning any archetypical image to her. Instead, when pressed, I tend to describe her as a very pretty, street-smart, confident, down-to-earth tomboy, who also happens to be a very talented and creative artist – which only reiterates how I view her first and foremost as an ordinary human being like you and me. Therefore, a fan seems to define the public image of the admired film star or celebrity – just like that of any other person on the street – by the physical appearance, style and beauty as well as the profession and social status as a known artist rather than the personification of a cultural archetype. In fact, it often is the film star's/celebrity's physical appearance, beauty, style and mediated personality that provide a particularly strong personal attraction to the individual fan once it happens to match one's inherently desired beauty ideal.

Moreover, the autoethnographic consumer narrative also shows quite strongly that Jena Malone's media appearances at her film premieres, at film festivals, at TV talk shows, in interviews or in magazine articles (and, nowadays, her official Facebook page) offer a strong personal attraction that encourage me to follow her latest news on a regular, though not quite daily, basis. But although the primary purpose of those media appearances is to promote a forthcoming film release, the attraction of the *'performer'* Jena Malone's public persona stems actually from four areas of personal interest to me:

(a) as a source of information for Jena Malone's forthcoming film releases, new film projects or any other new creative projects, like her initially home-made music project *Jena Malone and her Bloodstains* (2006–2007) and her present, more professionally self-managed alternative music project *The Shoe* (since 2008);

(b) as a means of staying up-to-date with how Jena Malone really looks like right now when she is not playing a particular character, with any professional and personal news as well as her relationship status;

(c) as a means of catching glimpses of Jena Malone's 'true' personality and 'private' person based on how she moves, speaks, argues, interacts with others and responds to various situations;

(d) as a means of obtaining news of whether there is an opportunity for me to see (or even meet) Jena Malone in person at a public event or performance, i.e. when she performs live on stage in a theatre play or with *The Shoe*, attends a film premiere or festival, participates in a public interview and/or autograph signing, etc.

Indeed, the autoethnographic data also reveal how I have constantly measured up the pros and cons of going to New York to watch Jena Malone's stage performance in the Broadway play <u>Doubt</u> (US 2006) or trying to catch a glimpse of her at a film premiere and, then, often tended to regret at the end that I have failed to follow up on it.

Contradicting the popular stereotype that fans would always consume indiscriminately every single product and piece of information associated with the admired film star or celebrity regardless of its nature, quality and source of origin (McCutcheon et al. 2002), the hermeneutic analysis of the autoethnographic data in this study is unambiguous in its finding that fans actually tend to be much more critical and highly selective in what source and type of information they trust than the average, more detached consumer. This should come to no surprise, as fans obtain over the years a detailed and thorough knowledge of the admired film star or celebrity and his/her creative performances, output and media appearances. Therefore, they have the necessary expertise to critically assess the trustworthiness of news and their sources. Indeed, the autoethnographic case study provides clear evidence that, although I enjoy watching and reading proper, informative articles, media clips and interviews with Jena Malone, I'm highly selective in paying only attention to those larger articles published in those 'arty' niche and arts scene magazines that are specialised in the kind of indie, arts and fashion world that Jena Malone seems to be interested in and associate herself with.

Nonetheless, I have also voiced my sheer contempt for the very kind of sensationalist fashion, gossip and tabloid press at the very heart of celebrity culture (Gabler 1998) with their obsession for what celebrities wear or should not wear,

what parties they attend, whom they supposedly date, how much they have supposedly earned and, of course, what saucy scandals they are supposedly involved
in. The principle reason for my contempt is simply that virtually all those articles
either contain superficially re-edited bits of generic information taken out of
context from other sources or, only too often, are entirely made-up to tell some
'saucy stories' in relation to some red carpet or paparazzi photos. For *'genuine
fans'* of a film star or celebrity like me, paparazzi are a particularly annoying
nuisance, since their selfish, scrupulous 'business' of harassing celebrities everywhere and invading their privacy just to catch them out for some 'exposing,
scandalous' photos is perceived to be a major reason why many film stars and
celebrities become increasingly reluctant to appear in public and/or to meet their
fans in person.

Adoring the celebrity as a 'private' person

The fan's desire to meet the admired film star or celebrity in person is at the
heart of the next constituent of the everyday lived fan experience. Opening the
door to a new perspective on consumers' fan relationships with their favourite
celebrities, I argue based on the analysis of the autoethnographic data that consumers value and consume their admired celebrities not only as *'the performer'*
or for their physical beauty, but also as the real *'private person'* behind the
public persona in the media. Especially the fan often craves for a look behind the
'performer' to learn more about the human nature, personality and private life of
the adored celebrity as a *'private person'*, when s/he is neither performing a
character nor standing in the spotlight of the media. Although Dyer (1998), as
discussed earlier, acknowledged that a film star is actually embodied by the
physical presence of a real-living person, who provides the celebrity with a
unique face, body, personality, voice and background story that differentiates
him or her from other film stars or celebrities, both the stardom and celebrity literatures have not only ignored, but fully *'erased'* the human side of the film star
or celebrity from the academic discourse when they conceptualised them as
'semiotic signifiers of cultural meaning'.

This scholarly view is quite unfortunate, since the film star's/celebrity's physical presence provides the individual consumer with the clear evidence that s/he
is not just a personified cultural archetype or human brand, but in fact a real
human being like you and me with personal feelings, dreams, political opinions,
personality, a private life and social relationships, who experiences joy and
sorrow or success and failure just like any other person. Indeed, the autoethnographic case study in Chapter 4 provides us with ample proof that my emotional
attachment to Jena Malone derives not only from her public persona and my
admiration for her skills, ability and flexibility as an actress to portray a wide
range of diverse characters, but even more importantly perhaps from actually
seeing her as a *'normal, ordinary'* young woman with all her personal views,
quirks, habits, strengths and weaknesses rather than as the semiotic personification of some cultural ideal, which is also evidenced by my romantic attraction to

her. In other words, Jena Malone is for me primarily an interesting, intelligent, naturally beautiful, quirky, imaginative, creative and talented young woman, who also has some flaws, 'bad habits' (i.e. her smoking) and makes mistakes from time to time – just like you, me and any other human being on earth.

You, the reader, may now wonder how the fan's attraction to the film star or celebrity as *'the private person'* and a human being is any different to how any other consumers may experience a certain physical attraction to the celebrity and/or have a certain interest in his/her private life. After all, as mentioned earlier, I have also related to other actresses as human beings and even been physically attracted to some of them, but did not become a fan. In other words, what is the difference in Jena Malone's *'private person'* and that of the others? Well, first, as we can see from the autoethnographic case study, besides her excellent acting talent and her incredible portrayal of Mary Cummings in the film *Saved!* (US 2004), Jena Malone has caught my eyes especially because her personal beauty, physical appearance, personality and quirkiness clearly meet my personal ideal of *'the girl I am always dreaming of'*. But this initial (physical) attraction in itself, as mentioned earlier, is still no different to other actresses or celebrities like Kristen Stewart, Ellen Page or even Jennifer Lawrence, who caught my attention in the same way, or any other woman I may see on the street, on a bus, in a pub or at a live gig.

If we, however, take a closer look again at the autoethnographic consumer narrative in Chapter 4, then it should become clear that the true moment, when I turned from a curious and a bit infatuated consumer into her fan, was when I read the LA Weekly article by Nancy Rommelmann (2000) and learnt some very insightful, interesting, but also sad details about Jena Malone's private life and background, her close but troubled relationship with her mother and her *'not so rosy'* experiences as a child actress in Hollywood. The article enabled me not only to take a curious look behind the curtain of *'the performer'* and get to know Jena Malone as *'the private person'*, but actually to relate to her on a more personal level, as it has revealed to me some intriguing similarities between her past and my own, such as our interest in acting from a young age, growing up in an impoverished working-class neighbourhood and having similar hope and dreams while using films and our imagination as a means of escape. Subsequently, I have not only been really impressed by her life-story and how she managed to stay true to herself despite her young age and the personal pressure she was under, but I could also empathise with her by *'sharing similar life experiences'*.

These feelings of empathy and infatuation are further strengthened by me engaging in out-of-text intertextuality (Hirschman 2000b; Wohlfeil & Whelan 2008, 2012), whereby I have linked Jena Malone's personal life-story to my own life experiences to the extent that I even partially identify with her. For example, by comparing my own personal experiences of growing up in an impoverished working-class neighbourhood to hers in trailer parks, *'I know only too well what it means to overcome the obstacles she had to face'* and, therefore, admire her courage and determination in following her dreams; especially, as I failed to do the same under less severe circumstances. In other words, *'sharing'* similar life experiences helps to strengthen the emotional bond and attachment that the consumer experiences towards the admired, and even adored, film star or celebrity (Wohlfeil & Whelan 2012).

Similarly, I have also been impressed by how Jena Malone, despite being legally emancipated since her 15th birthday, appears to have managed to resist so far the tempting pitfalls of the typical glamorous celebrity life-style and the associated excessive party-life, drugs- and sex-scandals, etc. and has instead remained apparently down-to-earth by maintaining a regular, non-glamorous life-style (Hastings 2004; Rotter 2003, 2004). And it is this perceived emotional connection based on perceived shared life experiences, dreams, ideals and ambitions why a consumer feels close to and becomes a fan of a specific celebrity instead of another one who, on the surface, may be equally talented, beautiful, attractive and (even more) successful, but just lacks this perceived connection. For that reason, it is one of the individual fan's biggest desires to gain backstage access to the adored celebrity's personal everyday life and to get to know him or her as the real person. But since the fan, at the same time, also wants to respect and not intrude the adored film star's/celebrity's right to privacy, s/he is constantly required to negotiate the fine line between the personal desire to meet the film star or celebrity in person and to respect the latter's privacy.

Nonetheless, the process of getting to know the real *'private person'* enables the fan to bring the adored but still *'distant, unreachable'* film star or celebrity down to an equal social level and, therefore, make him or her more *'accessible'* and *relatable'*. The film star or celebrity as *'the private person'* can thereby become a role model, an acquaintance, an ideal *'friend'* or even a potential love-interest – depending on the individual fan's personal needs, desires, hopes and dreams, as the following original autoethnographic extract shows:

> Jena Malone really caught my eye because she's the very type of girl I'm always falling for – a tomboy and natural beauty. And she comes across as extremely likeable, funny, highly intelligent, but also very independent and mature for her age … Since reading her interview today, I imagine what it would feel like to actually go out with her or even to date her.
>
> (Introspection, 26 December 2005)

As I have already pointed out a few times before, the autoethnographic data analysis provides clear evidence of how the film actress Jena Malone has at times appealed to me in particular as the personification of an ideal female mate for me. Indeed, she is, with regard to her physical appearance and beauty, but even more so in terms of her personality, her artistic nature, her intelligence and her life-style, the manifestation of the girl of my dreams, which has quite clearly distinguished her in my eyes from many other equally talented, interesting, beautiful and even popular female celebrities. But the insights obtained from a select numbers of detailed, insightful articles about her personal everyday life and as a private person (Brink 2008; Lyon 2008; Rems 2004; Sherwin 2004) have also helped me to form a much fuller picture of her as a human being and, subsequently, strengthened my emotional attachment to her. As a result, these insights into her private life have set the *'private person'* Jena Malone actually rather in competition with other females in my daily environment than with other distant film stars and celebrities. In fact, my infatuation with Jena Malone is really not much different to my infatuation with any other ('normal') females closer at home who are unavailable, in most cases just not interested in me, or I am just too shy to approach.

However, with very few exceptions, it is highly unlikely for the average consumer and, therefore, the fan ever to meet the adored film star or celebrity personally, never mind to really get to know him or her as a private person. As the autoethnographic case study shows, my own impression of Jena Malone's personality is essentially a personalised intertextual reading of those select media texts that I, as a fan, perceive to be relevant and *'reliable'*, such as her personal website and Facebook site, her print media and TV interviews and detailed articles in *'better'* magazines (Wohlfeil & Whelan 2011, 2012). But while Dyer (1998) argues that a consumer's image of a film star or celebrity is fixed and externally managed by the media, the presented autoethnographic fan narrative in Chapter 4 suggests instead that this image is actually constructed within the fan's mind and constantly evolving – similar to our impressions of the people we regularly encounter in our everyday lives. This is clearly evident in my deeply-engaged, very personal reading of Rommelmann's (2000) article, when I genuinely empathised with Jena Malone in how she *'handled so maturely all the problems she had to face at such a young age'* and admired how she developed, in my opinion, into *'such a smart, nice and interesting personality without losing her personal integrity'*.

Wohlfeil & Whelan (2012) theorise that the fan internalises the film star's/celebrity's private persona thereby psychically within oneself through a selective reading of reports, interviews, public photos and private photos taken by other people (i.e. during a chance encounter) and loads it with one's own thoughts, feelings, fantasies, values and meanings. Then, s/he projects the created personal impression back onto the film star or celebrity, just to internalise it once again with new imageries obtained from the media. This finding would also explain why my reported impression of Jena Malone's personality emphasises in particular those traits of her character and life-style that resonate strongly with my own private life experiences, ideals, dreams and desires and, as a result, strengthen my emotional attachment to her as a *'genuine person'*. More importantly, this continuous process of introjection and projection (Gould 1993) allows for the feelings to evolve of actually *'knowing'* the film star or celebrity like a close friend, whose career and life choices are empathetically followed in the same way as that of a fictional media character in an ongoing melodramatic narrative.

This experienced feeling of knowing the film star or celebrity personally, including his/her private thoughts, feelings, personality and way of life, can at times become strong enough to elicit an emotional feeling within the fan of *'personal friendship'* or even *'love'* towards the adored film star or any other celebrity;

a phenomenon that Horton and Wohl (1956) have termed parasocial interaction or, more precisely, parasocial relationship (Alperstein 1991). While the literature has acknowledged parasocial relationships with film stars, celebrities and any other media figures as quite a common phenomenon, especially among adolescents (Giles & Maltby 2004) and the elderly (Chory-Assad & Yanen 2005; Rubin et al. 1985), the term itself has become increasingly loaded with largely negative connotations in both academic and popular literature. This is not surprising, as a group of social psychologists (McCutcheon et al. 2003) have in recent years discussed parasocial relationships primarily as a mental illness that is associated with the individual's alleged impressionability, cognitive inflexibility, gullibility and pathological-obsessive behaviour.

However, this narrow but increasingly popular view is not only quite unfortunate, but also misleading, since Horton and Wohl (1956) have actually suggested the complete opposite by clearly highlighting the beneficial and healthy cathartic effects that parasocial relationships would offer the lonely and socially isolated, but otherwise *'mentally normal and healthy'* people. In their opinion, *'nothing could be more reasonable or natural than that people, who are isolated and lonely, should seek sociability and love wherever they think they can find it'* by forming a compensatory emotional attachment to a particular film star or any other celebrity, who is *'readily available as an object of love'* (Horton & Wohl 1956: 223). Parasocial relationships with film stars or celebrities would therefore provide lonely individuals with a cathartic experience that helps to restore their emotional well-being in times of psychological distress. Leets et al. (1995) also add that a parasocial relationship only turns into pathological and dangerous behaviour on those extremely rare occasions, when it proceeds into fanatical obsession and an absolute defiance of reality where the individual is completely convinced that the imagined relationship is real and mutual.

The collected autoethnographic data would indeed support Horton and Wohl's (1956) theory. One theme that has been dominant throughout my entire autoethnographic consumer narrative is the experienced feeling of loneliness deriving from my unfulfilled longing for a romantic, affectionate and loving relationship with a woman, which has failed to materialise in my life so far. Since any social relationship involves essentially two people mutually reciprocating their feelings for each other, experiencing constant rejections by women on their expressed grounds that I am not handsome, tall and interesting enough have resulted over time in low self esteem, extreme shyness (*'don't converse easily with women'*) and growing insecurity (*'don't know how to behave appropriately or to read her signals correctly'*) when interacting with women I fancy. With little opportunity for a (potential) romantic relationship with a woman available or to emerge in real life, Jena Malone has lent herself perfectly as a readily available object of love for me at a time of need and emotional distress to compensate for the experienced deficits; especially as her physical appearance and private persona match very closely *'the type of girl I'm always falling for'*.

The presented autoethnographic consumer narrative provides clear evidence that my impression of Jena Malone's personality is thereby a projection of my own unfulfilled desires and, especially, of what a potential girlfriend for me may be like as a normal person. My parasocial relationship fantasies with her essentially reflect how I imagine an ideal romantic relationship with a woman to be like in everyday life. However, that my parasocial fan relationship with Jena Malone is of a cathartic nature becomes apparent by the fact that is not constantly present, but develops and recedes as a direct psychological response to external events in my real-life relations to women. As the autoethnographic case study shows, the parasocial relationship with her declines to zero every time I am interested in or fancy a woman in my everyday life. Indeed, I engage most intensively in a parasocial relationship with Jena Malone in those particular moments, when I have just suffered another serious interpersonal disappointment or have been rejected again by a woman I fancy. My imagined relationship with Jena Malone, thereby, offers me a temporary means of coping with feelings of loneliness, perceived unattractiveness and the lack of romantic love that would otherwise eat me up from the inside. But every time a new chance emerges for me to develop a real-life relationship with a woman in my everyday life, the parasocial experience quickly recedes again.

Nonetheless, the hermeneutic analysis of the autoethnographic data also shows that the fan, unlike many other consumers, still experiences often this inherent craving for the opportunity to meet the beloved film star or celebrity in person – if only to have a chance for confirming whether one's personal image of the film star or celebrity as a *'private person'* and his/her private life actually corresponds with the reality.

> Several times by now, someone has already suggested that I should see first-hand how Jena Malone is really like. Of course, I'd love that. But how? … The response usually is that I should write her a personal letter to get (really) in contact with her … I don't know … Will she actually read it? Also, what impression will the letter give her about me? I don't want to sound dull and boring. … What if she responds negatively or doesn't care at all? It would destroy me! Maybe I should rather leave everything as it is …
>
> (Introspection, 14 December 2006)

This original extract from the autoethnographic data diaries reveals a quite surprising, but also very interesting personal ambivalence with regard to my own personal desire of meeting the film star or celebrity in person. Throughout much of the autoethnographic data transcripts, I have been expressing a strong longing and desire for meeting and getting to know Jena Malone in person and have spent some time on imaging how such a meeting – and even a relationship – would be like. However, when the opportunity arises to make this desire come true and to confront my personal image of Jena Malone with the actual reality, i.e. seeing her on stage in an Off-Broadway play or catching a glimpse of her on the red carpet of a film premiere, I have always backed away in fear of disappointment.

Taking possession of the celebrity

The intangible nature of the film star's/celebrity's creative performances, artworks and, especially, private everyday life is for the fan a constant and particularly strong reminder of the film star's/celebrity's personal inaccessibility and illusiveness as both the admired *'performer'* and, in particular, as the adored *'private person'*. Indeed, fans become particularly painstakingly aware of it, when their admired rock/pop star or celebrity does not perform a show in their area or even country and/or, even worse, when they are unable to procure one of the limited tickets – knowing that *'less devoted'* consumers may often be in the audience for *'a little bit of entertainment'* instead. And as it so happens, in the autoethnographic case study I have voiced my frustrations on several occasions that some of Jena Malone's films are never released in European cinemas – never mind my local cinemas – (or even on Region 2 DVDs) and, subsequently, have remained inaccessible to me, or that I am unable to watch her performance live on stage in an Off-Broadway play, as I do not live anywhere near New York. And because she is little known here in Europe, even some well-known global magazines have in their European editions often replaced elaborate articles about her with articles about a local reality TV star or socialite, which makes her even more inaccessible and, thus, annoys and saddens me even further. For that reason, the fan has a personal vested interest in making the film star's/celebrity's creative performances and his/her private persona accessible through the acquisition and tangible possession of relevant physical products, such as films on DVD, music on CD or vinyl, digital downloads, video clips, books, photos, autographs, clippings of magazine articles and other branded merchandise.

The possession of those products as the manifestation of the film star's/celebrity's creative artworks and performances in itself is no different between fans and any other, more detached consumers. What is different, however, is the personal meaning that the individual fan attaches to such products and their consumption. The ownership of the creative artworks and, thus, the creative performances recorded on CD, DVD or digital download enables the fan not only to enjoy them repeatedly whenever and wherever s/he likes, but also to share and to display one's appreciation, admiration and fandom as an extended self (Belk et al. 1989) to others as much as to oneself. Furthermore, possessing the recorded performance allows the fan to access and enjoy those of the film star's/celebrity's artworks at home and at one's leisure that would otherwise not be available. In a similar way, a T-shirt obtained at the live gig of the admired rock/pop star/band means more to the fan than just saying *'I was there!'* Instead, each T-shirt is worn and/or displayed to demonstrate one's allegiance to the admired and adored rock/pop star/band, film star or any other celebrity in public.

Indeed, the autoethnographic case study shows that I am often highly dependent on acquiring her films as digital downloads or on DVD in order to enjoy and admire both the film and her acting performances, as Jena Malone often features in those small, but more artistic and challenging independent film productions that are rarely screened in my local cinemas. The fact that some of her independent films are only available in the US DVD Region 1 format and, thus, unavailable in Europe, as many of the small independent film productions cannot find an international distributor these days, has obviously been a source of frustration for me. Nevertheless, it has also provided me with something of a *'hip'* insider knowledge (Holbrook 1986). What the autoethnographic consumer narrative also reveals is to what great lengths I have gone to access and enjoy watching those films released only in the US by buying an external DVD drive and locking it into the Region 1 area code, so that I can purchase, collect and watch those films on US DVDs instead. Thus, I have actually been able to overcome the major problem of access and availability by *'taking possession'* of her films and, by extension, of Jena Malone as *'the performer'*.

However, it is important for a fan to own not only the one or other recorded album, DVD or book, but as collectors to *'possess'* the complete creative work of the admired film star or celebrity and other relevant items associated with him or her. Indeed, the autoethnographic consumer narrative clearly shows how I have engaged in an extensive collection of Jena Malone photos, media reports and interviews in magazines or on video files and, especially, all of her films on DVD or, if absolutely necessary, on any other media formats. The ability to *'take tangible possession'* of the admired film star's/celebrity's recorded creative artworks and performances enables the fan not only to consume them whenever, wherever and how often one likes, but also to act like a *museum curator* in keeping them and, by extension, the film star or celebrity *'alive'* for eternity and giving him/her a touch of immortality (Radford & Bloch 2012), so that new generations of people would be able to enjoy and appreciate him/her in the future.

However, while I have made Jena Malone's creative performances and artworks as an actress tangible through the purchase her films on DVD or digital downloads and her public persona through the collection of video clips and articles of her interviews in the media, the physical presence of Jena Malone as a *'private person'* has also manifested herself over time in the photos and posters of her that have increasingly decorated both my living- and work-space. In other words, the fan uses certain types of products like photos (especially those that depict the film star or celebrity in his/her private life), posters, T-shirts and, in particular, personalised items like hand-signed autographs, personal artefacts, film props and costumes, which have once been owned or, at least, personally used by the film star or celebrity (Newman et al. 2011), as proxies to make the latter's illusive *'private person'* symbolically accessible and a part of one's everyday life. However, an interesting finding that has emerged from the hermeneutic analysis of the collected autoethnographic data is that, although I have acquired original hand-signed autographs from a select group of trusted professional traders and other collectibles on eBay, I still have not been happy with the way film stars and celebrities in general and Jena Malone in particular are commoditised and their *'kindness'* (they often volunteer their personal time to sign autographs for their fans) is exploited by profit-driven traders and, worse, fraudsters, as the following extract shows.

> On eBay, I discovered that this *(trader)* is bidding again for a signed Jena Malone autograph. He always buys autographs cheaply in order to resell them a week later on eBay for at least twice the price – and then often claims that he's collected the autograph himself supported by a fake 'proof candid' downloaded from the Internet. Thus, he is the last person, who deserves to get his dirty hands on her original autographs! I'll spoil it for him by raising the bid.
>
> (Introspection, 24 May 2006)

What this autoethnographic account demonstrates is that the individual fan sees it as one's duty as a devoted *'curator'* of the admired film star or celebrity to *'protect'* him/her as both *'the performer'* and *'the private person'*, his/her creative artworks and his/her personal items from *'falling into the wrong hands'*, such as those of speculators and second-hand autograph traders. However, the autoethnographic data also reveal a clear indicator of how a fan would place a very different value (and priority) on a film star's/celebrity's personal items and original autographs than a commercial trader or speculator would. In order to prevent the commercial trade with their autographs, many celebrities have started to dedicate them directly to a person by name, because a dedicated autograph has a significantly lower commercial market value than a *'generic'* one, as they are harder to sell on. Like most other fans and collectors, however, for me it is exactly the opposite, as those original hand-signed photos that Jena Malone has in person dedicated to me personally (see Figure 4.7) are still my most valued and cherished treasures – due to their (perceived and experienced) personal nature. In fact, as the autoethnographic consumer narrative shows, the personal dedication on these original autographs symbolise to me most strongly her *'physical presence'* in my everyday life. And how priceless and precious they are to me in my everyday life is evident in the following original extract from my autoethnographic diary.

> While I'm preparing and packing for my annual trip to Germany, I'm also a bit worried about having to leave my priceless and precious original hand-signed photos, especially the ones that she has personally dedicated to me (my most invaluable treasures), behind. What if something happens to them in my absence? That would surely destroy and kill me! Furthermore, I somehow need to have them with me – all the time. I've just invested too much into them. I need to find a way … *(A few hours later)* Well, I have finally decided to take my most precious Jena Malone autographs with me to Germany; placed in my hand luggage together with my laptop.
>
> (Introspection, 15 December 2006)

Sharing the celebrity

As I have already discussed in Chapter 2 of this book, much of the fan studies literature has conceptualised fandom as *'a subculture composed of like-minded fans, typified by a feeling of closeness to others with a shared interest'* (Thorne & Bruner 2006). For them, the fan community – whether offline in the form of traditional fan-clubs (Henry & Caldwell 2007; O'Guinn 1991) or online in the form of fan forums and fan-sites (Hewer & Hamilton 2012a; Kozinets 1997) – is the central site where fans negotiate their polysemic meanings of the film star or celebrity and his/her creative performances with the *'proper meanings'* championed by the fan community's *'canon'* (Duffett 2013; Hills 2002), which they supposedly share together in social discourse, rituals and the display or *'worship'* of valued artefacts (Henry & Caldwell 2007) and the co-creation of fan-fiction (Lanier & Schau 2007). Due to this nearly exclusive focus on the fan community as the legitimate site of fandom, several CCT and fan studies scholars have even implied that the participation in a fan community is the primary motivation for a consumer to be a fan in the first place (Hills 2002; Jenkins 1992). In strong contrast, however, the autoethnographic consumer narrative shows that I have had absolutely no interest or intention whatsoever to share my personal admiration and adoration for Jena Malone and what she, her creative artworks and performances mean to me within any online or offline fan community or with any other fans and consumers in general. Instead, irrespective of whether it is Jena Malone as *'the performer'* and her acting skills, whether it is her films and portrayed characters or whether it is Jena Malone as *'the private person'*, I still prefer to enjoy those personal fan experiences just by myself.

Nonetheless, the autoethnographic data reveal that, from time to time, I do actually browse a certain fan-site, which I believe to be *'run by a genuine fan'* like me, and the discussion forum on IMDb. But it is quite clearly the type of fan community discourse on the latter that strongly reinforces my aversion to sharing my personal admiration for Jena Malone with other consumers. In fact, the hermeneutic analysis strongly underlines that I am particularly annoyed by a very superficial and meaningless 'fan' discourse that, similar to the tabloid media I despise, consists primarily of uninformed gossip, half-truths and deliberate misinformation often left by trolls and visitors (= consumers with clearly no further interest), endless 6-degree-games and *'she looks like...'* posts. Hence, I have become convinced that fan communities have nothing to offer that would make it worthwhile to participate in them.

However, the collected autoethnographic data clearly indicate that I actually do like to share my admiration for Jena Malone's acting performances, talent and the quality of her (often little known) independent films with friends, close acquaintances and colleagues within my inner social circle – *but* not with other fans that I have never met in person. In this regard, I could be classified as a relatively self-contained fan, who does not participate in fan communities *because* I just do not want to negotiate *my* personal image, meaning(s) and views of the admired film star or celebrity and his/her creative work with that of other people. Nevertheless, in spite of recommending her films and praising her acting talent to other *'worthy'* potential viewers, I still tend to enjoy watching those films more by myself than in the company of others. More importantly, however, at no point am I ever willing to share my personal admiration and adoration for the *'private person'* Jena Malone – and especially not my parasocial romantic infatuation with her. This observation emerging from the autoethnographic data analysis quite clearly suggests that the individual fan, when interacting with other consumers and like-minded fans in particular, may not fully engage in a negotiated fan discourse of shared celebrity meaning, as the literature on fan studies and consumer tribalism often implies, but may actually be rather highly selective with regard to what specific attributes of the film star or celebrity s/he wants to share, how and with whom.

The explanation for this contradictory behaviour can be found by taking a closer look at which of the other three identified constituents of the film star's/celebrity's consumer appeal the individual fan would like to share and which s/he would not. The presented autoethnographic consumer narrative demonstrates quite clearly that the individual fan tends to enjoy sharing those attributes of the beloved film star or celebrity with other consumers that refer to the film star or celebrity as *'the performer'*, i.e. the talent, the public persona and the creative work, and their manifestation as *'tangible possession'*. But s/he appears to be less likely to share his/her emotional attachment to the film star or celebrity as *'the private person'* with others. The reason should be obvious. When I share my admiration for Jena Malone's acting talent and creative performances with friends and colleagues or recommend her films to them, I am actually promoting her work in order to give her exposure as an actress. My unwillingness to share *'the private person'* Jena Malone with others, on the other hand, stems from the fact that I may see them as competitors. After all, who wants to share one's desired flame, dream woman or ideal mate with other people – and especially with those that could be potential rivals?

Living with the celebrity

While these four presented fan relationship constituents correspond directly with the respective four constituents of the film star's/celebrity's polysemic consumer appeal to the individual fan and each, thus, forms an essential part of the personal everyday lived fan experiences, the presented autoethnographic consumer narrative in Chapter 4 also reveals that a consumer's fan relationship with a film star or celebrity is not static but in constant flux and, therefore, constantly evolving. Indeed, the fan relationship is a dynamic process that varies not only over time, but also on each single day in terms of its intensity and experienced significance. The hermeneutic analysis of my autoethnographic data collected between April 2005 and December 2006 suggests that I went during that period through six different phases. While I do not even pretend or argue that each individual fan goes through and experiences exactly the same six phases in exactly the same way and order that I have done, I am confident that most fans have gone in their own way through similar stages.

In my personal case, as the autoethnographic consumer stories shows, the first phase started in April 2005 after I had watched the film *Saved!* (US 2004) on DVD and discovered the actress Jena Malone in the process. It lasted until July

2005. The dominant feature of the first phase can thereby be characterised as the intensive search for more detailed information about the film star or celebrity and for his/her other artworks. Hence, this first phase of the fan relationship was obviously driven to a large extent by an initial feeling of curiosity, which had been triggered by my first encounter with Jena Malone on the screen, and the experienced desire to learn more about her, who she actually is and what other films she has featured in. However, my initial attraction, curiosity and motivation to search for more information about Jena Malone and her other films have not been much different to those that I have experienced with regard to other film actresses like Natalie Portman, Kristen Stewart, Ellen Page or Jennifer Lawrence. It could therefore be argued that the first phase is probably very similar not only for fans, but also for consumers in general. For that reason, I would suggest that this phase is actually a precursor that eventually determines – based on the outcome of the information search – whether the individual consumer just remains interested enough to enjoy the one or other creative artwork of the film star or celebrity or whether s/he becomes a fan because the uncovered information resonate with his/her inherent desires.

From August to October 2005, I had entered into the second phase in my fan relationship, which was characterised by the excessive acquisition and collection of films, articles, photos and video clips featuring Jena Malone. This is technically the stage, where the individual consumer either crosses the line towards turning into a fan or remains detached. At this point, the consumer/fan enjoys and admires the film star's/celebrity's creative performances as the *'performer'* in a number of relevant artworks, while some of the uncovered information about the film star or celebrity as the *'private person'* is likely to have touched a personal nerve with the individual. While the previous phase encouraged me to seek out and watch a few other films with her, I had now developed the desire to obtain, watch *and* possess *all* of her films. Since this was met with the added obstacle that many of her films were difficult to come by, being denied access to them had actually awoken a hunting instinct within me that I *'must'* find and obtain them. The even bigger scarcity of relevant, informative articles in Europe had added further fuel to the fire and I was on the prowl like a hunter.

However, due to their scarcity, I had been tempted to purchase the films and magazines immediately, and without further thought, in the very moment I had found them – often at higher than necessary prices. Some of the articles in the magazines purchased during the second phase have turned out to be extremely disappointing. And it is safe to say that I have never experienced this kind of *'desire to possess'* with regard to any other film star or celebrity before. In other words, it is the second phase, in which the individual fan is most likely to buy celebrity-related products, in terms of quality, most *'indiscriminately'* in an effort to get one's hands on the important, relevant information and recorded performances. But this does not mean that the emerging fan will buy everything – just because the film star or celebrity name and image is attached to it (Banister & Cocker 2014). Instead, the excessive acquisition is concentrated on recorded performances and more detailed articles, whereby the intensity is dependent on the accessibility of those items.

By October 2005, the second phase had eventually come to a sudden hold, when the excessive search and acquisition of films on DVD (or alternative formats like VHS and VCD) and articles had slowed down. The following third phase in my personal case, therefore, began in October 2005 and lasted until January 2006. One of the major reasons why the search and acquisition of her films suddenly stopped was simply that, by that time, I had already obtained all of her available films and, hence, nearly completed my collection of her back catalogue of creative artworks as *'the performer'*. From here on, it has primarily been a question of purchasing her latest film releases as soon as they became available or obtaining the one or other obscure little film that has not received its DVD (or even cinema) release yet. The more important facet of the third phase, however, is the fact the emphasis of my attention shifted from a strong admiration for Jena Malone the *'performer'* to Jena Malone the *'private person'*. It is at this particular point that I had actually developed my emotional attachment to her as an attractive, intelligent, interesting, exciting and desirable young woman in the aftermath of another date in my everyday life having gone wrong.

As a result, early signs of a parasocial relationship with the film actress had emerged that include a playful romantic infatuation with her as a potential, but idealised mate, which has always been more present in those moments when I felt lonely and isolated – especially after a failed date, being stood up or over the Christmas period. In those periods, I drew emotional comfort from watching her films, looking at her photo images obtained from the Internet on fan-sites and imagining in daydreams what it might be like if she was there with me. All the time I was consciously aware that this was just that – a fantasy! No more, no less! This behaviour is clearly in line with what Horton and Wohl (1956) argued, when they devised their parasocial interaction theory. Furthermore, in a similar manner, it is also a consumption experience and behaviour common among teenage fans of teen pop stars or reality TV stars, for whom the beloved celebrity often serves as the object of their first romantic affections in a *'safe, socially acceptable'* manner (Ehrenreich et al. 1992; Karniol 2001).

While my emotional attachment to the film actress Jena Malone was carried over into the next phase, which started in February 2006 and lasted until late-June 2006, the autoethnographic consumer narrative clearly reveals that Phase 4 was characterised by another series of excessive acquisitions. But this time, the purchases were much more targeted – and also much more expensive. Indeed, Phase 4 had started with an original hand-signed autograph of Jena Malone being offered for sale on eBay. It was the first one in a line of numerous original hand-signed autographs, which Jena Malone had signed during the six months she performed on stage in the Broadway play *Doubt* (US 2006), that have been collected and sold (alongside fakes) by professional autograph traders. For the individual fan, the original hand-signed autograph, especially those ones with a personal dedication to the individual, symbolises the tangible manifestation of the film star's/celebrity's *'physical presence'* as the *'private person'* in one's everyday life (Newman et al. 2011). As the autoethnographic case study in Chapter 4 highlights, I felt the sudden urge that I *'must have it'* – and not only the one but as many as I could afford.

A further driving force behind the excessive purchase of Jena Malone's original hand-signed autographs in this phase has been to *'prevent them from falling into unworthy hands'*. In other words, I instinctively felt the need to act as a self-appointed *'protector'* and *'curator'* of Jena Malone's personal heritage. In fact, it is not uncommon for fans to collect personal or personalised items of their beloved celebrity with a view of protecting them and the celebrity from misuse and commodification at the hands of speculators and fraudsters (O'Guinn 1991; Wohlfeil & Whelan 2012). At the same time, the film star or celebrity is increasingly manifesting his/her *'physical presence'* not only within the mental space, but also throughout the living space of the individual fan, as the much more expensive, valuable and personal items *'need'* to be displayed – or, at least, provided with a special place. In many cases, this can take the form of a shrine or a dedicated room that is turned into a personal *'mini-museum'*, as reported by O'Guinn (1991) or Henry & Caldwell (2007). In my personal case, as the autoethnographic consumer narrative shows, Jena Malone's *'physical presence'* slowly entered and indiscriminately took hold across my entire living space – similar to jazz music in Holbrook's case (1987). During this period I have also experienced the wish to see her in person … performing on stage, of course, and perhaps obtaining an autograph from her personally.

However, the autoethnographic consumer narrative in Chapter 4 also shows that the fourth phase in my personal case came to an abrupt end in late-June 2006, when the possibility of a real-life romantic relationship had arisen at the time and the romantic nature of my parasocial fan relationship with Jena Malone as the *'private person'* had ceased in response. The next phase that followed, the fifth phase, from late-June 2006 to the end of August 2006, was characterised by a period of complete calm and detachment. Moreover, I did not purchase a single item or even search eBay for anything during this phase. This does not mean that my fan relationship with the film actress Jena Malone had ended or been on some kind of hiatus. I was still admiring and praising her talent as an actress, even though I had not really watched a film with her. Furthermore, her images had still occupied the walls of my room, the background image and screensaver on my laptop and the original hand-signed autographs, especially the ones she has dedicated to me in person, have still been my *'most treasured possessions'*. But the parasociality with its daydreams of what it might be like to go out on date with her had disappeared completely. Instead, I was imaging – or better planning – in my head how I could spend the time with the young woman I fancied at the time the next time we meet and how a date might work out. In other words, the illusive, imaginary placeholder has stepped aside for a real person in my actual everyday life.

When, however, the hope of a real relationship with the person did not materialise and ended under negative external circumstances in a severe disappointment, my fan relationship with the actress Jena Malone had entered from September to December 2006 into its sixth phase, which was characterised by the return of my parasocial emotional attachment to her as *'the private person'* and potential love-interest. Essentially, the sixth phase was very similar to the third phase in terms of the nature and content, but due to the circumstances that dropped me into a severe emotional turmoil it was much more intense. Still, once again, the autoethnographic consumer narrative confirms Horton and Wohl's (1956) central argument that the parasocial relationship with a celebrity provides the individual fan in times of distress with a cathartic effect. In my own case, watching Jena Malone as *'the performer'* on screen and engaging with her as *'the private person'* through her hand-signed autographs and photo images has helped me to overcome a very painful depressive episode that, otherwise, would have made another already lonely Christmas much worse.

But as I said earlier, each individual fan will go through their very own phases often determined by the interplay between one's emphasis on the film star or celebrity either as *'the performer'*, as *'the private person'*, as *'the tangible possession'* and/or as *'the social link'* that results from a personal response to emotional desires and external events. Over a longer time, it is likely that the phases will settle down, become more consistent and vary mainly between two or three phases in response to emotional events in the individual fan's personal lives. My fan experiences with the actress Jena Malone have in recent years settled down largely in an interplay of the phases 3, 4, 5 and a newer phase of feeling emotionally attached to her as *'the performer'* only, without any stronger romantic feelings for her and a decreasing interest in her personal life – even though there has often been no woman, who has caught my eyes in my everyday life.

Either way, the changing dynamics within an individual's fan relationship with the admired film star or celebrity vary constantly with regard to the significance and the intensity that the personal fan experiences with each facet of the individual constituents have for the individual fan – not only over periods of time, but even during every single day. In other words, the fan may not think about or experience any feelings for the admired celebrity for a day or a week, while being heavily involved with them the next day or week – and vice versa. In fact, even during the same day, the personal fan experiences can vary heavily in response to the individual's emotional needs, desires and events in one's everyday life. For that reason, a consumer's everyday lived fan relationship with one's beloved film star must be understood as highly dynamic, ever-changing, personal and responsive to internal or external emotional events just like everything else in everyday life. In this regard, the fan is indeed living with the admired, adored and beloved film star, rock/pop star or any other celebrity in a mutual parasocial relationship in everyday life, as the celebrity's popularity, career and success depends on his/her engagement with fans as much as on their continuous flow of creative artworks and performances and their own mediated everyday lives (Hills 2016).

Note

1 The *Star Wars*-prequels and *Thor* in the case of Natalie Portman, the *Twilight*-films in the case of Kristen Stewart, *X-Men: The Last Stand* and *X-Men: Days of Future Past* in the case of Ellen Page, *The Hunger Games*-films in the case of Jennifer Lawrence as well as *Sucker Punch* and *The Hunger Games: Catching Fire* in the case of Jena Malone.

7 Sucker Punch(ed) or Saved?

Celebrity fan takeaways

Takeaway is for McDonalds! The hope is that someone, as an audience member, would be open enough to go on a personal journey, to be affected by it in a very personal way, to relate to things, to personalise them and pull from them.

Jena Malone, 16 September 2007

Inherent Vice

So, here we are, back again from our narrative journey into the world of celebrity fandom and the life of an actual celebrity fan – or, more precisely, the fan of a film actress. The aim, thereby, was to obtain a deeper and truly holistic understanding of how an individual consumer's everyday lived fan relationship with one's admired film star, rock/pop star, athlete or any other celebrity manifests itself in everyday consumption experiences and practices, and what personal meanings they have in that person's daily life. As the reader, probably, the question on your mind right now is what practical or theoretical lessons can the reader take away from this personal narrative journey. Well, in an interview at the press junket for the film <u>Into the Wild</u> (US 2007), Jena Malone was once asked what she hoped the audience could take away from watching the film. Her response to that question (see the quote at the top of this page) also offers a perfect answer in the present context of this book.

The reason why I have taken you, the reader, as a side-participant on a narrative journey into the life of a fan is for you to be affected personally by it, to relate to the presented autoethnographic narrative and experiences in a personal way, to personalise elements of it by sympathising, empathising or even identifying with the narrator and to pull your own lessons from it based on your own needs, thoughts, feelings and inherent desires. Furthermore, Holbrook (1995) repeatedly argued that *'the fundamental difference between **marketing research** and **consumer research** is that the former **should** whereas the latter **should not** be guided by the criterion of practical relevance and usefulness to marketing managers'*. Therefore, although this book and the presented findings – like any other *'piece of decent consumer research'* (Holbrook 2005) – may eventually become very useful to some marketers within the film, music, broadcast, media and other creative industries such as those working for film studios, record labels, publishing houses, TV/radio stations, talent agencies, publicists, the media or even the celebrities themselves, I went into the research project with the primary aim of advancing our knowledge on celebrity fandom itself – especially since much of the discourse surrounding the subject is driven to this day by popular stereotypes.

However, there are still some *'handy'* lessons we can take away from our research journey. As already mentioned, the aim of our research journey and, thus, this book is to gain a deeper, truly holistic understanding of what meaning(s) the everyday lived fan relationship with an admired film star or celebrity has for the individual consumer and how this emotional attachment manifests and expresses itself in everyday consumption practices and experiences from a genuine insider perspective. Due to the very special nature of film star and celebrity fandom, I have drawn on an interdisciplinary body of literature from a broad range of academic disciplines like marketing, consumer research, film studies, media studies, social psychology, sociology, sports studies and leisure research. Thus, despite its primary location within consumer culture theory, this book makes its overall contribution to the cross-disciplinary literatures on stardom, fandom, celebrity culture and film consumption by providing new insights from an insider perspective (Smith et al. 2007) into the actual substance of an individual film star's/celebrity's personal polysemic consumer appeal and introducing a reconceptualisation of fans that puts the emphasis back on the special emotional bond that consumers form, foster and sustain with their own favourite film stars, rock/pop stars, athletes and any other celebrities.

Apart from the clear evidence that the fan relates to the admired film star or celebrity as a real-living human being with a unique beauty, personality, talent, social background and life-style, the presented consumer narrative also reveals that the fan relationship with one's favourite film star/celebrity follows a logical transition from the admiration for the celebrity's creative performances and artworks as *'the performer'* to the adoration of his/her *'private person'*. This transition is thereby twofold. On the one hand, the narrative consumer story constitutes a personal journey in itself that reflects a gradual transition over time from the consumer's initial interest in a creative artwork over the admiration of the creative performer to an infatuation with the celebrity as a real person. After all, any fan interest in a film star, obviously, starts by actually watching him or her in a certain film or TV show that captures not only the attention but also the heart of the consumer and, in individual circumstances, gradually moves on from there towards fandom. On the other hand, the autoethnographic consumer narrative provides a kind of transition, too, in terms of covering the broad spectrum of consumer experiences that a fan relationship with a film star or celebrity usually entails and that are always in some form present with varying degrees of intensity, direction and significance. The various individual constituents of the film star's/celebrity's personal polysemic consumer attraction and their individual and/or symbiotic appeal to the individual fan have thereby come step-by-step to the fore.

Since autoethnography is still viewed as a controversial research methodology among more traditional scholars, because of its use of a sample of one who happens to be the researcher (me), and often unheard of outside academia, it might be a good idea to start here and get the elephant out of the room before I discuss what implications we may take away from the findings. But if you happen to be a non-academic reader and read this book because of your personal interest in the actual subject matter of celebrity fandom, i.e. by being a fan of a celebrity just like me, but have neither the interest nor the relevant background knowledge in the mechanics of academic research, then I would suggest that you skip the next section. Otherwise, if you are looking for a few valuable tips for your own autoethnographic research project, you may want to stick with me.

Implications for using an autoethnographic methodology

In order to gain a truly holistic understanding of how a consumer's everyday lived fan relationship with one's admired film star or celebrity manifests itself in everyday consumer behaviour and may even lead to the formation of a parasocial relationship, it requires a research methodology that gives the individual consumer a genuine voice (Stern 1998) and, at the same time, affords the researcher with a 24-hour access to the observed phenomenon of interest. Unfortunately, any research approach that seeks to deconstruct and compare the fan experiences of as many consumers as possible in order to make generalisable claims ultimately reduces not only consumers' fan relationships, but even the individual fan experience to the smallest common denominator and, subsequently, disenfranchises the individual consumer's everyday lived fan relationship with one's favourite film star or celebrity of its very essence.

In heeding Smith et al.'s (2007) call for an emic description of fandom *'as it is experienced'* by a real fan and without the researcher imposing any preconceived abstract frameworks onto it, this book's first major takeaway derives from the controversial nature of my research journey's methodology, whereby I occupy the dual role of the researcher and the sole informant. Indeed, in this book I have demonstrated how using autoethnography enables the researcher to explore first-hand the subjective nature of human thoughts, feelings, daydreams, creativity, spirituality, sensations and streams of consciousness related to consumption, fandom and even the human condition (Gould 1993; Holbrook 2006) in the very way they are experienced by the individual consumer, but have remained inaccessible through conventional *scientific* and *qualitative* research methods (Brown 1998b). Hence, I essentially make in this book three important sub-contributions to advancing the use of autoethnography as an appropriate research methodology of choice. First of all, much of the debate and controversy surrounding the *'scientific merits'* of autoethnography has revolved around the credibility and trustworthiness of the collected data (Ellis 1991; Gould 2006; Holbrook 1995). Yet, there has never been a real discussion in relation to the appropriate and rigorous analysis of autoethnographic data. After laying the groundwork in my earlier work (Wohlfeil & Whelan 2008, 2011, 2012), I have presented in this book an appropriate, rigorous autoethnographic data analysis strategy based on a detailed hermeneutic interpretation process, which I have adapted from Thompson's (1997) proposed phenomenological approach.

The second sub-contribution is the introduction of narrative transportation theory as a hermeneutic framework for examining autoethnographic consumer narratives like written texts. After all, if stardom scholars conceptualise film stars as semiotic sets of accumulated film and media texts and phenomenologists tend to interpret an individual's everyday life-world as a text (Thompson 1998), then it is only fair to suggest that a consumer's personal fan relationship with one's beloved film star or any other celebrity would not only represent a kind of narrative transportation experience, but can also be understood as a text in itself that allows for a thorough hermeneutic examination through a narrative transportation approach. Thus, by drawing on narrative transportation theory as a framework for hermeneutic analysis, autoethnography offers some genuine insights into the meaning that the emotional attachment to the admired film star or celebrity and the experiential consumption of his/her films, records, autographs, photos, articles and other associated products have for the fan beyond the hedonic pleasure value that can be observed during their immediate consumption.

The final sub-contribution to advancing autoethnographic research is heeding a call by Brown (1998b) for a more inspired and *'reader-engaging'* style of writing within marketing and consumer research; one that draws on the conventions of fictional literature in order to make the reading experience more enjoyable. Indeed, the academic marketing literature has been hampered by a certain, ever-increasing breed of uninspired academic texts that are written solely with the intention to get published in the academic field's top journals and, as a result, are only too often tedious to read – especially for anyone outside the author's tiny circle of peers. Hence, I have not only used autoethnography in this book to present you, the reader, with deeper insights into a consumer's personal everyday lived fan experiences with a film star or celebrity, but also in order to break down the traditional divide between the researcher, the text and the reader by speaking directly to you and encouraging you to follow me as a *'side-participant'* on a journey of discovery into the phenomenon of celebrity fandom. You are thereby encouraged to engage personally with the narrator's personal everyday lived fan experiences with and struggle of *'being-in-the-world'* (Heidegger 1927; Merleau-Ponty 1962) through use of a biographical consumer narrative. Moreover, you, the reader, are invited to develop your own understanding of film star and celebrity fandom through an active dialogue and an *'active mental immersion'* into the presented consumer narrative in a way that would not be possible by traditional means of academic research and scholarship. I would therefore be particularly grateful, if you could let me know how the narrative experience has worked for you.

As with any other academic research, there are obviously some limitations attached to the autoethnographic research in this book, too. What limitations there are, however, also depends to some extent on the expectations, ideology and epistemological grounding of the reader – in other words, yours. For example, if you, the reader, are deeply embedded in logical empiricism, then you may consider the book's reliance on a sample of one and the subsequent lack of generalisability as its biggest limitation. Indeed, the fact that the classic hallmarks of good *'scientific'* research just do not apply to the epistemological, ontological and methodological stance of my research might already be considered as a major limitation in this regard. In Chapter 1 of this book, however, I have already discussed some of the more common concerns raised against autoethnography and how I addressed them in the overall research design.

The fear of a distorted recall of events due to the reconstructive nature of human long-term memory has been addressed by collecting the lived fan experiences as contemporaneous data at the time of occurrence (or at least as close as possible), which ensures high data accuracy due to the very limited intervening time. So, here is a valuable *'takeaway'* from the practical lessons I have learnt along the way that I would recommend to anyone interested in pursuing an autoethnographic study. In addition, I have ensured data access for external review by recording the autoethnographic data in a specifically assigned diary. Sometimes, I thought that a digital voice recorder would have been handy at times. But after giving it a try recently, I found it of little use in a noisy environment and transcribing the recordings for the data analysis is a nightmare – unless you are senior enough as a researcher to have someone doing it for you. The contemporaneous data collection approach, finally, also ensures that the data specificity is not distorted by a primary focus on more memorable events, which often tend not to be remembered in the way they objectively happen anyway – and which is normally the case in research methods relying on retrospective recall of past events, such as interviews, surveys and focus groups.

You, the reader, may also be reminded that the phenomenological perspective views memories not as the recall of past events, but as an experience that takes place in the present but happens to involve an event in the past (Husserl 1986). A conceptual misunderstanding among many critics of autoethnography (Woodside 2004) has always been the case that these critics often tend to interpret autoethnographic accounts as a factual, objective witness account of the observed event or phenomenon itself that can be confirmed. However, this view is completely wrong, as the actual subject of autoethnographic research is not the factual description of a certain event itself, but the description of how the individual actually experiences this particular event as part of one's life-world. A fusion of horizons (Gadamer 1989), so to speak! You, the reader, may therefore also be reminded that the emphasis of the research in this book is on the consumer's everyday lived fan experiences with the beloved film star or any other celebrity, which include personal thoughts, feelings, desires, fantasies and daydreams, rather than the mere recollection of factual behaviour that could have been achieved by less controversial, but also by far less exciting research methods. Of course, I needed to tone down the presented autoethnographic consumer narrative in Chapter 4 to protect myself and other people involved, and to avoid any potential libel issues.

But even though autoethnography is the best, if not the only way to get access to the real world of human experiences, there are nonetheless some operational limitations attached to it that need to be mentioned. First, in order to record the experienced emotional feelings, dreams and fantasies, they need to be transferred and described in linguistic terms. Obviously, this holds the general problem that, despite a shared culture and negotiated meaning of language, the same word can have different mental imageries for different individuals due to their different personal backgrounds and life experiences. Second, even though the fan experiences have been recorded where and when they occurred, due to the complexity of human experiences, it is very difficult to record all relevant experiences in their entirety – especially in times of emotional turmoil, stress and excitement. A selective perception of events, though strongly reduced by the contemporaneous data collection approach, cannot be prevented completely.

Also, a problem especially at the beginning of the data collection is the issue of self-censorship. Recording your own feelings into the diary was a bit like talking to another person and, hence, required a period of building trust and becoming comfortable with revealing your explicit inner feelings and desires to the public – or even to yourself for that matter. Thus, the takeaway lesson here is that I would recommend practicing in advance of any project, so that you get in the right habit early on. Another related issue is that certain experiences are recorded in the heat of the moment and, therefore, can be perceived by (sensitive) outsiders as offensive and immoral or even lead to libel issues. To address this issue, I recommend recording everything in the diary as it occurs. During the transcription of the diaries, I have made some necessary alterations (i.e. taking out names and identifying marks of affected individuals other than myself, Jena Malone and any other textual media person, changing certain words and phrases to avoid potential libel issues, etc.).

A major problem with autoethnographic data is the issue of data credibility and confirmability (Wallendorf & Brucks 1993). Most traditional qualitative methods like grounded theory and case study research require their own hallmarks of good research, such as the triangulation between different informants or different researcher interpretations, member checks and external confirmations (Woodside 2004). However, it is the nature of human experiences that they are always unique to the individual and, therefore, cannot be described, measured and explained by quantitative means and methods. Indeed, as I pointed out earlier, any data interpretation that reduces human experiences to their smallest common denominator by focusing exclusively on the commonalities and similarities within the obtained responses, as scientific research methods and traditional qualitative methodologies like grounded theory generally do, is inadvertently disenfranchising them of their very essence. For that reason, it is also impossible for anyone to observe and confirm another person's inner emotional experiences. But while human experiences such as the nature of a fan's emotional attachment to one's adored film star or celebrity cannot be confirmed by a third person or observer, the individual's fan experiences, nonetheless, can be compared with those of another person (Gould 2008). Key is thereby *not* to focus on establishing the smallest common denominator, but actually to compare the individual consumer experiences for their similarities *and* differences.

Implications for understanding film consumption

Having dealt with the methodological elephant in the room, we can now focus our attention on the lessons we may take away from the insights into a consumer's everyday lived fan relationship with one's beloved celebrity gained in this book. It does not require much imagination to see that a fan's admiration for a film star is also intrinsically and inadvertently linked to an admiration of his/her creative work as an artist and performer, which is in essence the enjoyment of his/her films. Therefore, the second contribution of the research in this book is to the film consumption literature. Previous research on film consumption has focused either on a film's commercial success at the box office or on comparing the attractiveness of individual media formats (the film's *'packaging'*) and their trade-offs, while audience-response theory generally discussed film consumption as a proxy for advancing the scholar's own ideological agenda. In contrast, this research has taken an actual film viewer's and/or fan's perspective and has looked holistically at how a film is really consumed.

The first finding that has emerged from the case study is that the widely assumed rational trade-off between various film formats is virtually non-existent, since the consumer – and especially the fan – is primarily interested in the film itself and is actually most likely to watch the same film a number of times across various film formats (i.e. cinema, DVD and TV), which would render the conceptual research designs and findings of several earlier, mostly experimental studies (i.e. Basil 2001; Gazley et al. 2010) quite obsolete. The second finding is the previously overlooked fact that a consumer not only enjoys the consumption of a film holistically and in its entirety, but that it actually is a complex tapestry of interrelated factors that contribute to the individual's film enjoyment even long before and/or after watching the film – as my autoethnographic narrative has revealed to some extent with regard to *Saved!* (US 2004), *Cheaters* (US 2000) and, especially, *Pride & Prejudice* (UK 2005).

In taking a narrative transportation approach, however, the major contribution to the film consumption literature and *'takeaway'* is the important role of the consumer's (and especially the fan's) personal engagement with the film's storyline, characters and underlying philosophical message, which has in this form and complexity never been revealed before. This means that consumers may value the storytelling properties of films more than fancy gadgets. CGI spectacles may be eye-catching in the heat of the moment. But without a proper story to tell, good character development and acting, they are quickly forgotten. *Star Wars, Jurassic Park, Titanic* and *Avatar* are not global successes because of their CGI effects, but because they told stories audience members could relate to. Instead, it is the consumer's personal engagement that allows not only for a momentary escape from reality into the film world, but is even further enhanced through intertextuality, by which the consumer connects the film to one's personal life experiences (Wohlfeil and Whelan 2008). The nature and intensity of a consumer's immersion experience is exclusively determined by one's private motivations, interests and inherent desires. For that reason, it becomes apparent that, although it is possible to compare the immersion experiences of 2–3 consumers for their similarities and differences, comparing the immersion experiences of an increasing number of consumers with each other inadvertently reduces them to the smallest common denominator and disenfranchises the individual's film consumption experience of its very essence (Batat & Wohlfeil 2009).

Finally, the involvement of the admired film star obviously plays a major role in a fan's interest and enjoyment of the film. In fact, the admired film star is widely accepted as generating a fan's initial awareness and interest in a film in the first place. But while the role of the film star in attracting audiences for a film has already been considered by many earlier studies in marketing (Albert 1998; Elberse 2007; Ravid 1999) and film studies (Dyer 1998; Hollinger 2006), this was often done by considering merely the 2–3 leading film stars in the order of their billing on film posters and/or film credits (Kerrigan 2010; McDonald 2000, 2008). However, the autoethnographic consumer narrative in Chapter 4 offers clear evidence that the size of the admired film star's role actually is not an issue in capturing a fan's interest in those films at all. In fact, my awareness, interest and enjoyment of the three films that are discussed in some detail in the autoethnographic consumer narrative in Chapter 4 of this book have clearly emerged from the film actress's involvement in them; even though she is only featuring in a support role in one of them. And while her appearance and performance may have gone unnoticed to many other viewers, who have primarily been preoccupied with other facets of the film, her screen presence has been the key area of interest and attention for the fan.

This observation stands in clear contradiction to the vast body of literature on stardom, film consumption and consumer preferences in general and, thus, opens up an interesting area for further academic research. In terms of a managerial *'takeaway'*, it would be far too easy to suggest now that producers should advertise their film's forthcoming release well in advance through trailers in the cinema and press junkets, just like the authors of numerous studies published in top marketing journals have done over the years – since this has been common practice within the film industry since the birth of Hollywood (Kerrigan 2010), as we know only too well. Instead, based on the findings in the book, I recommend that producers and distributors (especially of smaller, independent films) consider involving their creative talents more strongly in the promotion efforts. Even lesser known actors, directors or screenwriters, as the autoethnographic case study has shown, have their followers. Hence, by interacting and keeping their fans updated with any film project they are involved in throughout the entire filmmaking process (including any early stages), actors and directors would be able to accumulate an audience for the film well in advance to create a pull effect that could ensure its release in cinemas and on DVD. Some already do, but too many do not.

Implications for understanding a celebrity's consumer appeal

The next major contribution of this book is to the stardom and celebrity literature by providing a deeper understanding of how a film star, rock/pop star, athlete, TV personality, model or any other celebrity appeals to the individual consumer that has emerged from the study's narrative transportation approach (Green et al. 2004). Until now, due to its origins within the fields of film and media studies, the stardom and celebrity literature has primarily relied on audience-response theory as a means of examining from a very specific ideology-informed perspective how film audiences, at least in theory, would interpret film stars as *'homogeneous sets of film textual images'* (Watson 2007a) and *'semiotic signifiers of cultural archetypes and values'* (Dyer 1998; McCracken 1989). But although the film star is thereby seen as the accumulation of various film and other off-screen media texts, film scholars put the emphasis primarily on the film star's on-screen persona with his/her mediated private persona serving merely as an extension to the former, while media scholars focus solely on the celebrity's public persona in the media. As a result, the portrayed characters on screen and the private persona of the film star off-screen tend to be seen as being virtually one-and-the-same person, whose personal image is designed and managed to fulfil universal cultural expectations (Dyer 1998; McDonald 2000; Thomson 2006).

However, the autoethnographic consumer narrative in this research clearly shows that the consumer and, especially, the fan does not mistake the film star for his/her portrayed characters and quite clearly distinguishes between them by enjoying the portrayed character as part of the overall film text and, at the same time, admiring the quality of the film star's personal acting skills and performance. The research and this book, therefore, have introduced narrative transportation theory as an alternative analytical lens to enhance our understanding of how consumers personally engage with film stars or any other celebrities in real life. In fact, unlike the critical audience-response theory, a narrative transportation approach examines actual consumer narratives to gain genuine insights into how consumers actually experience film stars and celebrities as self-constructed reflections of their own personal values, dreams and inherent desires.

Using a narrative transportation approach and drawing on my own fan relationship with a film actress, this book's most significant contribution to the stardom literature is the *'rehumanisation'* of the film star or celebrity and the deconstruction of his/her personal polysemic consumer attraction as a real human being. This book has thereby offered for the first time an explanation why a consumer may be attracted to one specific film star or celebrity but remains indifferent to other equally talented, beautiful, interesting and perhaps even more popular ones. The indisputable fact is that different consumers are attracted to very different film stars, rock/pop stars, TV personalities, athletes, novelists, models, reality TV stars or any other celebrities. And even if they actually do like the same ones, they may still be motivated by very different personal reasons and also apply different meanings to their relationships and experiences with individual film stars or celebrities.

The polysemy of personal meanings and the diversity of perspectives suggest that consumer-celebrity relationships solely seen through an ideology-informed semiotic lens, as the stardom and celebrity literature tend to do (Lovell 2003), only reduces and masks the co-creation of that (sometimes parasocial) relationship and the diversity of narratives that blossom in the daily cultural interaction not only between celebrities and their fans, but also between celebrities and consumers in general. In contrast to this traditional view that presents each film star and celebrity as a one-dimensional textual construct with a universal appeal that semiotically unites his/her recognisable canon of portrayed on-screen characters with the public media images of their private lives (Dyer 1998), I have argued in this book that each film star or celebrity is a real-living human being with a complex, multi-constituted *'media-textual allure'*, who offers each individual consumer a very personal appeal that elicits various kinds of personal emotional responses such as curiosity, interest, disgust, sexual attraction or emotional attachment.

A good metaphor to explain this personal polysemic consumer appeal that a particular film star or celebrity offers different individual consumers is perhaps that of fishing in a lake. Have you ever wondered why some fish bite while others of the same species do not? The reason why a fish eventually bites a specific hook thrown in by a particular fisherman after ignoring all the other fishermen's hooks in the lake is simply that this hook has offered something special as bait that this fish desired, while all the other hooks did not. But the next fish may be attracted to the bait of a very different hook, while another fish may not care for any of them at all. Since a film star or celebrity is a complex human being with a personal polysemic, multi-constituted consumer appeal, each attraction constituent represents such a specific *'hook'* with the celebrity's unique personal features, beauty, creative output, personality and private life-style as its *'bait'* in what could be described as a very big lake full of individual consumers.

When an individual consumer experiences certain unfulfilled needs, desires and/or aspirations, s/he starts looking for something that promises to satisfy those personal needs and desires. As a result, some can become *'hooked'* by the film star's/celebrity's creative performances, while others are more attracted to the *'hook'* of his/her personal beauty and/or personality. For some, it is the film star's/celebrity's tangible manifestation in products that offers the *'hook'* they are interested in, while others are primarily *'hooked'* by the promise of being part of a social community. The bigger those unfulfilled personal needs and desires and the more desperate the longing for something special, the more intensive the search for the perfect hook. And in a big lake that is not only filled with individual consumers, but also with a plethora of different *'hooks'* offered by many different film stars, rock/pop stars and many other celebrities with their own personal baits, a consumer looking for his/her *'personal hook'* is bound to find eventually the alluring one s/he has been longing for – even if it may require *'trying out'* a few other ones first. But once the right *'hook provider'* (a specific film star, rock/pop star or celebrity) with the right alluring bait (creative talent, beauty, personality, life-style, etc.) has been found, there is little need for the individual consumer to look any further. And this is usually the point, where the individual consumer experiences either a strong emotional attachment or a strong emotional repugnance towards the film star or celebrity – depending on the initial needs.

Hence, by rehumanising the film star or celebrity and deconstructing his/her allure as a human being, it has turned out that s/he offers each individual consumer a very personal attraction as (a) *'the performer'* and artist (including the creative artworks and other output), (b) *'the* (perceived) *'private' person'* hidden underneath the performer that gives the artist a *'physical human presence'* in real everyday life, (c) the physical products that enable the manifestation and *'tangible possession'* of the otherwise intangible performer and private person, and (d) *'the social link'* to other like-minded consumers as a site of either shared admiration or shared contempt. The individual consumer can thereby relate to only one individual consumer appeal constituent or to any given symbiotic combination of these consumer appeal constituents in order to feel at least temporarily attracted to a particular film star or celebrity. The conclusion of this finding is that a consumer's emotional fan relationship, but also just an initial interest or feeling of disgust, is determined and expressed by the personal attraction to the film star's/celebrity's consumer appeal constituents. The more of the film star's/celebrity's consumer attraction constituents appeal with growing intensity, either individually or symbiotically, to the consumer's – and especially the fan's – inherent needs, unfulfilled desires, ideals and dreams, the stronger s/he feels emotionally attached to the respective film star or celebrity.

Obviously, the *'takeaway'* of this contribution has some consequences for managing celebrity endorsements and, more importantly, for managing celebrities themselves. First, it is a popular, but ill-conceived myth that consumers would buy a product just because it is promoted or associated with a celebrity they like. Instead, celebrity endorsements only work, when the celebrity is known to have the relevant expertise to give the interested consumer *'informed professional'* advice as a *'competent spokesperson'* for the brand (i.e. a rock musician endorsing a guitar brand). In that case, the attraction of the celebrity as a performer or private person aligns with the consumer's personal interest in the endorsed brand. But it would be foolish to assume that a consumer purchases a brand because s/he likes the celebrity. Second, the findings also question the wisdom behind the popular *'blockbuster'*-strategy (Elberse 2014) of manufacturing pop stars and celebrities with a single universal appeal based on the mass audience's smallest common denominator. Since each individual consumer tends to look for something unique and special in a celebrity that speaks to their own inherent needs and desires, a manufactured celebrity designed to be everything to everybody is unlikely to encourage a genuine and sustainable emotional attachment. Thus, it might be wiser to let the celebrity's natural talent, beauty and personality speak for him/her instead.

Implications for understanding celebrity fandom

Apart from offering us a much better understanding of the actual consumer appeal of a film star or celebrity, this book's final and most significant *'takeaway'* or contribution is to the interdisciplinary fan studies literature by presenting you with a reconceptualisation of fans and fandom that puts the emphasis back on what should normally matter the most – the special emotional bond that fans form, build and experience with the admired subject of their fandom. This reconceptualised understanding of celebrity fans in particular provides us with some very interesting insights into the personal meanings that the emotional fan relationship with his/her beloved film star or celebrity has for the individual consumer and how it expresses itself in everyday consumer behaviour. In order to allow for such a reconceptualisation of fans, a clear and detailed overview of how fans have already been conceptualised across the literatures of the different academic disciplines so far is required. Unfortunately, despite the fandom phenomenon's interdisciplinary nature, most of those disciplines – perhaps with the exception of consumer research – have previously shown very little interest in crossing the boundaries of their own internal literature into those of other academic disciplines. Hence, this book's first sub-contribution to the fan studies literature is the development of a truly interdisciplinary taxonomy of how fans have been conceptualised across the literature of various academic disciplines so far. And since none of those conceptualisations of fans pays any attention to the fans' personal relationships with the subjects of their fandom, the most important contribution to the fan studies literature is a reconceptualisation of fans and fandom that addresses this particular conceptual deficit in the literature.

By following up and building on the research's finding of how celebrities appeal to consumers, I have argued, and provided evidence from my own parasocial relationship with the film actress Jena Malone as a site of meaning, that the nature and intensity of a fan's emotional attachment to one's beloved film star or celebrity are determined by the personal relevance, attraction and meaning that each of the latter's four major consumer appeal constituents has for the individual consumer, either individually or in symbiotic harmony with each other, based on one's personal values, interests, beauty ideals and, in particular, unfulfilled conscious and subconscious desires. I have thereby identified five fan relationship constituents that have emerged iteratively as themes from the hermeneutic analysis and interpretation of the autoethnographic data of my own personal fan experiences with the film actress Jena Malone presented in Chapter 4. In keeping with the personal autoethnographic nature of the research journey in this book I have labelled the five fan relationship constituents as follows.

- Admiring the celebrity as a performer.
- Adoring the celebrity as a private person.
- Taking possession of the celebrity.
- Sharing vs. non-sharing the celebrity.
- Living with the celebrity.

But although these theme labels for the five fan relationship constituents emerged from the autoethnographic case study of my personal everyday lived fan relationship with a film actress, they are equally applicable to any other consumers' personal fan relationships with their favourite film star, rock/pop star, athlete or any other celebrity. Indeed, as I have shown in this book, a fan is not attracted to the admired film star, rock/pop star or any other beloved celebrity as the unidimensional semiotic personification of some cultural archetype – as theorised by the stardom and celebrity literature. Instead, Jena Malone appeals to me not only as a very talented, imaginative and creative film actress, who portrays a variety of very different complex characters on screen or stage (even in support roles), but also as this very beautiful, intelligent, interesting, complex, but also ordinary young woman that s/he appears to be in her private life outside the media spotlight.

The first four identified fan relationship constituents are closely linked to those four major constituents that make up the film star's/celebrity's personal polysemic consumer appeal and explain his/her special attraction to the fan. *'Admiring the celebrity as a performer'* reflects the fan's strong interest in the film star or celebrity as a creative artist and performer, which involves the admiration for his/her acting skills and performances in portraying on-screen characters as much as enjoying the films themselves for the quality of their narrative storytelling. This should come to no surprise, since it usually is the enjoyment of a particular film that lays the foundation for such a relationship to form in the first place – just like it is a particular album or live performance that lays the foundation for a fan relationship with a rock/pop star or a sports performance for fan relationship with an athlete, etc. Moreover, it is often because of the admired film star or celebrity that a fan is interested in a film, album, etc. in the first place. Whether the performance is a lead or support role is thereby irrelevant, which clearly contradicts the stardom literature. For instance, my interest and desire to watch <u>Pride & Prejudice</u> (UK 2005) was awoken by Jena Malone featuring in it, even though she is only playing a support role. Yet, while I have admired her acting performances and how she brought her characters to life, I also enjoyed watching the film in itself. But according to Dyer (1998), Jena Malone would not be a film star anyway – just a character actress. So, why am I fascinated by her and enjoy her presence in those films more than, let's say, leading lady and film star Keira Knightley? The answer is that her acting performance made her stand out *for me* by not imposing herself onto the film.

'Adoring the celebrity as a private person', on the other hand, reflects the fan's emotional attachment to the film star or celebrity as a real-living human being with a private life outside the media spotlight. This emotional attachment often involves an inherent curiosity and desire to *'access the backstage'* (Beeton 2015; MacCannell 1973) in order to get to know the real person behind the adored film star, rock/pop star or any other celebrity. However, there is also the secret hope that s/he might acknowledge an awareness of the fan's existence in return. The individual film star or celebrity can thereby serve as the reflection of the fan's desire for a role model, a hero/heroine (Henry & Caldwell 2007;

O'Guinn 1991; Radford & Bloch 2012), a friend (Kanai 2015; Stacey 1994), an *'ideal'* partner (Wohlfeil & Whelan 2012) or even an idealised lover (Karniol 2001). But because it is highly unlikely for the fan ever to meet the adored film star, rock/pop star or any other celebrity in person and get to know the real private person behind the public media persona, the fan's impression of the celebrity is essentially one's own mental construction that emerges from a personal and highly selective intertextual reading of what the fan perceives to be relevant and *'reliable'* media texts or *'witness accounts'* by those individuals, who know the film star or celebrity either personally or may have met him/her by chance in a public space.

Thus, the film star or celebrity as *'the 'private' person'* is essentially a polysemic mental creation of the individual fan in accordance with one's personal needs, ideals, desires and aspirations – and, hence, a paradox. But in drawing on narrative transportation theory, we are now able to obtain insights into how this personal impression of the film star or celebrity is constantly evolving within the fan's mind through an ongoing process of introjection and projection (Gould 1993; Wohlfeil & Whelan 2011, 2012). The fan, thereby, internalises both the film star's/celebrity's off-screen and private persona psychically within oneself, loads it with one's private thoughts, feelings, fantasies, meanings and desires and, then, projects this personal impression back to the film star or celebrity; just to introject the new image and project it again and again. My personal impression of Jena Malone's personality, therefore, emphasises especially those facets of her character and personal life-style that resonate strongly with my own private life experiences, ideals, dreams and desires and, subsequently, strengthen my emotional attachment to her as a *'real'* person.

The continuous process of introjection and projection allows for the feeling of *'knowing'* the beloved film star or any other celebrity like a *'personal friend'* – including his/her thoughts, feelings, hopes, dreams, personality and way of life – to develop. In fact, this experienced *'bond of emotional closeness'* can be strong enough at times to elicit within the fan a real feeling of *'personal friendship'* or even *'love'* towards the adored film star or celebrity. Just like a traditional social or romantic relationship, a fan's parasocial relationship with one's beloved film star or celebrity represents a dynamic process that evolves over time in response to situational circumstances and emotional feelings. Hence, the parasocial relationship with the film star or celebrity can actually provide lonely individuals with a cathartic experience that helps to restore their emotional well-being in times of personal psychological distress.

Next, *'taking possession of the celebrity'* is obviously not meant to be taken literally, but refers instead to those fan activities, whereby the individual fan seeks to establish and signify a tangible presence of the admired and adored film star, rock/pop star or any other celebrity as either the *'performer'* or the *'private person'* or often even both in one's personal life through the acquisition and display of the relevant and suitable products, such as DVDs, CDs, vinyl records, photos, posters, badges, T-shirts, original hand-signed autographs, items previously owned or used as props on stage/screen by him/her and so on. Furthermore, in case of less famous film actors, musicians or other celebrities, the possession of their less accessible creative output, such as independently produced films or albums, articles in scene publications with limited print runs and/or regional distribution, affords the individual fan with something of a *'hip'* insider knowledge (Holbrook 1986, 1995) that could be shared with *'worthy others'*.

Finally, *'sharing vs. non-sharing the celebrity'*, obviously, refers to the fan's actual willingness to share one's fandom, one's admiration and one's adoration with other like-minded consumers. As Jenkins (1992), Kozinets (2001) or Hills (2002) argue, the main reasons why socially alienated, isolated and lonely consumers tend to participate actively in fan communities is not only to interact socially with like-minded people, but also to co-create and share with each other the meanings and understanding they have of the celebrity, his/her work and life, and to express their creativity together with an appreciative audience (Lanier & Schau 2007). In contrast to this dominant view, however, I have argued in this book that the central facet in one's fandom is the personal meaning and relationship one has with the admired subject. Some fans may want to share it with others on a fan forum or while screaming together as part of a crowd at a premiere or live show (Ehrenreich et al. 1992), other fans rather prefer to enjoy their personal fan experiences by themselves – just like I do.

Of course, I am mindful of the paradox of my researcher reflexivity in writing this book about my parasocial fan relationship with the film actress Jena Malone – just in case you, the reader, may wonder and raise this point. Well, the *'fan me'* that has been studied in the autoethnographic case study is a relatively self-contained fan and does not participate in either virtual or analogue fan communities *because* I simply do not want to negotiate *my* personal image, meaning(s) and views of the film star Jena Malone with that of other people. Hence, the *'fan me'* in this book still does not share or negotiate his fandom with others. It is instead the *'scholar me'* (Rambo 1992) who reports on his observations and, more precisely, his interpretation of the collected autoethnographic data and *shares* his findings on the nature of my fandom (and even my private *'fan me'*) with the reader and a wider academic as well as non-academic audience – but not really my Jena Malone fandom itself. That said, there is inextricably a certain inescapable reflexivity between myself and readers such as you with regard to my research design, ever-continuing hermeneutic readings and interpretations by all parties involved. In the end, the scholar-fan is informed by two co-creating streams – that of the fan and that of the scholar (Gould 1991; Hills 2016; Rambo 1992).

Notwithstanding this, drawing on the autoethnographic consumer narrative of my own personal everyday lived fan relationship with the film actress Jena Malone, I have also argued in this book that an individual fan's willingness to share one's personal fan experiences with the admired and adored film star, rock/pop star or any other celebrity is rather selective and highly dependent on what exactly is actually shared with others. The individual fan usually tends to be happy to share one's admiration for the film star or celebrity as a performer and, subsequently, his/her creative performances, artworks and public appearances with like-minded fans and even other consumers. Much of this sharing can be interpreted as the fan seeking to promote the film star's/celebrity's creative work in order to stimulate demand and, therefore, to ensure a supply of future creative performances and artworks to enjoy.

However, the individual fan tends to be much more reluctant and unwilling to share one's emotional attachment to the adored film star or celebrity as a private person; in particular when this emotional attachment derives from a romantic attraction. After all, who wants to share a friend or even (potential) girlfriend/boyfriend with others – especially with potential rivals for his/her (*'imagined'*) affection? And it does not matter that this *'crush'* is only a conscious daydream, and unlikely to become reality. But even this secret infatuation and the romantic daydream attached to it can help the individual to deal meaningfully with mundane daily issues or emotional problems, such as loneliness, stress, social rejection or bullying, in a cathartic manner (Horton & Wohl 1956; Wohlfeil & Whelan 2012). And before you consider it *'not normal'* and feel uncomfortable by the idea, it might be a good idea to reflect first how all this may also relate to yourself. Have you never had a crush on a celebrity? Or, have you ever fancied someone secretly and imagined what it would be like to go out on a date and more with this person, just because you were too shy to talk to him or her? How did it make you feel? Would that really be any different to what I am arguing here? Now, that is a *'take-away'* for you to think about. And here is another one: before looking down on some teenage girls and boys falling in love with a certain pop star, film star or reality TV star or sneering at those adult fans that still follow their favourite rock band, pop star, sports team or film star with the same devotion as a teenager, we would do well to have a careful look at ourselves, as we may have in the past actually done – and, only too often still do – the same, because this kind of consumer behaviour may actually be quite *'natural'* and *'normal'*.

Nonetheless, an underlying key theme and vital fan relationship constituent, which most forcefully emerged iteratively from the hermeneutic analysis of the autoethnographic data and the presented case study in this book, is the issue of temporality that I have labelled *'living with the celebrity'*. Indeed, just like any other social or romantic relationship in real life, a consumer's everyday lived fan relationship with the beloved film star, rock/pop star or any other celebrity is far from being the static characteristic or personality trait it is only too often presented in the fan studies, social psychology and marketing literatures. Instead, I have provided in this book clear evidence that a consumer's fan relationship is not only parasocial in nature, but also a dynamic process that constantly develops, evolves and changes over time in response to a constant, never-ending flow of incoming information, personal emotional experiences, changing personal circumstances and, especially, because of the individual fan's own changing needs, values, desires, aspirations, fantasies, daydreams, romantic or sexual attraction to the beloved film star or celebrity and each of his/her personal polysemic consumer appeal constituents.

It is also this same dynamic process, however, that allows the fan to develop, foster, reinforce and experience this personal feeling of actually *'knowing'* the film star, rock/pop star or any other celebrity like a personal friend and even to experience true feelings of *'love'* for him or her. Indeed, the individual's fan experience must be understood as a dynamic process of introjecting the film star's/celebrity's persona, loading it with one's personal feelings, inherent desires and aspirations and projecting this new imagery back onto the beloved film star or celebrity; just to introject this newly created imagery together with new incoming information again and again. As a result, the mentally created imagery of the film star or celebrity *'becomes'* a real-living person in the fan's mind that corresponds with one's personal desires, hopes, dreams and aspirations. Figure 6.1 in the previous chapter of this book outlines how the other four fan relationship constituents interact with, feed into, drive and reinforce the *'living with the celebrity'* constituent and, thereby, enable fans to experience the mentally created, personal film star or celebrity persona as an organic, ever-evolving part of one's personal life-text.

The Ruins ... or a few last words

If you, the reader, still wonder whether the findings in this book are generalisable and represent the absolute truth, no they are not. The findings, however, are comparable and transferable, which means that the reader is invited to compare my fan relationship and the presented everyday lived experiences to your own fan or general consumption experiences with celebrities and transfer the presented findings in the book to explain them. Moreover, I do not pretend that my presented hermeneutic interpretation of the complex autoethnographic data would be the only possible one; far from it. As Heidegger (1927) has pointed out, the existential-phenomenological perspective holds that any interpretations that emerge through a hermeneutic analysis never represent the final and absolute findings, but only one set of possible explanations (Goulding 2005). Any interpretation of a phenomenon, therefore, has to be understood as being merely a snapshot that has been taken at a particular moment in time from a particular perspective.

But it is the nature of both any given phenomenon and the knowledge of the same given phenomenon that they constantly evolve and develop further in response to every piece of newly obtained information or following a re-reading of the same old material under altered personal and situational circumstances. And the same is true for the presented study in this book, which represents merely a snapshot of an ongoing research journey into the phenomenon of celebrity fandom – a territory that still has lots of potential for further research. A good starting point would be to bury the old sociological-theoretical stereotypes about celebrities and fans forever and look at them with fresh eyes. An important part, thereby, is to look at and treat both celebrities and fans as real-living human beings just like you and me. In this book, I have taken a major step in this direction and have deconstructed the personal polysemic consumer appeal of a celebrity to identify four major constituents. Each of the celebrity's personal consumer appeal constituents provides consumers with a *'hook'* that may encourage one to experience an emotional attachment. And based on this model, I have also presented in this book a model of a consumer's everyday lived fan relationship with a celebrity, which offers a newly emerging picture of how fans relate to their beloved celebrity in their personal everyday life and how this parasocial relationship organically evolves over time – just like any other social or romantic relationship would.

Obviously, the main finding and contribution of this book is that a consumer's fan experiences revolve around one's personal engagement with the celebrity as a real-living human being – both as a creative performer and as a private person. The latter is essentially the fan's own mental construction that evolves from the personal intertextual reading of what one perceives to be relevant and *'reliable'* media texts and/or witness accounts, and is determined by the fan's inherent desires, aspirations, hopes and dreams. This is why drawing on narrative transportation theory can help to explain in particular how and why fans often develop and experience the feeling of knowing the celebrity personally, including his/her personal thoughts, feelings, personality and everyday way of life, despite having actually never met the real person. This experienced *'bond of emotional closeness'* can sometimes be strong enough to elicit feelings of *'personal friendship'* within the fan or, in a way, even a feeling of *'love'* towards the beloved celebrity that can express itself in a parasocial relationship.

It also provides an explanation as to why consumers sometimes feel enormously disappointed, when their most desired dream of actually meeting the beloved celebrity in person comes true, because the celebrity turns out to be a very different person in his/her real private life or s/he just cannot live up to the (perhaps unrealistic) imaginary person that the consumer has created in his/her mind. Hence, it would be a very good idea to explore in form of autoethnographic consumer narratives the personal fan experiences of other consumers and how their everyday lived fan relationships with the beloved film star, rock/pop star, athlete or any other celebrity express themselves in their everyday lives. The key concern should thereby be a comparison between those fan experiences and relationships in terms of their similarities *and* differences – and *not* to identify their smallest common denominator. Every fan experience and relationship is unique to the individual consumer and must always be treated, understood and cherished as such.

There are two potentially interesting features in a consumer's everyday lived fan relationship with a film star, rock/pop star, athlete, reality TV star or any other celebrity that have not been addressed in this book, primarily because they have not emerged iteratively as an issue from the hermeneutic analysis of my autoethnographic data, but may actually warrant further research in the future. First, since separation, break-ups and divorce, though unfortunate and generally not sought after, represent common occurrences within many types of social, romantic and even professional relationships, even a consumer's (parasocial) fan relationship with a celebrity may at some stage come to an end and dissolve. It is clearly worthwhile, therefore, to take a closer look at how and why the dissolution of an emotional attachment occurs and how they play out within the fan's relationship with the (previously) beloved film star or celebrity. Parmentier and Fischer (2015) provide some interesting groundwork with their recent exploration of how and why audiences fall out of love with their favourite TV shows. Perhaps some of their findings may also be applicable or transferable to explain the decline and dissolution of a fan-celebrity relationship.

Second, although a consumer's parasocial fan relationship is purely imaginary, there is still the valid question of what happens when the beloved film star or celebrity is either dating or even involved in a serious real-life relationship with a long-term partner or, *'worse'*, is even getting married. How does such a development, if at all, affect the nature of the consumer's personal fan relationship with that film star or celebrity? While the popular tabloid media are filled with the stereotype of the jealous fan stalking the celebrity and threatening the perceived rival, empirical field data – whether quantitative or qualitative – are still non-existent, since the interdisciplinary stardom and celebrity literatures have never concerned themselves so far with such *'human'* questions.

Last but not least, it seems to me that you, the reader, may still want to know what has happened to my own personal fan relationship with the film actress Jena Malone ever since, whether I am still her fan and whether I have had in the meantime the chance to meet her in person. At least, these are questions I am getting asked quite regularly at conferences by colleagues or in the lecture theatre by students, who have come across my JBR paper on the Internet. After all, nearly 10 years have since passed. Well, the short answer is: *'Yes, I am still a fan of Jena Malone. And yes, I've had the opportunity to meet her briefly.'* Well, I have always regretted that I failed to see Jena Malone performing live on stage in the Broadway play <u>Doubt</u> (US 2006). Therefore, when she was cast to play the lead character in the Off-Broadway play <u>Mourning Becomes Electra</u> (US 2009) from February to June 2009, I planned and booked this time a short 5-day trip to New York in April 2009 as a birthday present to myself. Unfortunately, following some mixed critical reviews, the show was cancelled. If it were not for the opportunity to meet finally my academic idol Professor Morris B. Holbrook in person, I would have had a miserable time in New York as a result.

Anyway, the nature of my fan relationship and emotional attachment to Jena Malone has settled over time. The experienced strength and intensity of my parasocial attraction to the actress Jena Malone as a beautiful, intelligent, interesting, imaginative and talented young woman continued to fluctuate in response to social events, experienced rejections and feelings of loneliness. But an episode similar to Phase 6 from September to December 2006 has only occurred once more in 2012 under nearly identical circumstances – even though I was not in quite such a dark place on that occasion. Moreover, I experienced twice a repeat of Phase 3 with its targeted purchase of Jena Malone's original hand-signed autographs – first, in relation to the film release of <u>Sucker Punch</u> (US 2011) in 2011 and, then, in relation to the film release of <u>The Hunger Games: Catching Fire</u> (US 2013) in 2013 – but with a much lower intensity.

In 2011, however, I eventually received the news that Jena Malone was now involved in a serious relationship with a graphic designer she had supposedly met at an arts-fair. My initial response was to ignore this information just like I have always ignored previously that she smoked. When this relationship began to last longer than previous ones and she began to appear regularly with him publicly at premieres and public events, which she has never done before, I found it increasingly difficult to ignore and must admit that I experienced a feeling of jealousy, but even more a feeling of sadness and resignation in me. And although I have continued to admire her acting skills and performances while watching her in films like *Five Star Day* (US 2010), *In Our Nature* (US 2011), *The Wait* (US 2012), *The Hunger Games: Catching Fire* (US 2013), *The Hunger Games: Mockingjay – Part 2* (US 2015) or *Neon Demon* (US 2016), strangely enough, the parasocial nature of my fan relationship with Jena Malone, which was until then mainly driven by the *'adoring Jena Malone as a private person'* constituent, has since 2013 begun to decline steadily and, nowadays, nearly disappeared – and with it also my interest in her original hand-signed autographs or articles in US magazines. In fact, I haven't been on eBay ever since. Yet, I am still collecting her films and watch them in the cinema, if possible, or purchase them on DVD *and* iTunes download in the moment they are released.

It was exactly at this moment in time, when my long-held wish to see and meet Jena Malone finally did come true. When Jena Malone released the album *'I'm Okay'* of her music project *The Shoe*, she also came to London in July 2014 to play a free, RSVP-only live gig in the Belgraves Hotel. As my (parasocial) romantic feelings for her have already been declining, I thought that, if I meet Jena Malone in person and she turns out to be very different to the person that I have imagined her to be, it might help to close this chapter in my life – even though she was apparently single again. Hence, I organised to stopover in London on my return from a conference and to stay in this hotel for the weekend. Unfortunately, the plan did not work out as I intended. Instead, besides being enamoured with her live performance in the hotel bar, I have actually managed to meet her briefly in person and to take a personal photograph with her. Well, to my surprise, the real Jena Malone I have met is not only lovely, beautiful and charming, but has also turned out to be *exactly* the person that I have imagined her to be during all those years. Sadly, as always in those situations when I meet a girl that I fancy, I was so nervous that, even though she was very nice to me, I could barely speak a word and mainly mumbled a few, probably inaudible words – at best. I am not sure what impression I left, if any at all. But that is typically me, I guess.

Nonetheless, even months later, I am still stunned to learn that the real Jena Malone I have met that day is nearly identical to the Jena Malone I have created in my imagination over the years as a result of my selective reading of her interviews and trustworthy articles and watching her media appearances. So, what does this mean? You might wonder or even ask. Well, that is a good question! But at the moment, I do not know the answer. However, while I will continue thinking about it, I would like to invite you, the reader, to share with me your interpretation or your own personal experiences with meeting your favourite celebrity. After all, fan stories are constantly developing and evolving, aren't they?

References

Addis, Michela and Morris B. Holbrook (2010), "Consumers' Identification and Beyond: Attraction, Reverence and Escapism in the Evaluation of Films", *Psychology & Marketing*, 27(9), 821–845.

Adorno, Theodor W. and Max Horkheimer (2006), "The Culture Industry: Enlightenment as Mass Deception", in *Stardom and Celebrity: A Reader*, (Eds.) Redmond, Sean and Su Holmes, London: Sage, 34–43.

Alberoni, Francesco (2006), "The Powerless 'Elite': Theory and Sociological Research on the Phenomenon of the Stars", in *The Celebrity Culture Reader*, (Ed.) Marshall, P. David, New York: Routledge, 108–123.

Albert, Steven (1998), "Movie Stars and the Distribution of Financially Successful Films in the Motion Picture Industry", *Journal of Cultural Economics*, 22(2), 249–270.

Alperstein, Neil M. (1991), "Imaginary Social Relationships with Celebrities Appearing in Television Commercials", *Journal of Broadcasting & Electronic Media*, 35(1), 43–58.

Argo, Jennifer, Rhui Zhui and Darren W. Dahl (2008), "Fact or Fiction: An Investigation of Empathy Differences in Response to Emotional Melodramatic Entertainment", *Journal of Consumer Research*, 34(3), 614–623.

Arsena, Ashley, David H. Silvera and Mario Pandalaere (2014), "Brand Trait Transference: When Celebrity Endorsers Acquire Brand Personality Traits", *Journal of Business Research*, 67, 1537–1543.

Baltin, Steve (2004), "Jena Malone's Learning Curve: The Former Child Star Graduates to Leading Lady in *Saved!*", *Venice: Los Angeles Arts & Entertainment*, 15(May), 54–60.

Banister, Emma N. and Hayley L. Cocker (2014), "A Cultural Exploration of Consumers' Interactions and Relationships with Celebrities", *Journal of Marketing Management*, 30(1–2), 1–29.

Barbas, Samantha (2001), *Movie Crazy: Fans, Stars and the Cult of Celebrity*, New York: Palgrave Macmillan.

Barron, Lee (2015), *Celebrity Cultures: An Introduction*, London: Sage.

Basil, Michael D. (2001), "The Film Audience: Theater versus Video Consumers", *Advances in Consumer Research*, 28, 349–352.

Basuroy, Suman and Subimal Chatterjee (2008), "Fast and Frequent: Investigating Box Office Revenues of Motion Picture Sequels", *Journal of Business Research*, 61(8), 798–803.

Basuroy, Suman, Subimal Chatterjee and S. Abraham Ravid (2003), "How Critical Are Critical Reviews? The Box Office Effects of Film Critics, Star Power and Budgets", *Journal of Marketing*, 67(1), 103–117.

Batat, Wided and Markus Wohlfeil (2009), "Getting Lost *'Into the Wild'*: Understanding Consumers' Movie Enjoyment Through a Narrative Transportation Approach", *Advances in Consumer Research*, 36, 372–377.

Baudrillard, Jean (1970/2017), *The Consumer Society: Myths and Structures, Revised Edition*, London: Sage.

Beckwith, Douglas C. (2009), "Values of Protagonists in Best Pictures and Blockbusters: Implications for Marketing", *Psychology & Marketing*, 26(5), 445–469.

Beeton, S. (2015), *Travel, Tourism and the Moving Image*, Bristol: Channel View.

Belk, Russell W., Melanie Wallendorf and John F. Sherry Jr. (1989), "The Sacred and the Profane in Consumer Behavior: Theodicy from the Odyssey", *Journal of Consumer Research*, 16(1), 1–38.

Beltran, Mary C. (2006), "The Hollywood Latina Body as Site of Social Struggle: Media Constructions of Stardom and Jennifer Lopez's 'Cross-Over Butt'", in *Stardom and Celebrity: A Reader*, (Eds.) Redmond, Sean and Su Holmes, London: Sage, 275–286.

Benjamin, Walter (2006), "The Work of Art in the Age of Mechanical Reproduction", in *Stardom and Celebrity: A Reader*, (Eds.) Redmond, Sean and Su Holmes, London: Sage, 25–33.

Bielby, Denise D., C. Lee Harrington and William T. Bielby (1999), "Whose Stories Are They? Fans' Engagement with Soap Opera Narratives in Three Sites of Fan Activity", *Journal of Broadcasting & Electronic Media*, 43(1), 35–45.

Boorstin, Daniel J. (1961), *The Image: A Guide to Pseudo-Events in America*, New York: Schuster & Schuster.

Bourdieu, Pierre (1984/2010), *Distinction: A Social Critique of the Judgement of Taste*, New York: Routledge.

Brink, Rob (2008), "Jena Malone and her Orgy of Talents", *MissBehave*, 6, 60–62.

Briscoe, Joanna (2005), "A Costume Drama with Muddy Hems", *Culture (Sunday Times Supplement)*, 31 July 2005, 6–7.

Brooker, Will (2005), "It Is Love: The Lewis Carroll Society as a Fan Community", *American Behavioral Scientist*, 48(7), 859–880.

Brower, Sue (1992), "Fans as Tastemakers: Viewers for Quality Television", in *The Adoring Audience: Fan Culture and Popular Media*, (Ed.) Lewis, Lisa A., London: Routledge, 163–184.

Brown, Stephen (1998a), "Romancing the Market: Sex, Shopping and Subjective Personal Introspection", *Journal of Marketing Management*, 14(7–8), 783–798.

Brown, Stephen (1998b), "The Wind in the Wallows: Literary Theory, Autobiographical Criticism and Subjective Personal Introspection", *Advances in Consumer Research*, 25, 25–30.

Brown, Stephen (2002), "Who Moved My Muggle? Harry Potter and the Marketing Imaginarium", *Marketing Intelligence & Planning*, 20(3), 134–148.

Brown, Stephen (2005), *Wizard! Harry Potter's Brand Magic*, London: Cyan.

Brown, Stephen (2006), "Rattles from the Swill Bucket", in *Consuming Books: The Marketing and Consumption of Literature*, (Ed.) Brown, Stephen, Abingdon, Oxon: Routledge, 1–17.

Brown, Stephen (2007), "Harry Potter and the Fandom Menace", in *Consumer Tribes*, (Eds.) Cova, Bernard, Robert V. Kozinets and Avi Shankar, Oxford: Butterworth-Heinemann, 177–193.

Brown, Stephen, Lorna Stevens and Pauline Maclaran (1999), "I Can't Believe It's Not Bakhtin!: Literary Theory, Postmodern Advertising, and the Gender Agenda", *Journal of Advertising*, 28(1), 11–24.

Browne, Jeffrey A. (1997), "Comic Book Fandom and Cultural Capital", *Journal of Popular Culture*, 30(4), 13–31.

Calhoun, Dave (2003), "From *Stepmom* to *Donnie Darko*: Jena Malone's LA Story", *Dazed & Confused*, 2(3), 66–69.

Cashmore, Ellis (2006), *Celebrity/Culture*, Abingdon, Oxon: Routledge.

Chen Yu (2009), "Possession and Access: Consumer Desires and Value Perceptions Regarding Contemporary Art Collection and Exhibit Visits", *Journal of Consumer Research*, 35(6), 925–940.

Chory-Assad, Rebecca M. and Ashley Yanen (2005), "Hopelessness and Loneliness as Predictors of Older Adults' Involvement with Favorite Television Performers", *Journal of Broadcasting & Electronic Media*, 49(2), 182–201.

Cicioni, Mirna (1998), "Male Pair-Bonds and Female Desire in Fan Slash Writings", in *Theorizing Fandom: Fans, Subculture and Identity*, (Eds.) Harris, Cheryl and Alison Alexander, Cresskill, NJ: Hampton, 153–177.

Cocker, Hayley L., Emma N. Banister and Maria Piacentini (2015), "Producing and Consuming Celebrity Identity Myths: Unpacking the Classed Identities of Cheryl Cole and Katie Price", *Journal of Marketing Management*, 31(5–6), 502–524.

Cohen, Jonathan (2001), "Defining Identification: A Theoretical Look at the Identification of Audiences with Media Characters", *Mass Communication & Society*, 4(3), 245–264.

Cohen, Scott Lyle (2002), "Jena Malone: Emancipated at 15, Can She Do the Same for the Movies?", *Interview*, March, 128–133.

Cooper-Martin, Elizabeth (1991), "Consumers and Movies: Some Findings on Experiential Products", *Advances in Consumer Research*, 18, 372–378.

Cousins, Mark (2011), *The Story of Film*. London: Anova Pavilion.

Cova, Bernard (1998), "From Marketing to Societing: When the Link Is More Important than the Thing", in *Rethinking Marketing: Towards Critical Marketing Accountings*, (Eds.) Brownlie, Douglas, Michael Saren, Robin Wensley & Richard Whittington, London: Sage, 64–83.

Cova, Bernard, Stefano Pace and David J. Park (2007), "Global Brand Communities across Borders: The Warhammer Case", *International Marketing Review*, 24(3), 313–329.

Cuadrado, Manuel and Marta Frasquet (1999), "Segmentation of Cinema Audiences: An Exploratory Study Applied to Young Consumers", *Journal of Cultural Economics*, 23, 257–267.

Cusack, Maurice, Gavin Jack and Donncha Kavanagh (2003), "Dancing with Discrimination: Managing Stigma and Identity", *Culture & Organisation*, 9(4), 295–310.

De Certeau, Michel (1984/2002), *The Practice of Everyday Life*, Berkeley: University of California Press.

De Cordova, Richard (1991), "The Emergence of the Star System in America", in *Stardom: Industry of Desire*, (Ed.) Gledhill, Christine, London: Routledge, 17–29.

De Cordova, Richard (2006), "The Discourse on Acting", in *The Celebrity Culture Reader*, (Ed.) Marshall, P. David, New York: Routledge, 91–107.

Derbaix, Christian, Alain Decrop and Olivier Cabossart (2002), "Colors and Scarves: The Symbolic Consumption of Material Possessions of Soccer Fans", *Advances in Consumer Research*, 29, 511–518.

De Vany, Arthur (2004), *Hollywood Economics: How Extreme Uncertainty Shapes the Film Industry*, New York: Routledge.

De Vany, Arthur and W. David Walls (2002), "Does Hollywood Make Too Many R-Rated Movies? Risk, Stochastic Dominance and the Illusion of Expectation", *Journal of Business*, 75(3), 425–451.

Dickson, Paul (1989), *The Dickson Baseball Dictionary*, New York: Facts on File Inc.

Dietz, Park Elliot, Daryl B. Matthews, Cindy van Duyne, Daniel Allen Martell, Charles D. H. Parry, Tracey Stewart, Janet Warren and J. Douglas Crowder (1991), "Threatening and Otherwise Inappropriate Letters to Hollywood Celebrities", *Journal of Forensic Sciences*, 36(1), 185–209.

Dietz-Uhler, Elizabeth, Elisabeth A. Harrick, Christian End and Lindy Jacquemotte (2000), "Sex Differences in Sport Fan Behaviour and Reasons for Being a Sport Fan", *Journal of Sport Behaviour*, 23(3), 219–231.

Droste, Wiglaf (1995), *Die Schweren Jahre ab 33*, Berlin: Frühstyxradio.

Duffett, Mark (2013), *Understanding Fandom: An Introduction to the Study of Media Fan Culture*, New York: Bloomsbury.

Dyer, Richard (1998), *Stars, New Edition*, London: British Film Institute.

Dyer, Richard (2000), "Introduction to Film Theory", in *Film Studies: Critical Approaches*, (Eds.) Hill, John and Paula Church Gibson, Oxford: Oxford University Press, 4–19.

Eagar, Toni and Andrew Lindridge (2014), "Becoming Iconic: David Bowie from Man to Icon", *Advances in Consumer Research*, 42, 302–306.

Ehrenreich, Barbara, Elizabeth Hess and Gloria Jacobs (1992), "Beatlemania: Girls Just Want to Have Fun", in *The Adoring Audience: Fan Culture and Popular Media*, (Ed.) Lewis, Lisa A., London: Routledge, 84–106.

Elberse, Anita (2007), "The Power of Stars: Do Star Actors Drive the Success of Movies?", *Journal of Marketing*, 71(1), 102–120.

Elberse, Anita (2014), *Blockbusters: Why Big Hits – and Big Risks – Are the Future of the Entertainment Business*, London: Faber & Faber.

Eliashberg, Jehoshua, Anita Elberse and Mark A. A. M. Leenders (2006), "The Motion Picture Industry: Critical Issues in Practice, Current Research and New Research Directions", *Marketing Science*, 25(6), 638–661.

Eliashberg, Jehoshua, Sam K. Hui and Z. John Zhang (2007), "From Story Line to Box Office: A New Approach for Green-Lighting Movie Scripts", *Management Science*, 53(6), 881–893.

Eliashberg, Jehoshua and Mohanbir S. Sawhney (1994), "Modelling Goes to Hollywood: Predicting Individual Differences in Movie Enjoyment", *Management Science*, 40(9), 1151–1173.

Eliashberg, Jehoshua and Steven M. Shugan (1997), "Film Critics: Influencers or Predictors?", *Journal of Marketing*, 61(1), 68–78.

Ellis, Carolyn (1991), "Sociological Introspection and Emotional Experience", *Symbolic Interaction*, 14(1), 23–50.

Ellis, Carolyn (1995), "The Other Side of the Fence: Seeing Black and White in a Small Southern Town", *Qualitative Inquiry*, 1(2), 147–167.

Ellis, Carolyn (2002), "Shattered Lives: Making Sense of September 11th and Its Aftermath", *Journal of Contemporary Ethnography*, 31(4), 375–410.

Ellis, Carolyn and Tony E. Adams (2014), "The Purposes, Practices and Principles of Autoethnographic Research", in *The Oxford Handbook of Qualitative Research*, (Ed.) Leavy, Paul, New York: Oxford University Press, 254–276.

Epstein, Edward J. (2005), *The Big Picture: Money and Power in Hollywood*, New York: Random House.

Epstein, Edward J. (2012), *The Hollywood Economist 2.0: The Hidden Financial Realities behind the Movies*. Brooklyn, NY: Melville House.

Erdogan, B. Zafer (1999), "Celebrity Endorsement: A Literature Review", *Journal of Marketing Management*, 16(4), 291–314.

Escalas, Jennifer Edson (2004), "Imagine Yourself in the Product: Mental Simulation, Narrative Transportation and Persuasion", *Journal of Advertising*, 33(2), 37–48.

Escalas, Jennifer Edson and Barbara B. Stern (2003), "Sympathy and Empathy: Emotional Responses to Advertising Dramas", *Journal of Consumer Research*, 29(4), 566–578.

Ferguson, Brooks (2009), "Creativity and Integrity: Marketing the 'In Development' Screenplay", *Psychology & Marketing*, 26(5), 421–444.

Fillis, Ian and Craig Mackay (2014), "Moving Beyond Fan Typologies: The Impact of Social Integration on Team Loyalty in Football", *Journal of Marketing Management*, 30(3–4), 334–363.

Fiske, John (1992), "The Cultural Economy of Fandom", in *The Adoring Audience: Fan Culture and Popular Media*, (Ed.) Lewis, Lisa A., London: Routledge, 30–49.

Fornerino, Marianela, Agnes Helme-Guizon and David Gotteland (2008), "Movie Consumption Experience and Immersion: Impact on Satisfaction", *Recherche et Applications en Marketing*, 23(3), 93–109.

Gabler, Noel (1998), *Life: The Movie – How Entertainment Conquered Reality*, New York: Vintage.

Gadamer, Hans-Georg (1989/2004), *Truth and Method, 2nd Edition*, London: Continuum.

Gaines, Jane M. (2000), "Dream/Factory", in *Reinventing Film Studies*, (Eds.) Gledhill, Christine and Linda Williams, London: Arnold, 100–113.

Gamson, Joshua (2006), "The Assembly Line of Greatness: Celebrity in Twentieth Century America", in *Stardom and Celebrity: A Reader*, (Eds.) Redmond, Sean and Su Holmes, London: Sage, 141–155.

Gazley, Aaron, Gemma Clark and Ashish Sinha (2010), "Understanding Preferences for Motion Pictures", *Journal of Business Research*, 64, 854–861.

Geertz, Clifford (1973/2000), *The Interpretation of Cultures, New Edition*, New York: Basic Books.

Geraghty, Christine (2000), "Re-Examining Stardom: Questions of Texts, Bodies and Performance", in *Reinventing Film Studies*, (Eds.) Gledhill, Christine and Linda Williams, London: Arnold, 183–201.

Geraghty, Christine (2003), "Performing as a Lady and a Dame: Reflections on Acting and Genre", in *Contemporary Hollywood Stardom*, (Eds.) Austin, Thomas and Martin Barker, London: Arnold, 105–117.

Gerrig, Richard J. (1993), *Experiencing Narrative Worlds: On the Psychological Activities of Reading*, New Haven, CT: Yale University.

Giles, David C. (2006), "The Quest for Fame", in *The Celebrity Culture Reader*, (Ed.) Marshall, P. David, New York: Routledge, 470–486.

Giles, David C. and John Maltby (2004), "The Role of Media Figures in Adolescent Development: Relations between Autonomy, Attachment and Interest in Celebrities", *Personality & Individual Differences*, 36, 813–822.

Glass, Loren (2016), "Brand Names: A Brief History of Literary Celebrity", in *A Companion to Celebrity*, (Eds.) Marshall, P. David and Sean Redmond, Oxford: Wiley, 39–57.

Gould, Stephen J. (1991), "The Self-Manipulation of My Pervasive, Perceived Vital Energy through Product Use: An Introspective-Praxis Perspective", *Journal of Consumer Research*, 18(2), 194–207.

Gould, Stephen J. (1993), "The Circle of Projection and Introjection: An Introspective Investigation of a Proposed Paradigm Involving the Mind as 'Consuming Organ'", *Research in Consumer Behaviour*, 6, 185–230.

Gould, Stephen J. (1995), "Researcher Introspection as a Method in Consumer Research: Applications, Issues and Implications", *Journal of Consumer Research*, 21(4), 719–722.

Gould, Stephen J. (2006), "Unpacking the Many Faces of Introspective Consciousness: A Metacognitive-Poststructuralist Exercise", in *Handbook of Qualitative Research Methods in Marketing*, (Ed.) Belk, Russell W., Cheltenham: Edward Elgar, 186–197.

Gould, Stephen J. (2008), "An Introspective Genealogy of My Introspective Genealogy", *Marketing Theory*, 8(4), 407–424.

Goulding, Christina (2005), "Grounded Theory, Ethnography and Phenomenology: A Comparative Analysis of Three Qualitative Strategies for Marketing Research", *European Journal of Marketing*, 39(3–4), 294–308.

Green, Melanie C. and Timothy C. Brock (2000), "The Role of Transportation in the Persuasiveness of Public Narratives", *Journal of Personality & Social Psychology*, 79(5), 701–721.

Green, Melanie C., Timothy C. Brock and Geoff F. Kaufman (2004), "Understanding Media Enjoyment: The Role of Transportation into Narrative Worlds", *Communication Theory*, 14(4), 311–327.

Grossberg, Lawrence (1992), "Is There a Fan in the House? The Affective Sensibility of Fandom", in *The Adoring Audience: Fan Culture and Popular Media*, (Ed.) Lewis, Lisa A., London: Routledge, 50–65.

Hackley, Chris and Rungpaka Amy Hackley (2015), "Marketing and the Cultural Production of Celebrity in the Era of Media Convergence", *Journal of Marketing Management*, 31(5–6), 461–478.

Hansen, Miriam (1986), "Pleasure, Ambivalence, Identification: Valentino and Female Spectatorship", *Cinema Journal*, 25(4), 6–32.

Hart, Andrew, Finola Kerrigan and Dirk von Lehm (2016), "Experiencing Film: Subjective Personal Introspection and Popular Film Consumption", *International Journal of Research in Marketing*, 33(2), 375–391.

Haskell, Molly (1999), "Female Stars in the 1940s", in *Film Theory and Criticism: Introductory Readings, 5th Edition*, (Eds.) Braudy, Leo and Marshall Cohen, New York: Oxford University, 562–575.

Hastings, Michael (2004), "This Isn't a Guy's World: Jena Malone's Declarations of Independence", *Venus*, 19(June), 54–56.

Hede, Anne-Marie and Maree Thyne (2010), "A Journey to the Authentic: Museum Visitors and Their Negotiation of the Inauthentic", *Journal of Marketing Management*, 26(7–8), 686–705.

Heidegger, Martin (1927/2001), *Sein und Zeit*, Tübingen: Max Niemeyer.

Hennig-Thurau, Thorsten, Victor Henning and Henrik Sattler (2007), "Consumer File Sharing of Motion Pictures", *Journal of Marketing*, 71(1), 1–18.

Hennig-Thurau, Thorsten, Gianfranco Walsh and Matthias Bode (2004), "Exporting Media Products: Understanding the Success and Failure of Hollywood Movies in Germany", *Advances in Consumer Research*, 31, 633–638.

Hennig-Thurau, Thorsten and Oliver Wruck (2000), "Warum wir ins Kino gehen: Erfolgsfaktoren von Kinofilmen", *Marketing: Zeitschrift für Forschung und Praxis*, 22(3), 241–256.

Henry, Paul and Marylouise Caldwell (2007), "Imprinting, Incubation and Intensification: Factors Contributing to Fan-Club Formation and Continuance", in *Consumer Tribes*, (Eds.) Cova, Bernard, Robert V. Kozinets and Avi Shankar, Oxford: Butterworth-Heinemann, 163–173.

Hermes, Joke (2006), "Reading Gossip Magazines: The Imagined Communities of 'Gossip' and 'Camp'", in *The Celebrity Culture Reader*, (Ed.) Marshall, P. David, New York: Routledge, 291–310.

Hermes, Joke and Jaap Kooijman (2016), "The Everyday Use of Celebrities", in *A Companion to Celebrity*, (Eds.) Marshall, P. David and Sean Redmond, Oxford: Wiley, 483–496.

Herrmann, Andrew F. (2012), "Never Mind the Scholar, Here's the Old Punk: Identity, Community and the Ageing Music Fan", *Studies in Symbolic Interaction*, 39, 153–170.

Hewer, Paul and Kathy Hamilton (2012a), "On Consuming Celebrities: The Case of the Kylie E-Community", *Advances in Consumer Research*, 38, 274–280.

Hewer, Paul and Kathy Hamilton (2012b), "Exhibitions and the Role of Fashion in the Sustenance of the Kylie Brand Mythology: Unpacking the Spatial Logic of Celebrity Culture", *Marketing Theory*, 12(4), 411–425.

Hills, Matthew (2002), *Fan Cultures*, London: Routledge.

Hills, Matthew (2016), "From Parasocial to Multisocial Interaction: Theorizing Material/Digital Fandom and Celebrity", in *A Companion to Celebrity*, (Eds.) Marshall, P. David and Sean Redmond, Oxford: Wiley, 463–482.

Hirschman, Elizabeth C. (1987), "Movies as Myths: An Interpretation of Motion Picture Mythology", in *Marketing & Semiotics: New Directions in the Study of Signs for Sale*, (Ed.) Umiker-Sebeok, Jean, Berlin: Mouton de Gruyter, 335–374.

Hirschman, Elizabeth C. (1988), "The Ideology of Consumption: A Structural-Syntactical Analysis of Dallas and Dynasty", *Journal of Consumer Research*, 15(3), 344–359.

Hirschman, Elizabeth C. (1992), "Mundane Consumption: The Cinematic Depiction of Cocaine Consumption", *Advances in Consumer Research*, 19, 424–428.

Hirschman, Elizabeth C. (1993), "Consumer Behaviour Meets the Nouvelle Femme: Feminist Consumption at the Movies", *Advances in Consumer Research*, 20, 41–47.

Hirschman, Elizabeth C. (1999), "Applying Reader-Response Theory to a Television Program", *Advances in Consumer Research*, 26, 549–554.

Hirschman, Elizabeth C. (2000a), *Heroes, Monsters and Messiahs: Movies and Television Shows as the Mythology of American Culture*, Kansas City: Andrews McMeel.

Hirschman, Elizabeth C. (2000b), "Consumers' Use of Intertextuality and Archetypes", *Advances in Consumer Research*, 27, 57–63.

Hirschman, Elizabeth C. and Morris B. Holbrook (1992), *Postmodern Consumer Research: The Study of Consumption as Text*, London: Sage.

Hirschman, Elizabeth C. and Barbara B. Stern (1994), "Women as Commodities: Prostitution as Depicted in *The Blue Angel, Pretty Baby* and *Pretty Woman*", *Advances in Consumer Research*, 21, 576–581.

Holbrook, Morris B. (1986), "I'm Hip: An Autobiographical Account of Some Musical Consumption Experiences", *Advances in Consumer Research*, 13, 614–618.

Holbrook, Morris B. (1987), "An Audiovisual Inventory of Some Fanatic Consumer Behavior: The 25-Cent Tour of a Jazz Collector's Home", *Advances in Consumer Research*, 14, 144–149.

Holbrook, Morris B. (1988), "Consumption Symbolism and the Meaning in Works of Art: A Paradigmatic Case", *European Journal of Marketing*, 22(7), 19–36.

Holbrook, Morris B. (1991), "From the Log of a Consumer Researcher: Reflections on the Odyssey", in *Highways and Buyways: Naturalistic Research from the Consumer Behavior Odyssey*, (Ed.) Belk, Russell W., Duluth, MN: Association for Consumer Research, 14–33.

Holbrook, Morris B. (1993), "Nostalgia and Consumption Preferences: Some Emerging Patterns of Consumer Tastes", *Journal of Consumer Research*, 20(2), 245–256.

Holbrook, Morris B. (1995), *Consumer Research: Introspective Essays on the Study of Consumption*, Thousand Oaks, CA: Sage.

Holbrook, Morris B. (1999), "Popular Appeal versus Expert Judgements of Motion Pictures", *Journal of Consumer Research*, 26(2), 144–155.

Holbrook, Morris B. (2005), "Customer Value and Autoethnography: Subjective Personal Introspection and the Meanings of a Photograph Collection", *Journal of Business Research*, 58(1), 45–61.

Holbrook, Morris B. (2006), "Photo Essays and Mining of Minutiae in Consumer Research: 'bout the Time I got to Phoenix'", in *Handbook of Qualitative Research Methods in Marketing*, (Ed.) Belk, Russell W., Cheltenham: Edward Elgar, 476–493.

Holbrook, Morris B. (2011), *Music, Movies, Meanings and Markets: Cinemajazzamatazz*, New York: Routledge.

Holbrook, Morris B., Stephen Bell and Mark W. Grayson (1989), "The Role of the Humanities in Consumer Research: Close Encounters and Coastal Disturbances", in *Interpretive Consumer Research*, (Ed.) Hirschman, Elizabeth C., Duluth, MN: Association for Consumer Research, 29–47.

Holbrook, Morris B. and Mark W. Grayson (1986), "The Semiology of Cinematic Consumption: Symbolic Consumer Behaviour in *Out of Africa*", *Journal of Consumer Research*, 13(3), 374–381.

Holbrook, Morris B. and Elizabeth C. Hirschman (1982), "The Experiential Aspects of Consumption: Consumer Fantasies, Feelings and Fun", *Journal of Consumer Research*, 9(2), 132–140.

Holbrook, Morris B. and Elizabeth C. Hirschman (1993), *The Semiotics of Consumption: Interpreting Symbolic Consumer Behaviour in Popular Culture and Works of Art*, New York: Mouton de Gruyter.

Hollinger, Karen (2006), *The Actress: Hollywood Acting and the Female Star*, New York: Routledge.

Holt, Douglas (1998), "Does Cultural Capital Structure American Consumption?", *Journal of Consumer Research*, 25(1), 1–26.

Horton, Donald and R. Richard Wohl (1956), "Mass Communication and Parasocial Interaction", *Psychiatry*, 19(1), 215–229.

Houlberg, Rick (1984), "Local Television News Audience and the Parasocial Interaction", *Journal of Broadcasting*, 28(4), 423–429.

Huffer, Ian (2003), "What Interest Does a Fat Stallone Have for an Action Fan?: Male Film Audiences and the Structuring of Stardom", in *Contemporary Hollywood Stardom*, (Eds.) Austin, Thomas and Martin Barker, London: Arnold, 155–166.

Hunt, Kenneth A., Terry Bristol and R. Edward Bashaw (1999), "A Conceptual Approach to Classifying Sports Fans", *Journal of Services Marketing*, 13(6), 439–452.

Husserl, Edmund (1985), *Die Phänomenologische Methode: Ausgewählte Texte I*, Stuttgart: Reclam.

Husserl, Edmund (1986), *Phänomenologie der Lebenswelt: Ausgewählte Texte II*, Stuttgart: Reclam.

Hyman, Michael R. and Jeremy J. Sierra (2010), "Idolizing Sport Celebrities: A Gateway to Psychopathology?", *Young Consumers*, 11(3), 226–238.

Jaeckel, Anne (2003), *European Film Industries*, London: British Film Institute.

James, Jeffrey D. and Lynn L. Ridinger (2002), "Female and Male Sport Fans: A Comparison of Sport Consumption Motives", *Journal of Sport Behaviour*, 25(3), 261–278.

Jankovich, Mark (2002), "Cult Fictions: Cult Movies, Subcultural Capital and the Production of Cultural Distinctions", *Cultural Studies*, 16(2), 306–322.

Jansen, Christian (2005), "The Performance of German Motion Pictures, Profits and Subsidies: Some Empirical Evidence", *Journal of Cultural Economics*, 29, 191–212.

Jenkins, Henry (1992), *Textual Poachers: Television Fans and Participatory Culture*, London: Routledge.

Jenkins, Henry (2000), "Reception Theory and Audience Research: The Mystery of the Vampire's Kiss", in *Reinventing Film Studies*, (Eds.) Gledhill, Christine and Linda Williams, London: Arnold, 165–182.

Jenson, Joli (1992), "Fandom as Pathology: The Consequences of Characterization", in *The Adoring Audience: Fan Culture and Popular Media*, (Ed.) Lewis, Lisa A., London: Routledge, 9–29.

Jindra, Michael (1994), "Star Trek Fandom as a Religious Phenomenon", *Sociology of Religion*, 55(1), 27–51.

Kanai, Akane (2015), "Jennifer Lawrence, Remixed: Approaching Celebrity through DIY Digital Culture", *Celebrity Studies*, 6(3), 322–340.

Karniol, Rachel (2001), "Adolescent Females' Idolization of Male Media Stars as a Transition into Sexuality", *Sex Roles*, 44(1–2), 61–77.

Kerrigan, Finola (2010), *Film Marketing*, Oxford: Elsevier Butterworth-Heinemann.

Kerrigan, Finola and Mustafa F. Özbilgin (2004), "Film Marketing in Europe: Bridging the Gap Between Policy and Practice", *International Journal of Non-Profit & Voluntary Sector Marketing*, 9(3), 229–237.

King, Barry (1991), "Articulating Stardom", in *Stardom: Industry of Desire*, (Ed.) Gledhill, Christine, London: Routledge, 167–182.

King, Barry (2011), "Stardom, Celebrity and the Para-Confession", in *The Star and Celebrity Confessional*, (Ed.) Redmond, Sean, Abingdon: Routledge, 7–24.

King, Geoff (2003), "Stardom in the Willennium", in *Contemporary Hollywood Stardom*, (Eds.) Austin, Thomas and Martin Barker, London: Arnold, 62–73.

Kirkland, Ewan (2003), "Peter Pan's My Dad?!? The Man-Child Persona of Robin Williams", in *Contemporary Hollywood Stardom*, (Eds.) Austin, Thomas and Martin Barker, London: Arnold, 243–254.

Kochberg, Searie (2007), "The Industrial Contexts of Film Production", in *An Introduction to Film Studies, 4th Edition*, (Ed.) Nelmes, Jill, London: Routledge, 24–58.

Kozinets, Robert V. (1997), "I Want to Believe: A Netnography of The X-Philes' Subculture of Consumption", *Advances in Consumer Research*, 24, 470–475.

Kozinets, Robert V. (2001), "Utopian Enterprise: Articulating the Meanings of Star Trek's Culture of Consumption", *Journal of Consumer Research*, 28(1), 67–88.

Krämer, Peter (2003), "A Woman in a Male-Dominated World: Jodie Foster, Stardom and 90s Hollywood", in *Contemporary Hollywood Stardom*, (Eds.) Austin, Thomas and Martin Barker, London: Arnold, 201–214.

Kreimeier, Klaus (1996), *The UFA Story: A History of Germany's Greatest Film Company 1918–1945*, München: Carl Hanser Velag.

Lacey, Joanne (2003), "A Galaxy of Stars to Guarantee Ratings: Made-For-Television Movies and the Female Star System", in *Contemporary Hollywood Stardom*, (Eds.) Austin, Thomas and Martin Barker, London: Arnold, 187–198.

Lanier Jr., Clinton D. and Hope Jensen Schau (2007), "Culture and Co-Creation: Exploring Consumers' Inspirations and Aspirations for Writing and Posting On-Line Fan Fiction", *Research in Consumer Behaviour*, 11, 321–342.

Larsen, Gretchen, Rob Lawson and Sarah Todd (2010), "The Symbolic Consumption of Music", *Journal of Marketing Management*, 26(7–8), 671–685.

Leets, Laura, Gavin de Becker and Howard Giles (1995), "Fans: Exploring Expressed Motivations for Contacting Celebrities", *Journal of Language & Social Psychology*, 14(1–2), 102–123.

Lehmann, Donald R. and Charles B. Weinberg (2000), "Sales through Sequential Distribution Channels: An Application to Movies and Videos", *Journal of Marketing*, 64(1), 18–33.

Levin, Aaron M., Irwin P. Levin and C. Edward Heath (1997), "Movie Stars and Authors as Brand Names: Measuring Brand Equity in Experiential Products", *Advances in Consumer Research*, 24, 175–181.

Levy, Emanuel (1989), "The Democratic Elite: America's Movie Stars", *Qualitative Sociology*, 12(1), 29–54.

Lewis, Lisa A. (1992), "Something More Than Love: Fan Stories on Film", in *The Adoring Audience: Fan Culture and Popular Media*, (Ed.) Lewis, Lisa A., London: Routledge, 135–159.

Liu Yong (2006), "Word of Mouth for Movies: Its Dynamics and Impact on Box Office Revenue", *Journal of Marketing*, 70(1), 74–89.

Lovell, Alan (2003), "I Went in Search of Deborah Kerr, Jodie Foster and Julianne Moore But Got Waylaid…", in *Contemporary Hollywood Stardom*, (Eds.) Austin, Thomas and Martin Barker, London: Arnold, 259–270.

Lowenthal, Leo (2006), "The Triumph of Mass Idols", in *The Celebrity Culture Reader*, (Ed.) Marshall, P. David, New York: Routledge, 124–152.

Luo Lan, Chen Xinlei, Jeanie Han and C. Whan Park (2010), "Dilution and Enhancement of Celebrity Brands Through Sequential Movie Releases", *Journal of Marketing*, 74(6), 1114–1128.

Lyon, Josh (2008), "Miss Independence: Quirky, Charming Actress Jena Malone Has Never Followed Anyone's Rules", *Page Six Magazine*, 1 June, 14–17.

MacCannell, Dean (1973), "Staged Authenticity: Arrangements of Social Space in Tourism Settings", *American Journal of Sociology*, 79(3), 357–361.

Maltby, John, Liza Day, Lynn E. McCutcheon, Raphael Gilett, James Houran and Diane D. Ashe (2004), "Personality and Coping: A Context for Examining Celebrity Worship and Mental Health", *British Journal of Psychology*, 95, 411–428.

Marchand, Andre, Thorsten Hennig-Thurau and Sabine Best (2015), "When James Bond Shows off his Omega: Does Product Placement Affect Its Media Host?", *European Journal of Marketing*, 49(9–10), 1666–1685.

Marshall, P. David (1997), *Celebrity and Power: Fame in Contemporary Culture*, Minneapolis, MN: University of Minnesota.

Marwick, Alice E. (2016), "You May Know Me from YouTube: (Micro-)Celebrity in Social Media", in *A Companion to Celebrity*, (Eds.) Marshall, P. David and Sean Redmond, Oxford: Wiley Blackwell, 333–350.

McAlexander, James H., John W. Schouten and Harold F. Koenig (2002), "Building Brand Community", *Journal of Marketing*, 66(1), 38–54.

McCracken, Grant (1989), "Who is the Celebrity Endorser? Cultural Foundations of the Endorsement Process", *Journal of Consumer Research*, 16(3), 310–321.

McCutcheon, Lynn E., Diane D. Ashe, James Houran and John Maltby (2003), "A Cognitive Profile of Individuals Who Tend to Worship Celebrities", *Journal of Psychology*, 137(4), 309–322.

McCutcheon, Lynn E., Rense Lange and James Houran (2002), "Conceptualization and Measurement of Celebrity Worship", *British Journal of Psychology*, 93(1), 67–87.

McCutcheon, Lynn E., Vann B. Scott Jr., Mara S. Arugate and Jennifer Parker (2006),

"Exploring the Link Between Attachment and the Inclination to Obsess About or Stalk Celebrities", *North American Journal of Psychology*, 8(2), 289–300.

McDonald, Paul (2000), *The Star System: Hollywood's Production of Popular Identities*, London: Wallflower.

McDonald, Paul (2003), "Stars in the Online Universe: Promotion, Nudity, Reverence", in *Contemporary Hollywood Stardom*, (Eds.) Austin, Thomas and Martin Barker, London: Arnold, 29–44.

McDonald, Paul (2008), "The Star System: The Production of Hollywood Stardom in the Post-Studio Era", in *The Contemporary Hollywood Film Industry*, (Eds.) McDonald, Paul and Janet Wasko, Oxford: Blackwell, 167–181.

McLeod, Kembrew (2006), "The Private Ownership of People", in *The Celebrity Culture Reader*, (Ed.) Marshall, P. David, New York: Routledge, 649–665.

Merleau-Ponty, Maurice (1962/2002), *Phenomenology of Perception*, New York: Routledge.

Mick, David G. (1986), "Consumer Research and Semiotics: Exploring the Morphology of Signs, Symbols and Significance", *Journal of Consumer Research*, 13(2), 196–213.

Miller, Ken (2006), "Jena Malone: I Find Inspiration in the Weirdest and Strangest Places", *Tokion*, 53 (June/July), 34–39.

Mills, Scott, Anthony Patterson and Lee Quinn (2015), "Fabricating Celebrity Brands via Scandalous Narrative: Crafting, Capering and Commodifying the Comedian Russell Brand", *Journal of Marketing Management*, 31(5–6), 599–615.

Misra, Shekhar and Sharon E. Beatty (1990), "Celebrity Spokesperson and Brand Congruence: An Assessment of Recall and Affect", *Journal of Business Research*, 21(2), 159–173.

Mulvey, Laura (1975), "Visual Pleasure and Narrative Cinema", *Screen*, 16(3), 6–18.

Munsterberg, Hugo (1916), *The Photoplay: A Psychological Study*, New York: Appleton.

Murrell, Audrey J. and Elizabeth Dietz (1992), "Fan Support of Sport Teams: The Effect of a Common Group Identity", *Journal of Sport & Exercise Psychology*, 14(1), 28–39.

Newman, George E., Gil Diesendruck and Paul Bloom (2011), "Celebrity Contagion and the Value of Objects", *Journal of Consumer Research*, 38(2), 215–228.

Nichols, Bill (2000), "Film Theory and the Revolt against Master Narratives", in *Reinventing Film Studies*, (Eds.) Gledhill, Christine and Linda Williams, London: Arnold, 34–52.

Nowell-Smith, Geoffrey (2000), "How Films Mean, or, from Aesthetics to Semiotics and Half-Way Back Again", in *Reinventing Film Studies*, (Eds.) Gledhill, Christine and Linda Williams, London: Arnold, 8–17.

Oatley, Keith (1999), "Meeting of Minds: Dialogue, Sympathy and Identification in Reading Fiction", *Poetics*, 26(5–6), 439–454.

Obst, Lynda (2013), *Sleepless in Hollywood: Tales from the 'New Abnormal' in the Movie Business*, New York: Simon & Schuster.

O'Guinn, Thomas C. (1991), "Touching Greatness: The Central Midwest Barry Manilow Fan Club", in *Highways and Buyways: Naturalistic Research from the Consumer Behaviour Odyssey*, (Ed.) Belk, Russell W., Duluth, MN: Association for Consumer Research, 102–111.

O'Reilly, Daragh and Finola Kerrigan (2013), "A View to a Brand: Introducing the Film Brandscape", *European Journal of Marketing*, 47(5–6), 769–789.

Pachelli, Sarah (2011), "Jena Malone: The Thinking (Wo)Man's Muse", *944*, March, 28–31.

Parmentier, Marie-Agnes and Eileen Fischer (2015), "Things Fall Apart: The Dynamics of Brand Audience Dissipation", *Journal of Consumer Research*, 41(5), 1228–1250.

Patterson, Anthony (2005), "Processes, Relationships, Settings, Products and Consumers: The Case for Qualitative Diary Research", *Qualitative Market Research: An International Journal*, 8(2), 142–156.

Patterson, Anthony (2009), "Art, Ideology and Introspection", *International Journal of Culture, Tourism & Hospitality Research*, 4(1), 57–69.

Patterson, Anthony (2012), "Social-Networkers of the World, Unite and Take Over: A Meta-Introspective Perspective on the Facebook Brand", *Journal of Business Research*, 65(4), 527–534.

Pearce, Garth (2005), "Their Naughty Little Sister", *Culture (Sunday Times Supplement)*, 11-September-2005, 16–17.

Perkins, Tessa (2000), "Who (and What) Is It For?", in *Reinventing Film Studies*, (Eds.) Gledhill, Christine and Linda Williams, London: Arnold, 76–95.

Phillips, Patrick (2007), "Spectator, Audience and Response", in *An Introduction to Film Studies, 4th Edition*, (Ed.) Nelmes, Jill, London: Routledge, 143–171.

Pollack, Sydney (2006), "The Director", in *The Movie Business Book, 3rd International Edition*, (Ed.) Squire, Jason E., Maidenhead, Berks: McGraw-Hill, 25–38.

Puttnam, David (2006), "The Producer", in *The Movie Business Book, 3rd International Edition*, (Ed.) Squire, Jason E., Maidenhead, Berks: McGraw-Hill, 14–24.

Radford, Scott K. and Peter H. Bloch (2012), "Grief, Commiseration and Consumption Following the Death of a Celebrity", *Journal of Consumer Culture*, 12(2), 137–155.

Rambo, Carol (1992), "The Reflexive Self Through Narrative: A Night in the Life of an Erotic Dancer/Researcher", in *Investigating Subjectivity: Research on the Lived Experience*, (Eds.) Ellis, Carolyn and Michael G. Flaherty, London: Sage, 102–124.

Rambo, Carol (1996), "My Mother is Mentally Retarded", in *Composing Ethnography: Alternative Forms of Qualitative Writing*, (Eds.) Ellis, Carolyn and Arthur P. Bochner, Walnut Creek, CA: Alta-Mira, 109–131.

Rambo, Carol (2005), "Impressions of Grandmother: An Autoethnographic Portrait", *Journal of Contemporary Ethnography*, 34(5), 560–585.

Rapp, David N. and Richard J. Gerrig (2002), "Readers' Reality-Driven and Plot-Driven Analyses in Narrative Comprehension", *Memory & Cognition*, 30(5), 779–788.

Ravid, S. Abraham (1999), "Information, Blockbusters and Stars: A Study of the Film Industry", *Journal of Business*, 72(4), 463–492.

Redmond, Sean (2014), *Celebrity and the Media*, Basingstoke, Hants: Palgrave Macmillan.

Rems, Emily (2004), "Girl Uncorrupted: Jena Malone – Our Fave Screen Teen", *Bust*, Summer, 42–47.

Richardson, Brendan and Darach Turley (2006), "Support Your Local Team: Resistance, Subculture and the Desire for Distinction", *Advances in Consumer Research*, 33, 175–180.

Richardson, Brendan and Darach Turley (2008), "It's Far More Important than That: Football Fandom and Cultural Capital", *European Advances in Consumer Research*, 8, 33–38.

Rojek, Chris (2006), "Celebrity and Religion", in *The Celebrity Culture Reader*, (Ed.) Marshall, P. David, New York: Routledge, 389–417.

Rommelmann, Nancy (2000), "Jena at 15: A Childhood in Hollywood", *LA Weekly*, June 16–22, available on: www.nancyrommelmann.com/jena.html.

Rotter, Jeffrey (2003), "Goodbye Girl: Why Jena Malone Said 'So Long' to Hollywood and 'Hello' to Homemade Hairdos", *Nylon*, April, 86–89.

Rotter, Jeffrey (2004), "What Would Jena Do? Love, Death and Drywall: Actress Jena Malone Solves Life's Enduring Mysteries", *Nylon*, May, 82–85.

Rubin, Alan M., Elisabeth M. Pearse and Robert A. Powell (1985), "Loneliness, Parasocial Interaction and Local Television News Viewing", *Human Communication Research*, 12(2), 155–180.

Rubin, Rebecca B. and Michael P. McHugh (1987), "Development of Parasocial Interaction Relationships", *Journal of Broadcasting & Electronic Media*, 31(3), 279–292.

Russell, Cristel A. and Barbara B. Stern (2006), "Consumers, Characters and Products: A Balance Model of Sitcom Product Placement Effects", *Journal of Advertising*, 35(1), 7–21.

Sandvoss, Cornel (2005), "One Dimensional Fan: Toward an Aesthetic of Fan Texts", *American Behavioral Scientist*, 48(7), 822–839.

Sandvoss, Cornel (2007), "The Death of the Reader?: Literary Theory and the Study of Texts in Popular Culture", in *Fandom: Identities and Communities in a Mediated World*, (Eds.) Gray, Jonathan, Cornel Sandvoss and C. Lee Harrington, New York: New York Press, 19–32.

Schau, Hope Jensen and Albert M. Muniz Jr. (2007), "Temperance and Religiosity in a Non-Marginal, Non-Stigmatised Brand Community", in *Consumer Tribes*, (Eds.) Cova, Bernard, Robert V. Kozinets and Avi Shankar, Oxford: Butterworth-Heinemann, 144–162.

Schickel, Richard (1985), *Intimate Strangers: The Culture of Celebrity*, New York: Doubleday.

Schmidt-Lux, Thomas (2010), "Geschichte der Fans", in *Fans: Soziologische Perspektiven*, (Eds.) Roose, Jochen, Mike S. Schäfer and Thomas Schmidt-Lux, Wiesbaden: Verlag fur Sozialwissenschaften, 47–68.

Schroeder, Jonathan E. (2005), "The Artist and the Brand", *European Journal of Marketing*, 39(11–12), 1291–1305.

Scott, Linda M. (1994), "The Bridge from Text to Mind: Adapting Reader-Response Theory to Consumer Research", *Journal of Consumer Research*, 21(3), 461–480.

Shefrin, Elana (2004), "Lord of the Rings, Star Wars and Participatory Fandom: Mapping New Congruencies between the Internet and Media Entertainment Culture", *Critical Studies in Media Communication*, 21(3), 261–281.

Sherwin, Skye (2004), "I'm Not That Kind of Girl", *I-D*, 242(April), 214–219.

Sinclair, Gary and Todd Green (2016), "Download or Stream? Steal or Buy? Developing a Typology of Today's Music Consumer", *Journal of Consumer Behaviour*, 15(1), 3–14.

Smith, Scott, Dan Fisher and S. Jason Cole (2007), "The Lived Meanings of Fanaticism: Understanding the Complex Role of Labels and Categories in Defining the Self in Consumer Culture", *Consumption, Markets & Culture*, 10(2), 77–94.

Sood, Sanjay and Xavier Drèze (2006), "Brand Extensions of Experiential Goods: Movie Sequel Evaluations", *Journal of Consumer Research*, 33(3), 352–360.

Speidel, Suzanne (2007), "Film Form and Narrative", in *An Introduction to Film Studies, 4th Edition*, (Ed.) Nelmes, Jill, London: Routledge, 60–89.

Spry, Amanda, Ravi Pappu and T. Bettina Cornwell (2011), "Celebrity Endorsement, Brand Credibility and Brand Equity", *European Journal of Marketing*, 45(6), 882–909.

Stacey, Jackie (1994), *Star Gazing: Hollywood Cinema and Female Spectatorship*, London: Routledge.

Staiger, Janet (1991), "Seeing Stars", in *Stardom: Industry of Desire*, (Ed.) Gledhill, Christine, London: Routledge, 3–16.

Staiger, Janet (2003), "Authorship Approaches", in *Authorship and Film*, (Eds.) Gerstner, David A. and Janet Staiger, London: Routledge.

Stern, Barbara B. (1989), "Literary Criticism and Consumer Research: Overview and Illustrative Analysis", *Journal of Consumer Research*. 16(3), 322–334.

Stern, Barbara B. (1998), "The Problematics of Representation", in *Representing Consumers: Voices, Views and Visions*, (Ed.) Stern, Barbara B., London: Routledge, 1–23.

Stern, Barbara B., Christel A. Russell and Dale W. Russell (2005), "Vulnerable Women on Screen and at Home: Soap Opera Consumption", *Journal of Macromarketing*, 25(2), 222–225.

Stever, Gayle S. (1991), "The Celebrity Appeal Questionnaire", *Psychological Reports*, 68(3), 859–866.

Studlar, Gaylyn (2016), "The Changing Face of Celebrity and the Emergence of Motion Picture Stardom", in *A Companion to Celebrity*, (Eds.) Marshall, P. David and Sean Redmond, Oxford: Wiley, 58–77.

Swami, Sanjeev, Jehoshua Eliashberg and Charles B. Weinberg (1999), "Silver Screener: A Modelling Approach to Movie Screen Management", *Marketing Science*, 18(3), 352–372.

Thompson, Craig J. (1997), "Interpreting Consumers: A Hermeneutical Framework for Deriving Marketing Insights from the Texts of Consumers' Consumption Stories", *Journal of Marketing Research*, 34(6), 438–455.

Thompson, Craig J. (1998), "Living the Texts of Everyday Life: A Hermeneutic Perspective on the Relationships Between Consumer Stories and Life-World Structures", in *Representing Consumers: Voices, Views and Visions*, (Ed.) Stern, Barbara B., London: Routledge, 127–155.

Thompson, Craig J., William B. Locander and Howard R. Pollio (1989), "Putting Consumer Experience Back into Consumer Research: The Philosophy and Method of Existential-Phenomenology", *Journal of Consumer Research*, 16(2), 133–146.

Thompson, John O. (1991), "Screen Acting and the Commutation Test", in *Stardom: Industry of Desire*, (Ed.) Gledhill, Christine, London: Routledge, 183–197.

Thomson, Matthew (2006), "Human Brands: Investigating Antecedents to Consumers' Strong Attachments to Celebrities", *Journal of Marketing*, 70(1), 104–119.

Thorne, Scott and Gordon C. Bruner (2006), "An Exploratory Investigation of the Characteristics of Consumer Fanaticism", *Qualitative Market Research: An International Journal*, 9(1), 51–72.

Thorp, Margaret (1939), *America at the Movies*, New Haven, CT: Yale Press.

Tuchinsky, Jessica (2006), "The Talent Agent", in *The Movie Business Book, 3rd International Edition*, (Ed.) Squire, Jason E., Maidenhead, Berks: McGraw-Hill, 222–229.

Turner, Graeme (2004), *Understanding Celebrity*, London: Sage.

Unwin, Elinor, Finola Kerrigan, Kathryn Waite and David Grant (2007), "Getting the Picture: Programme Awareness amongst Film Festival Customers", *International Journal of Nonprofit & Voluntary Sector Marketing*, 12(2), 231–245.

Wallace, Timothy, Alan Seigerman and Morris B. Holbrook (1993), "The Role of Actors and Actresses in the Success of Films: How Much is a Movie Star Worth?", *Journal of Cultural Economics*, 17(1), 1–28.

Wallendorf, Melanie and Merrie Brucks (1993), "Introspection in Consumer Research: Implementation and Implications", *Journal of Consumer Research*, 20(3), 339–359.

Wasko, Janet (2008), "Financing and Production: Creating the Hollywood Film Commodity", in *The Contemporary Hollywood Film Industry*, (Eds.) McDonald, Paul and Janet Wasko, Oxford: Blackwell, 43–62.

Watson, Paul (2007a), "Stardom and Hollywood Cinema", in *An Introduction to Film Studies, 4th Edition*, (Ed.) Nelmes, Jill, London: Routledge, 128–142.

Watson, Paul (2007b), "Approaches to Cinematic Authorship", in *An Introduction to Film Studies, 4th Edition*, (Ed.) Nelmes, Jill, London: Routledge, 90–108.

Weber, Max (2006), "The Sociology of Charismatic Authority", in *The Celebrity Culture Reader*, (Ed.) Marshall, P. David, New York: Routledge, 55–71.

Wei Liyuan (2006), "Making Sense of These Million Dollar Babies: Rationale Behind Superstar Profit Participation Contracts", *Marketing Science*, 25(6), 678–680.

Weiss, Andrea (1991), "A Queer Feeling When I Look at You: Hollywood Stars and Lesbian Spectatorship in the 1930s", in *Stardom: Industry of Desire*, (Ed.) Gledhill, Christine, London: Routledge, 283–299.

Wiles, Michael A. and Anna Danielova (2009), "The Worth of Product Placement in Successful Films: An Event Study Analysis", *Journal of Marketing*, 73(1), 44–63.

Williams, Rebecca (2006), "From 'Beyond Control' to In Control: Investigating Drew Barrymore's Feminist Agency/Authorship", in *Stardom and Celebrity: A Reader*, (Eds.) Redmond, Sean and Su Holmes, London: Sage, 111–125.

Winston, Andrew S. (1995), "Simple Pleasures: The Psychological Aesthetics of High and Popular Art", *Empirical Studies of the Arts*, 13(2), 193–203.

Wohlfeil, Markus and Susan Whelan (2008), "Confessions of a Movie-Fan: Introspection into a Consumer's Experiential Consumption of *'Pride & Prejudice'*", *European Advances in Consumer Research*, 8, 137–143.

Wohlfeil, Markus and Susan Whelan (2011), " *'The Book of Stars'*: Understanding a Consumer's Fan Relationship with a Film Actress through a Narrative Transportation Approach", *European Advances in Consumer Research*, 9, 290–296.

Wohlfeil, Markus and Susan Whelan (2012), " *'Saved!'* by Jena Malone: An Introspective Study of a Consumer's Fan Relationship with a Film Actress", *Journal of Business Research*, 65(4), 511–519.

Woodside, Arch G. (2004), "Advancing from Subjective to Confirmatory Personal Introspection in Consumer Research", *Psychology & Marketing*, 21(12), 987–1010.